A JOURNAL OF
CONSCIOUSNESS AND TRANSFORMATION

ReVision

I0118618

CONTENTS

Transformative Leadership
Alfonso Montuori & Urusa Fahim, Editors

Cover image: Whirling Dervishes by Mariana Castro de Ali

Winter 2010 • Volume 30 • Nos. 3 & 4

What is ReVision?

For almost thirty years ReVision has explored the transformative and consciousness-changing dimensions of leading-edge thinking. Since its inception ReVision has been a vital forum, especially in the North American context, for the articulation of contemporary spirituality, transpersonal studies, and related new models in such fields as education, medicine, organization, social transformation, work, psychology, ecology, and gender. With a commitment to the future of humanity and the Earth, ReVision emphasizes the transformative dimensions of current and traditional thought and practice. ReVision advances inquiry and reflection especially focused on the fields presently identified as philosophy, religion, psychology, social theory, science, anthropology, education, frontier science, organizational transformation, and the arts. We seek to explore ancient ways of knowing as well as new models of transdisciplinary, interdisciplinary, multicultural, dialogical, and socially engaged inquiry. It is our intention to bring such work to bear on what appear to be the fundamental issues of our times through a variety of written and artistic modalities. In the interests of renewal and fresh vision, we strive to engage in conversation a diversity of perspectives and discourses which have often been kept separate, including those identified with terms such as Western and Eastern; indigenous and nonindigenous; Northern and Southern; feminine and masculine; intellectual; practical, and spiritual; local and global; young and old.

Artwork: Mariana Castro de Ali

Volume 30, Nos. 3&4 (ISBN 978-0-9819706-2-2)

ReVision (ISSN 0275-6935) is published as part of the *Society for the Study of Shamanism, Healing, and Transformation.*

Manuscript Submissions

We welcome manuscript submissions. Manuscript guidelines can be found on our webpage http://revisionpublishing.org.

POSTMASTER: Send address changes to
ReVision Publishing, P.O. Box 1855, Sebastopol, CA 95473.

Subscriptions

For subscriptions mail a check to above address or go to
www.revisionpublishing.org.

Individual Subscriptions

Subscription for one year: $36 online only,
$36 print only (international $72),
$48 print and on-line (international $84).

Subscription for two years: $60 online only,
$60 print only (international $96),
$79 print and online (international $115).

Subscription for three years: $72 online only,
$72 print only (international $108),
$96 print and online (international $132).

Institutional Subscriptions

$98 online only (international $134),
$134 print and online (international $155).

Please allow six weeks for delivery of first issue.

EDITORIAL BOARD

ReVision Abstracts

Vol. 30 No. 3 & 4   *Winter 2010*

Cowan, D. A. (2010). Embedded spirituality as a leadership foundation for sustainable innovative learning. *ReVision*, *30*(3&4), 89-97. doi:10.4298/REVN.30.3.4.89-97

In response to leaders being challenged to handle chronic dilemmas with increasingly scarce resources, I resurface important findings of a worldwide study conducted by Botkin, Elmandjra, and Malitza (1979). Commissioned by the Club of Rome, the study illuminates a critical need for innovative learning, serving as a call for leaders – if not for everyone – to become more anticipatory and participatory. My argument enriches the call by describing how indigenous notions of embedded spirituality provide a more sustainable foundation for today's troubled world. By promoting practical stewardship for all life on earth, an embedded spirituality naturally promotes anticipation and participation. Drawing upon these connections, I outline leadership competencies to accompany the Botkin, Elmandjra, and Malitza prescription.

Durant, A. (2010). Leadership and lace. *ReVision*, *30*(3&4), 79-88. doi:10.4298/REVN.30.3.4.79-88

This essay employs a roundabout weaving of themes, including leadership, feminism, discourse, and stories, in order to create a pattern of open spaces. With various meanings of lace opening the document, I lace my observations of being a female scholar with verbal attacks on the system that prefers closed and linear logic, in large part in order to add zest to my story and observations. At heart, I hope to intertwine opposite edges of logic/emotions, male/female, theory/practice, truth/fiction, abstractions/bodies, and so forth. I gratefully acknowledge Marja Flory's (2008) courageous dissertation as a quilting, inspired by Ann Rippin's (2007) willingness to open herself to learning from threads.

Eisler, R. & Carter, S. (2010). Transformative leadership: From domination to partnership. *ReVision*, *30*(3&4), 98-106. doi:10.4298/REVN.30.3.4.98-106

In this time when change has become a powerful political rallying cry, critical question are: Change from what to what? What kind of leadership can bring about transformative rather than simply surface change? These questions are explored from the perspective of a new conceptual framework for cultural transformation. We show that the struggle for our future is between the regressive pull of a system of domination and a strong movement toward a partnership system. We describe both systems with specific examples historically and cross-culturally, show how traditions of domination in both the private sphere of families and other intimate relations and the larger national and international arena lie behind our mounting economic, environmental, and social crises. We highlight how students are empowered to become "partnership leaders" and help create positive, transformative social change.

Hampden-Turner, C. (2010). Teaching innovation. *ReVision*, *30*(3&4), 69-78. doi:10.4298/REVN.30.3.4.69-78

Starting in 2002 and extending until 2007 over two hundred students took a 4-month, post-graduate course at the Nanyang "Technnopreneurship" Center at Nanyang Technological University in Singapore. The purpose of the course was to produce high tech entrepreneurs at ease with complexity. This paper evaluates the pedagogy as designed and taught by Prof. Tan Teng-Kee and his associates. The aim was to create an entrepreneurial "ecosystem" with highly contrasting values, past and present, triumph and disaster, doubt and certainty etc. A methodology was devised which measured not simply the salience of various values but the extent to which contrasting values had been integrated, the hypothesis being that innovation requires values to be fused. The results were highly positive for the Technopreneurship program.

Harrison, B. (2010). Bringing your spiritual practice into your work. *ReVision*, *30*(3&4), 107-117. doi:10.4298/REVN.30.3.4.107-117

The author explores the barriers against speaking of one's spiritual practices in work settings and advocates bringing work and spiritual life into congruence. He describes his own journey towards such integration, which includes communicating and partnering with non-physical guides and allies, various forms of meditation and prayer. Practices are described that can be of value to leaders, consultants and any member of an organization for working with the being, soul or essence of an organization in spiritual ways. Examples of such work from the author's practice are given, and ways in which the work may be approached are suggested. The difficult question of when and how to enter into dialogue with others about spiritual issues is addressed, with suggestions for doing so and some guidelines for making such conversations safe.

Jones, C. A. & Mason, W. (2010). Leadership among spiritual teachers. *ReVision*, *30*(3&4), 28-36. doi:10.4298/REVN.30.3.4.28-36

This conversation between Constance A. Jones, Ph.D and Wendy Mason, MSN, ARNP, offers insight into issues surrounding spiritual leadership in East and West. The interaction between spiritual teacher and student in Eastern contexts (particularly Hinduism and Buddhism) derives from a worldview in which ontological being and a sense of relationship are paramount. Because this worldview differs significantly from Western notions of teacher and disciple, challenges arise in identifying the salient characteristics of successful spiritual leaders and communities. Jones and Mason explore the roles of epistemology and open inquiry in the process of spiritual leadership in both East and West.

Keeney, B. (2010). N/om and transformative leadership: Shaking things up with the Kalahari Bushmen N/om-Kxaosi. *ReVision*, *30*(3&4), 51-56. doi:10.4298/REVN.30.3.4.51-56

The Ju/'hoan Bushmen have a radically different way of knowing that highlights the importance of n/om, what they regard as the source of creative transformation. Based on fieldwork with Bushmen elders and leaders, this theoretical study proposes alternative questions, concerns, ideas, and practices for transformative leadership that arise from the Bushman cultural preference for "shaking things up." Here the importance of understanding and textuality is tempered, favoring a more improvisational presence that emphasizes never ceasing change in all aspects of experience, interaction, and community.

Montuori, M. (2010). Transformative leadership for the 21st century: Reflections on the design of a graduate leadership curriculum. *ReVision*, *30*(3&4), 4-14. doi:10.4298/REVN.30.3.4.4-14

This paper outlines the philosophical and pedagogical underpinnings of a masters degree in Transformative Leadership with a specific focus on the role of creativity and self-creation. It uses the design of the degree as a way of address some of the considerable complexities of the field of leadership, but also the larger planetary and personal challenges facing individuals who are committed to contributing to positive social change.

ReVision Abstracts

Montuori, A. & Fahim, U. (2010). Transformative leadership. *ReVision*, *30*(3&4), 1-3. doi:10.4298/REVN.30.3.4.1-3

The discourse and practice of leadership is undergoing great changes that reflect global changes. Traditional images of "strong man" and "heroic" leadership are inadequate in this age of transition. Members of traditionally under-represented populations are taking key leadership roles and new approaches to leadership are emerging from a variety of sources. They often explicitly incorporate dimensions such as spirituality and creativity that were mostly omitted from traditional models of leadership.

Low, A. (2010). What is Leadership? *ReVision*, *30*(3&4), 20-27. doi:10.4298/REVN.30.3.4.20-27

Most studies in leadership concentrate upon traits that leaders should supposedly have to be effective as leaders. It is suggested that this approach has limited value. A radically new approach is suggested: that the leader is the incarnation of a dynamic center. The paper expands upon what the expression 'dynamic center' means, and shows that it is not a psychological phenomenon but a 'transcendent one.

Ogilvy, M. (2010). Theses on Michael Murphy and Esalen. *ReVision*, *30*(3&4), 37-50. doi:10.4298/REVN.30.3.4.37-50

By changing just a few words in each of Marx's "Eleven Theses on Feuerbach," this article shows how Michael Murphy and Esalen exercised leadership in the human potentials movement. Just as Marx and Feuerbach before them turned Hegel on his head, Murphy and Esalen revolutionized both psychology and spirituality. In place of Freud's somewhat pessimistic focus on sickness and pathology, they feature Maslow's more optimistic focus on self-realization. In place of other worldly religions, both eastern and western, that take flight toward the transcendent, Murphy and Esalen return us to an earthly "religion of no religion," an earthy, incarnate spirituality.

Petranker, M. (2010). Leading from within the whole of time. *ReVision*, *30*(3&4), 57-62. doi:10.4298/REVN.30.3.4.56-62

Leadership is about change: initiating it, sustaining it, and guiding it. This article explores the potential to initiate and bring about change by focusing on the leader's relationship to time. The leader who hopes to transform a situation or organization must be ready to engage the whole of what is happening in each moment. In words and deeds, the leader must enter into each situation free from the burdens of past positions and conditionings, and present needs and concerns. Present to their own intentions, their own vision, they must be ready to make each moment the decisive point for action.

Simons, M. (2010). The Heart of hearing: A story of transformative leadership and sustainable development in a small New England City. *ReVision*, *30*(3&4), 63-68. doi:10.4298/REVN.30.3.4.63-68

We are living in the "Obama Age" of participatory democracy. However, participatory and sustainable approaches to government are not new. This article explores the role of transformative leadership in creating sustainable social development through the lens of a successful long-term partnership between the citizenry and local government of the City of Burlington Vermont. I focus on the story of one unusual leader, Yiota Ahladas, Director of The Center for Community and Neighborhoods (C-CAN), whose approach to leading emerged from the unique geographic and sociopolitical backdrop of Burlington.

Slater, P. (2010). Why democracy is taking over global culture. *ReVision*, *30*(3&4), 15-19. doi:10.4298/REVN.30.3.4.15-19

Democratic systems are replacing authoritarian systems throughout the world for two reasons: First, they are more natural to our genetic programming, given that we spent millions of years as hunter-gatherers and only a few thousand as warrior agriculturalists; second, they are more adaptable and more efficient under conditions of chronic change.

Transformative Leadership

Alfonso Montuori & Urusa Fahim, Editors

These are challenging and awe-inspiring days for leadership. At the beginning of the 21st century, the discourses and practices of leadership are being challenged in radical, fundamental ways (Hatch, Kostera, & Kozminski, 2006; Northouse, 2004; Rost, 1993; Western, 2008). President Barack Obama, the first African-American to be President of the United States of America, is leading the country and arguably the world through a period of tremendous change. In early 2010, this change is still being characterized as a largely economic one. But it is clear the repercussions and implications extend far beyond economics. Not just the economy, but the dreams and aspirations of a certain form of techno-industrial, consumer mentality of late modernity have proved to be unsustainable as well as ultimately unjust.

The rapid collapse of the global economy has not only shown the bankruptcy of a kind of late-industrial capitalism. It

For **Alfonso Montuori** see next article.
Urusa Fahim is a faculty in the Transformative Leadership (TLD) Program at the California Institute of Integral Studies (CIIS). She is interested in leadership in its many forms, identity development, intercultural communication, group process and spirituality among other things.

has also highlighted the terrible limitations of looking at the economy—and human wellbeing--solely from a quantitative, "purely" economic perspective with little or no accounting for values, culture, psychology, and more ultimate questions about what all this activity means (Morin & Kern, 1999). The trivialization of everyday life through the increasing use of metaphors and terms

In strange and uncertain times such as those we are living in, sometimes a reasonable person might despair. But hope is unreasonable, and love is greater even than this. May we trust the inexpressible benevolence of the creative impulse.

Robert Fripp (Public Talk, February 13, 2008, San Francisco)

from commerce and management, has threatened to reduce all human exchanges to economic, instrumental transactions between "consumers." The neat and tidy business-like language of cost benefit analyses, branding, and return on investment gives the illusion that it somehow cuts through the complexity of life. In the world of industry, this lan-

guage is often backed by "metrics" that give the impression of an edifice built on solid quantitative data. The reality is that the data are often little better than the "hypothetical future value" accounting that allowed Enron to thrive during the years its vicious Ponzi scheme made Fortune magazine hail it as the most innovative company in America for six years in a row. We seem to forget that numbers can hide as much as they illuminate, that sometimes they literally stand for nothing, and that, to paraphrase Humberto Maturana, everything that's counted is counted by somebody (Maturana & Varela, 1987).

What the bloodless and bloodcurdling actions of the Jeff Skillings, Ken Lays, and Bernie Madoffs of this world succeeded in doing for a while was to hide the underlying fundamental assumptions that drove them. Scientists still regularly debate whether human beings are fundamentally selfish and egotistical or cooperative and altruistic. But there is little doubt that regardless of any innate essence, human beings are capable of behaving in ways that represent the entire spectrum of behavior, and that they can institutionalize a set of beliefs and create self-fulfilling prophecies through culture and interactions over time. Given human adaptability, we can aspire to create Social Darwinian nightmares or fair and "pro-social" communities and organizations.

The cold but oddly hyperbolic language of facts and figures hid another

politicians simply do not understand the reality or the complexity of the situation. They seem to be adrift without a moral compass, and lacking in empathy as they muddle through (Mardell, 2009). We know what has happened in many countries during times of great change

thought will tell us that the establishment is the source of our present predicament. It is bankrupt both morally and practically, and given its dismal record it is certainly not in a position to tell us what qualities a leader should have. Remember George Bush was such an in-your-face-guy, and that is surely a dubious recommendation for these troubled times.

Transformative Leadership begins with a drastic rethinking of the who, what, where, when, and how of leadership.

kind of language, namely the culture of "big swinging dicks" at Goldman Sachs, and Skilling's "selfish gene"-inspired Enron culture of evaluation through "rank and yank." These have proved not only morally bankrupt but also economically bankrupt. It is at times of crisis, of profound systemic destabilization, when existential questions also reappear in public consciousness. The last 8 years of the Bush administration have taken the world to the brink of disaster but the ensuing crisis has made the often rapacious underlying assumptions very clear. It has unveiled the crumbling philosophical infrastructure that drew loosely on Social Darwinism and Anti-Democratic Straussian Platonism. Spurred by the deflation of hypertrophied egos and the death of one set of hyper-acquisitive dreams, we begin to ask again what the good life is, and Vanity Fair runs an article wondering what happened to the American dream. We begin to ask, in Kant's well known formulation, these fundamental questions: What we can hope for? What we can know? What we can do? It is these kinds of fundamental questions that lie at the heart of Trans-formative Leadership.

As the world undergoes a tremendous transformation, a leadership vacuum has emerged. In the USA, Barack Obama has stepped up to the plate, with a promise of hope and change. His election is itself an indication of change, and of the desire for change. At this early stage it is unclear whether there is a vision for which we can have the audacity of hope, let alone the will and skill to make it a reality. In Europe, the vacuum is painfully present, and interestingly it appears that one of the key issues is that

and economic hardship. All too often we have succumbed to heroic leaders who have promised to save us—and doom others in the process. The challenge for Obama is that old fashioned "great man," "heroic" leadership is not what we need in the emerging world. Unfortunately, that is the only kind of leadership the crumbling establishment seems to know, and he is being critiqued for not being an in your face tough guy (Fineman, 2009).

Indeed in a recent article in News-week Howard Fineman points to the "establishment's" emerging doubts about Barack Obama's leadership style two months after his inauguration. Obama, who is after all a surfer, seems too mellow and judicious. "A genial, amenable

It is to be expected the crumbling establishment's pundits believe that the President should follow a well-worn tough-guy style of leadership. In times of trouble, we know there will be calls for what they believe worked in previous times. But the present situation calls for an entirely different kind of leadership. One of the main reasons Obama was elected was precisely the hope that he would usher in a new form of leadership. Accusing Obama of not being the kind of black-and-white, my-way-or-the-highway style of leadership is viewing the situation through the mindset that got us into this trouble in the first place, and asking for more of the same.

The reality is that it is not so much what Obama is actually doing or not doing that is troubling the establishment. He doesn't look like the traditional savior-leader. He is too intellectual: "A busy, industrious overachiever," Fineman writes, "he likes to check off boxes

Obama's form of leadership is counter-intuitive for the establishment looking for coach John Wayne to knock this country into shape. It knows the days of cowboy posturing are over. We are now in an age of complexity and transformation.

guy, he likes to appeal to every constituency, or at least not write off any," Fineman writes. Obama doesn't have what the establishment considers to be "a central trait of the president's character: he's not really an in-your-face guy."

It's no wonder that the establishment is having its doubts about Obama. He is clearly not one of them. A moment's

on a long to-do list. A beau ideal of Harvard Law, he can't wait to tackle extra-credit answers on the exam." What the establishment and Feinman want is this: "a blunt-spoken coach." Perhaps Obama should yell "bring 'em on," and have a "Mission Accomplished" banner waiting backstage rather than be so damn smart.

Obama's task is a complex and precarious one. It is not one that will benefit from macho posturing. The fact that he "likes to appeal to every constituency" is clearly part of a larger effort to bring all the voices that should be heard to the table, and, as part of his stress on responsibility, to make sure we can have substantive contributions from all sectors of society. Unlike his predecessor, Obama's administration does not want to function as a closed system mired in groupthink and go it alone, a convict of the alleged courage of its own convictions. This will mean more reflection, more dialogue, more exploration, more inquiry, and no snap judgments about "evil-doers."

Obama's form of leadership is counter-intuitive for the establishment looking for coach John Wayne to knock this country into shape. It recognizes the complexity of our predicament. It knows the days of cowboy posturing are over. We are now in an age of complexity and transformation. We need a President who acknowledges this, does not offer simplistic solutions, and approaches the issues with the requisite degree of reflection, complexity, and intelligence. New ways of leading must be created and embodied, and Obama's task to do so in the middle of a "perfect storm" is not an easy one.

To say that every crisis offers an opportunity has become a cliché, in today's information saturated society. But information is not knowledge, let alone wisdom. Turning crisis into opportunity is not a cliché, at this point: it is an imperative. The breakdown of an old system has indeed opened up possibilities, and an increasing number of individuals are stepping up to the plate. The great transformation ahead of us cannot occur at the hands of one or two great leaders. While undoubtedly there will be key figures, and figures in positions of great power, the real source of innovation and creativity will come from individuals who have taken up President Obama's challenge to take responsibility not just for their lives and their communities, but for the future of the world.

Individuals who have chosen to lead to create, and create to lead.

Transformative Leadership begins with a drastic rethinking of the who, what, where, when, and how of leadership. In this sense, President Obama is only the tip of the iceberg. He is a leader in an age when the very definition and concept of leadership undergoing transformation. In an age of transition such as ours, Transformative Leaders are emerging everywhere. They are people from

Turning crisis into opportunity is not a cliché, at this point: it is an imperative.

all walks of life who are not satisfied standing on the sidelines and want to make a difference (Godin, 2009). They realize that the world is changing rapidly, and that they can contribute. They also realize that we can't transform the world without transforming ourselves, and yet we can't transform ourselves without transforming the world. They know how to reframe this apparently vicious cycle into a virtuous one because they understand the dynamics of creation. And there is no doubt that creativity is at the core of Transformative Leadership.

Whereas MacGregor Burns's Transformational Leadership stresses the importance of charisma (Burns, 2004), Transformative Leadership focuses centrally on Leaders as Creators and Creators as Leaders. Creators of new possibilities, of new ways of Being, Relating, Knowing, and Doing (Montuori & Conti, 1993). Transformative Leaders want to be creators of actions in the world that reflect a desire to make a difference inspired by a mutually beneficial, win-win view of the world. Transformative Leadership is also an act of self-creation: an individual who makes a commitment to make a difference in this changing and challenging transforming world knows that he or she has to be prepared, transform him or herself, and develop the necessary attitudes and skills to achieve the desired goal.

In this special double issue of ReVision our contributors will look at leadership from a multiplicity of perspectives, from the micro to the macro. We will meet leaders, explore their global and local contexts, assess their challenges and the complexity of the tasks ahead. These essays contribute to the emerging articulation of Transformative Leadership, which is clearly still a work in progress. The diversity of perspectives reflects a plurality of sources, contributors, perspectives, contexts, and disciplinary backgrounds. As the traditional image of the heroic leader is found wanting (but cf. (Fletcher, 2002), we will likely not return to one overriding image of an "in your face" tough guy. There may still be room for such leaders, but theirs will by no means be the dominant style in the public imagination, or in practice. The possibilities and opportunities are many. Transformative Leadership is re-creating leadership as Transformative Leaders re-create themselves to help our world re-create itself.

References

Burns, J. M. (2004). *Transforming leadership: The pursuit of happiness*. New York: Grove.

Fineman, H. (2009, March 10). A turning tide? *Newsweek*.

Fletcher, J. K. (2002). The greatly exaggerated demise of heroic leadership: Gender, power, and the myth of the female advantage. *CGO Insights(13)*. PAGE NUMBERS MISSING

Godin, S. (2009). *Tribes. We need you to lead us*. New York: Portfolio.

Hatch, M. J., Kostera, M., & Kozminski, A. K. (2006). The three faces of leadership: Manager, artist, priest. *Organizational Dynamics, 35*(1), 49-68.

Mardell, M. (2009). Angry Europeans look for direction, BBC News. http://news.bbc.co.uk/go/pr/fr/-/2/hi/programmes/from_our_own_correspondent/7955686.stm

Maturana, H., & Varela, F. (1987). *The tree of knowledge*. Boston: New Science Library.

Montuori, A., & Conti, I. (1993). *From power to partnership. Creating the future of love, work, and community*. San Francisco: Harper San Francisco.

Morin, E., & Kern, B. (1999). *Homeland Earth: A manifesto for the new millennium*. Cresskill, NJ: Hampton Press.

Northouse, P. G. (2004). *Leadership. Theory and practice*. Thousand Oaks Sage.

Rost, J. C. (1993). Leadership for the twenty-first century. Westport, CT: Praeger.

Western, S. (2008). *Leadership. A critical text*. Thousand Oaks: Sage.

Transformative Leadership for the 21st Century

Reflections on the Design of a Graduate Leadership Curriculum

Alfonso Montuori

A t the dawn of the 21st century, barely into its first decade, the planet is facing tremendous challenges. As I write this in the Spring of 2009, there is a global economic crisis that is predicted to get considerably worse before it gets better. It is truly planetary in scope in the sense that its effects are not limited to one country. It is felt all over the world. More importantly, it shows in stark relief the extent to which human beings live in an interdependent and interconnected planetary system. Since 1492, the connections between continents and cultures have increased enormously, of course: it is not *that* we are interconnected that is being highlighted as much as *how*, in an information technology driven era, the compression of time and space means we are connected at far greater speeds than ever before—indeed almost instantaneously. And most dramatically, the complex, interdependent and intercon-

Dr. Alfonso Montuori, is Professor and Department Chair of the Transformative Studies Ph.D. and Transformative Leadership M.A. at California Institute of Integral Studies. In 2003-2004, he was Distinguished Professor in the School of Fine Arts at Miami University, in Oxford Ohio, and in 1985-1986 he taught at the Central South University in Hunan, China. A former professional musician, he is the author of several books and numerous articles on creativity, complexity, and education. Alfonso is also a consultant focusing on creativity and leadership development. He lives in San Francisco with his wife Kitty Margolis, the noted jazz singer, and has co-produced her award-winning recordings.

nected relationship between humans and Nature is in desperate need of revision.

The crisis is forcing a radical reassessment of established economic models—not just the presently dominant neoliberal models, but the very foundations of the global economy, and, arguably, the very worldview of Modernity (Bauman, 2001; Ogilvy, 1989). The environmental crisis is deeply connected to this economic crisis, and the calls for sustainability all point to the fundamental un-sustainability of economic growth along its present lines, driven as it is by lifestyles and values that are founded in lack—in the need to always have more but never be satisfied. What we are witnessing is arguably the end of Modernity, and of late capitalism or Post-modernity (Lyotard, 1984). Ironically, the very engines of progress in Modernity, most notably technology, science, economic growth, and industry have now become sources of the problems we are trying to extricate ourselves from. Tellingly, the talk is of exit-strategies: exit strategies from the environmental crisis, from the war in Iraq, from the economic crisis.

The election of US President Barack Obama on a mandate of hope is tremendously symbolic. In his inaugural address, President Obama pointed out how 60 years earlier, his black father would not even have been allowed to eat in some restaurants in Washington. Obama's election win surprised many, not least civil rights advocates who

could not have imagined 40 years earlier that an African-American man would become President of the United States in their lifetime. Obama's achievement is itself a source of hope, showing that, as Edgar Morin has often said, the unexpected nature of life can also be a source of hope (Morin & Kern, 1999).

In his inaugural speech, the President argued for a new era of responsibility. The United States, and indeed humanity as a whole, should leave "childish things" behind. The clear message is that the world is in a tremendous period of transition. This transition is not going to be an easy one, and we should leave childish selfishness, greed, and the ambition to dominate others behind. Many of the industrial bastions of Modernity in the US—such as the auto and banking industries--are in dire straits. The blows dealt to society by the more Post-Modern phenomenon of computer-assisted financial corruption and the Byzantine complexity of derivatives and other ways of making money from the sizzle rather than the steak have also hit home, with dramatic results. The displays of greed, selfishness, and arrogance in industry and government have been colossal. In truth, perhaps no more than in previous ages. But the sums are bigger, the stakes are higher, and the news gets around the globe in seconds.

Any number of other challenges face humanity—from global terrorism to droughts to human rights to education.

The list is extensive and deeply troubling. If we are leaving one era behind, if we are witnessing the end of Modernity, where we are going is far less clear. The challenge of responsibility is complex: in this paper I explore how this call for responsibility is also a challenge of leadership for the 21st century, and how it is addressed in an educational context in the online Masters Degree in Transformative Leadership offered at the California Institute of Integral Studies (CIIS).

Overview

The Transformative Leadership MA at CIIS was designed to meet the increasing demand for a program that would support and prepare students interested in taking action and making a positive contribution in a rapidly changing world increasingly overwhelmed by social, political, economic, and environmental crises. We found many individuals wanted an opportunity to reflect on the state of the world and their communities, and on their own possibilities and potentials for contributing to addressing pressing issues. Since the start of the program the students have ranged from individuals transitioning in mid-life from a career in the private sector in order to make a contribution to social or environmental justice, to Millennials a few years out of college who want to explore how to address an issue they are passionate about.

Most if not all of these students do not identify with the traditional model of the heroic leader (Western, 2008). In fact, the majority are women. They are searching for new ways to express their desire to take the initiative and develop a leadership role. The program offers an opportunity to spend two years assessing their motivations and capacities, building skills, and most of all, accessing their creativity so that they can both create themselves as leaders in ways that reflect their own unique backgrounds, potentials, and missions, and to create the changes they want to see. Precisely

because our students are mostly what we might call non-traditional leaders, they want to be leaders *in their own way*. They do not resonate with most traditional leadership programs and the discourse of leadership. If anything they are, like most people, sorely disappointed with what generally passes for leadership. The program is designed to prepare individuals who want to lead by mobilizing their own creativity to help shape a more positive future. Students explore their Ways of Being, Doing, Relating, and Knowing, and develop both the conceptual framework and practical skills to engage in a process of self-creation: they create themselves as leaders with a view to contributing to creating a future that goes beyond exit strategies.

The Transformative Leadership MA is designed to address our world in transition (Morin & Kern, 1999; Slater, 2008) through the development of new interpretive frameworks, personal skills, competencies, and practices. The degree also to addresses the transition that the students themselves face entering the program. Generally our students face two types of personal transition. Students in their mid-twenties to early thirties with relatively little experience are still in a fundamental process of self-creation: they feel they want to make a contribution to an issue they are passionate about, and the program offers them an opportunity to assess their own aspirations, skills, assumptions, and beliefs. They learn about how they need to develop in order to be the kind of leader they want to be in the specific context they have chosen. Mid-career professionals, face the challenge of self-re-creation. They may have successful careers in the corporate world or government behind them, and are finding that they now want to immerse themselves in work they are really passionate about.

They know they are capable, they know they can make money, and they now want their mission to become transpersonal. In other words, they seek higher goals, beyond the self. Self-(re-)creation towards these higher goals is a central dimension of Transformative Leadership. Self-creation as a leader offers an opportunity for self-reflection, a deep exploration of our values and goals, at the personal, local, and global level, an awareness and articulation of the context in which we are creating ourselves, and the practices through which we can make this possible.

In an age of transition, one of the key dimensions of leadership education is not just learning but *un*learning. Many of us were brought up with the images of leadership (implicit theories) of Modernity. Even if we wholeheartedly embrace the new vision, and see ourselves as creative leaders of tribes, our implicit assumptions about leadership may still derive from a past age. For example, Pfeffer and Vega research (Pfeffer & Vega, 1999) show that many organizations are still pervaded by "perverse norms," most notably the idea that good leaders and managers are mean and tough and that their work consists mainly of detached analysis (formulation) backed up by muscle (implementation and enforcement), with some charisma thrown in to differentiate the leaders from the managers. Gabriel (2001, p.140) found that organizations are still largely represented as "orderly places where people behave in a rational, business-like way." Strati (1999) has similarly critiqued the discourse of organization theory and management studies as putting forth an ideal type that is fundamentally rational, logical, mental, and deeply disembodied.

If students who are enthused about Transformative Leadership still have implicit theories of leadership that the leader *ultimately* has to be mean and tough (for instance, "when the chips are down"), that organizations should be

> ## The Transformative Leadership MA is designed to address our world in transition through the development of new interpretive frameworks, personal skills, competencies, and practices.

orderly and factory-like, then this will clearly be an obstacle for them as they seek to create alternatives. The vision of themselves as Transformative Leaders may then end up seeming like nothing but "happy talk" with little relation to the "real world." Self-creation therefore involves addressing limiting beliefs about ourselves, about leadership, and about the larger shifts occurring in the world. On a very fundamental level, this means addressing questions about the nature of human nature, about how human beings relate, what motivates us, about what is and is not possible, and the human ability to create and re-create self and world.

The extensive research on creativity offers numerous insights into the process of self-creation. The characteristics of creative individuals can be cultivated (Barron, 1995): independence of judgment, tolerance of ambiguity, and integrative complexity, can be fostered during the coursework, as can an understanding of the nature of the creative process, with its alternating periods of divergence (idea-generation) and convergence (idea-selection) (Montuori, 2006). For instance, intolerance of ambiguity leads to the premature imposition of pre-established solutions to relieve anxiety. The ability to live with that anxiety to produce a potentially more appropriate solution (tolerance of ambiguity) allows for time to explore alternatives. As students work on group projects, it becomes clear when there is a tendency to jump to a decision prematurely to relieve anxiety. This tendency to premature action is particularly common in North American "doing," action-oriented culture: Don't just sit there—do something! (Stewart & Bennett, 1991). Leaders are often tempted to make decisions prematurely. But fostering creativity sometimes requires the opposite approach: Don't just do something—sit there! (and develop a more thoughtful and creative approach). The students' group projects can offer endless opportunities to reflect on and develop a creative attitude. The process of developing this creative attitude to work and self is a large part of the process of self-creation.

Students also receive a 360 feedback, coupled with a number of leadership and personality assessments. The combination of the assessments and the feedback from 8 or so colleagues about decision-making style, ability to handle stress, team work, and other leadership dimensions, provides a rich picture of areas requiring development. Along with this assessment, students write their autobiography from the perspective of age 80. They are invited to think creatively about what they would like to do with their lives, what contribution they want to make, and specifically how they intend to apply their work in the program. This is a playful step towards exploring possibilities they might otherwise not have considered, engaging their creativity and applying it to their own lives, and beginning the process of aligning their own abilities and contributions with their desired goals. Students are encouraged to Think Globally *and* Locally, and to Act Globally *and* Locally. The local and the global are inextricably intertwined (Morin & Kern, 1999).

Reinventing Leadership

For our purposes here I will begin my discussion of leadership very simply by asking, Who can be a leader? A brief review of the history of the world's great leaders shows that widely recognized celebrated as well as despised leaders have been overwhelmingly male representatives of the dominant culture,

In an age of transition, one of the key dimensions of leadership education is not just learning but *un*learning.

embodying characteristics that can be summarized (but are of course not limited to) the "heroic" model. It is becoming increasingly apparent that leaders are now emerging from traditionally under-represented groups, such as women and "minorities." President Obama is perhaps the most dramatic case in point. In the global "social imaginary" there is now an African-American President of the United States. This does not mean that leadership opportunities have now opened up to everybody. It does signal the beginning of a tremendous shift towards greater openness towards traditionally under-represented groups in leadership roles.

But the shift in the "who" of leadership extends in other areas: it is not confined to the position of arguably the most powerful man in the world. As an example, the Goldman Environmental Prize is handed out every year to individuals described as "grassroots environmentalists" from all over the world who have made a considerable and often courageous contribution to protecting the environment. The winners are not individuals who strike one as "heroic leaders" in the dramatic General Patton mold. They are not great warlike leaders, orchestrating armies of soldiers or engineering corporate take-overs. They are ordinary men and women who prove they are also quite *extra*-ordinary when circumstances require.

These individuals *are* heroic in the sense that they often take on multinationals or governments or both. They are involved in struggles against deforestation, privatization of water supplies and other projects that affect the well-being of their communities or involve the destruction of nature. One of these leaders and Goldman Prize recipients, Ken Saro-Wiwa of Nigeria, was hanged by a corrupt government on trumped up charges because his work put multi-million dollar deals at risk. The Goldman Prize winners are not individuals who had ambitions to be CEOs, generals, or elected officials. They did not see themselves in the traditional mold as "leaders of men." They simply responded passionately and thoughtfully to what they perceived to be an outrage. They felt they had to do something beyond their own personal survival and well-being. They became leaders because they felt they had to develop a coalition of people to fight injustice.

The message is clear. The "who" of leadership has changed: if leadership is about making a contribution to the global transition, making a contribution by taking the initiative, then the field is wide open. And as members of traditionally underrepresented groups become leaders, we can safely say that the concept of leadership will be irrigated by new streams of creativity and culture, new perspectives and potentials. Eventually it will not be the case that now underrepresented groups can also join the leadership club and play the game. The very definition of leadership, the rules of game themselves, will be changed, and are already changing.

The "who" of leadership also ties in directly with a central concern of the Transformative Leadership program: *self-creation*. The assumption is not that leadership is a fixed characteristic one either has or doesn't have. In an era of transition, there are few certainties, and great opportunities for creativity. We are not bound by fixed roles or destinies. It is possible to *create* oneself as a person, and as a leader. We can tap into, as President Obama wrote in a 2005 essay, "a larger, fundamental element of American life — the enduring belief that we can constantly remake ourselves to fit our larger dreams" (Obama, 2005). In an era of transition, we need to dream a new world together, and Transformative Leadership requires the creativity both to dream and to make our dreams a reality.

Tribes and Factories

Seth Godin's little book *Tribes* provides us with two useful images that can orient us to the emerging understanding of leadership (Godin, 2009). His argument is that we are moving out of the age of the Factory and are now in an age of Tribes. "A tribe," he writes, "is a group of people connected to one another, connected to a leader, and connected to an idea" (p.1). The term tribe might strike one as amorphous, as "pre-modern" as the word "factory" seems quintessentially "modern." The crucial difference now is in the word "connected." The new social media have connected individuals all across the globe. Whereas in pre-modern times a tribe was a local phenomenon strongly defined by physical proximity, it is now possible to be part of a planetary tribe—whether fans of some obscure indie band, coming together to support earthquake victims in Abruzzo, or, in the shadow side of this phenomenon, a terrorist organization

like Al-Qaida. And tribes are not only the most important new form of social organization and social change, they also drastically change the who, what, where, and how of leadership.

Factories are large, hierarchical, unwieldy, inflexible, and generally not prone to innovation. In a factory, leadership is confined to a few. Command and control are the central features of leadership in factories. Factories are like armies. But as we have seen, the US army defeated the Iraqi army in a matter of days, but that was hardly "Mission Accomplished." A distributed network of terrorists living all over the world cannot be defeated by an army in a head-on battlefield confrontation. It is not a hostile nation in the traditional sense. The 7/7 bombers in London were actually living in England, and the 9/11 bombers were living in the US. They were "a group of people connected to one another, connected to a leader, and connected to an idea."

Tribes are networked, flexible, and heterarchical, allowing leadership to emerge a plurality of sources (Ogilvy, 1989; Taylor, 2003). In fact, if in the Modern factory world there was only one leader, in the world of Tribes, everybody can be a leader, and that is Godin's point. That is also the foundation for the Transformative Leadership program. The democratization of leadership is becoming an increasingly mainstream perspective. Joseph Nye (2008) of the Kennedy School of Government at Harvard sums it up this way:

> Almost anyone can become a leader. Leadership can be learned. It depends on nurture as well as nature. Leadership can exist at any level, with or without formal authority. Most people are both leaders and followers. They "lead from the middle." (p. 147)

A far cry from the heroic, "great man" leadership picture, the captain of industry, Jack Welch, General Patton, Napoleon, and the classic figures associated with leadership, or even the nerdie but no less commanding figures of Bill Gates and Steve Jobs.

Leadership Jazz

One might compare a factory and a tribe to a symphony orchestra and a jazz ensemble respectively. In the symphony

orchestra, the score is already written, and the musicians know their parts. They also know not to deviate from them. When they are featured during a particular passage, such as the flute part in Debussy's *Prélude à l'après-midi d'un faune*, they still play the written notes. The hierarchy is very clear, and starts with the composer, to the conductor, the soloist, the first violin, and so on.

In a jazz ensemble, the key to the performance is improvisation on a song's theme/chord progression. Improvisation is central to the art of being a good jazz musician (Berliner, 1994). This means that there is a framework, provided by the song and the overall way the song is interpreted by the ensemble (as a ballad, up-tempo, medium swing), and the real challenge is to make the journey from a to b, from beginning to end of the song, interesting.

If the symphony orchestra was a dramatic expression of the creativity of modernity, traceable to the lone genius composer, and isomorphic to the industrial factory, the jazz ensemble is in many ways isomorphic to tribes, virtual teams, and the collaborative, networked creativity of an emerging age (Attali, 1985; Montuori, 2003). In the symphony, the main source of creativity lies outside the orchestra, with the individual composer. In the jazz ensemble creativity is an emergent property of the interaction of the musicians, their environment, and the composition they are performing. The degree of *discretion* accorded the individual jazz musicians is much greater than that of classical musicians, as they each get to improvise and make their own contribution to the piece. This also increases the degree of self-expression that is possible in a jazz context. Particularly interesting is the role of leadership. A jazz group may be led by one, or two or more individuals, and it can also be a collective. During performance, it is typical for every individual band-member to take one or more solos. During that time, the soloist leads, and guides the band in her or his direction, within the larger context of the leader's vision. The genius of certain jazz band leaders like Miles Davis or Duke Ellington was precisely that they knew their musicians well, and created an environment in which both individuals and the collective would shine (Crouch, 2007). If in the factory/symphony organization creativity is with the "man at the top," in the tribe/jazz, creativity is an emergent property of the interaction between the members/players.

The Davis/Ellington style of leadership involves a particularly important feature: the emphasis on creating a system (a band) that allows the musicians to thrive and achieve their highest potential, in function of the band as a whole. The system supports the individuals who support the system in a virtuous cycle, rather than the more typical vicious cycle where the system drains the individual, and the individual's growth and direction are not aligned with the system ("I need to do my solo album to express myself!") Particularly in the Miles Davis quintet of the early sixties, we find Davis putting together a team that, under his mentorship, explored new directions in music (Chambers, 1998). Davis did not know where the band would lead him, but he had parameters and carefully selected the members of his now classic quintet. Tenor sax player Wayne Shorter wrote many compositions that became classics of the jazz repertoire, and gave the band a sound and a direction. This is significant because while Miles was unquestionably the band leader, the band's tremendous innovation emerged because he managed to give the band members a great deal of discretion, and encouraged the spontaneous emergence of new material by insisting that the band practice on stage. In other words, he explicitly wanted the musicians to take enormous risks, to stretch and explore in front of an audience. The band was essentially a self-organizing system (Borgo, 2006). Davis did not tell

the band members what to do so much as what *not* to do.

But was Miles Davis simply a facilitator, using "soft power?" A close assessment of his leadership style shows that he did give enormous discretion, but he also had the final say on the band's direction. He did not stand by and let the band go in any direction they wanted. Even though he did not tell the band what to do, he set clear parameters by telling the band what he did *not* like, and that created parameters in the form of an aesthetic sensibility (Chambers, 1998).

The Miles Davis example highlights some important features of transforma-

Photo: Graham Harvey

tive leadership: 1) He created a generative environment that allowed the individual band members to blossom; 2) he stressed the importance of the interaction between the individuals, their roles and relations in the band, to create a unique combination; 3) he combined his nurturing, supportive work in "growing" the musicians, but his was no "laissez faire" leadership: he used smart power in a very subtle way, never making a big deal out of it, but at the same time clearly establishing ground rules and criteria for the journey. Not a map with a clear, predetermined outcome, but guidelines for an improvisational journey.

We can learn from Miles Davis, and his example offers a new set of choices for leaders. But there is no hard and fast

rule that these are the "ingredients" of Transformative Leadership. As Nye suggests, a leader must be able to combine "soft power," which is more facilitative, and "hard power," which is more directive. What we can say, though, is that Davis displayed both *emotional intelligence* (Goleman, 2000), through his self-awareness and his understanding of his own role as a leader, and *contextual intelligence* (Nye, 2008), as he understood the dynamics of his group, of the culture of jazz, and the larger societal changes in the shift from the 50s to the 60s, most notably when, in the mid-60s, he incorporated rock and psychedelic elements in his music, starting with controversial recordings such as *In A Silent Way* and *Bitches Brew*. These recordings were very risky because they alienated the hard-core straight-ahead acoustic jazz fans, but also created an entirely new, and younger audience that listened to Jimi Hendrix and the Grateful Dead. Bob Dylan made a similar, and equally controversial transition when he started working with an electric group (The Band), at the Newport Folk Festival on Sunday July 25, 1965. Like Davis, he was initially seen as a traitor to the music. Ultimately his vision prevailed, and folk music took a back seat and became marginalized in popular music.

Traditionally, most of the metaphors for leadership and organization have come from the military and from machines. Transformative Leadership explores the immensely generative potential in metaphors and exemplars from the arts, which often provide a radically different perspective. Particularly since creativity is such a central dimension of Transformative Leadership—in the creation of self, vision, relationships, implementation, and more—metaphors and examples from the arts are instructive and illuminating in ways that machine metaphors simply cannot be, because a machine performs a function, but is not in and of itself creative: the creativity resides in the creator of the machine.

Transdisciplinarity, and the Construction of Leadership

Leadership is now an established area of study, with departments and degrees. The literature on leadership is extensive, confusing and often contradictory (Maccoby, 2001; Rost, 1993). Bennis and Nanus (Bennis & Nanus, 1985) wrote that

A remarkable number of empirical investigations of leaders have been conducted in the last seventy-five years alone, but no clear and unequivocal understanding exists as to what distinguishes leaders from nonleaders, and perhaps more important, what distinguishes effective leaders from ineffective leaders. (p.4)

Not very much has changed in the last 25 years (Western, 2008). One of the reasons why there is so much confusion about what constitutes leadership is because, as I have already argued, we are moving out of one era and into a new era (Montuori, 1989; Montuori & Conti, 1993; Morin & Kern, 1999; Slater, 2008). In this transitional period, we see the demise of one form of leadership and the birth of new forms of leadership (Wren, 2007). The underlying transdisciplinary philosophical assumptions of Transformative Leadership draw extensively on process-relational and cybernetic and complexity-based ways of thinking. The four central assumptions are that Leadership is Constructed, Contextual/Relational, Emergent, and Paradoxical.

Leadership is Constructed. An overview of the research and of the history of the concept of leadership shows that it *constructed* (Ospina & Sorenson, 2006). By this I mean that there is no univocal timeless understanding of what constitutes leadership. Different times and cultures have different understandings of what leadership means, and of what constitutes good leadership (Bennis &

Nanus, 1985). Likewise, we see individuals as capable of constructing their own unique leadership philosophy and style. There is no "essence" of leadership, and leadership can indeed be learned (Nye, 2008). Construction is a creative process, and the challenge of leadership in the 21st century is therefore framed essentially as a creative one.

Leadership is Contextual-Relational. Leadership is not merely the function of the characteristics of a lone individual, but occurs in, and in fact arguably can be said to be, a network of interactions in a context. A leader can be a nexus, a systemic attractor, a catalyst, a facilitator, a leader can push and pull, but always in the context of a set of relationships, and these are by no means simply defined in the mode of instrumental transactional, tit-for-tat relations. The relationship between leaders and followers is not just mutually constitutive. The whole frame of leader and follower is problematized. Increasingly, for better or worse, in the age of the opinion poll, the leaders follow the followers—or their perception of the "followers."

Leadership is an Emergent Process. Leadership emerges through a process of interactions, with unpredictable, holistic, systemic properties and qualities. The whole that emerges—actions by leaders and followers in context—can be more than the sum of its parts, but it can also be less than the sum of its parts. The role of *organization* is key in this process (Morin, 2008a). The organization of interactions is always confronted with the dialogic of Order and Disorder. Too much order and the system becomes ossified, inflexible and incapable of change. Too much disorder and the system descends into utter chaos. Creativity can emerge as we navigate the edge of chaos. Transformative Leadership involves the ability to recognize, catalyze, and wisely inform this process of navigation. The Transformative Leader organizes the emergent relationships in a specific tribe, and may, like Miles Davis, focus on creating a tribe that is itself not simply a collection of followers but a generative, creative environment.

Leadership is Paradoxical. Transformative leaders combine "soft" and "hard" power, emotional intelligence and analytical intelligence, "hard" (orga-

nizational, task) and "soft" ("people") skills. They can lead but also follow, inspire but also listen, be decisive but also reflective. In more traditional ways of thinking we are often impaled on the horns of either/or thinking, whether in decision-making or in our self-creation as leaders, choosing either hard or soft, decisive or reflective. Transformative leaders must develop the ability to embrace paradox, where paradox refers to going beyond accepted ways and drawing on a wider spectrum of choices which may include combining what has traditionally been viewed as opposed (either/or) (Hampden-Turner, 1999; Hampden-Turner & Trompenaars, 2001; Handy, 1994; Low, 2008).

Another reason why leadership is a contested and somewhat confused term is *disciplinary fragmentation*. There are leadership studies grounded in management, political theory, education, psychology, sociology, history among others. But there is little or no consensus, and certainly no grand unifying theory (Goethals & Sorenson, 2006).

The fact that leadership has been studied from the perspective of different disciplines is itself of course not problematic. Leaders have come from the ranks of politicians, businesspersons, social activists, and so on, and it should not surprise us that they are therefore studied in the disciplines that traditionally study politics, business, and social change. But it does leave the field as a whole, as well as the student and practitioner, in a difficult position because there is a lack of coherence and integration in this proliferation of information.

Leadership has been described as inherently multidisciplinary (Wren, 2006) precisely because it draws on so many already existing disciplines. The problem with multidisciplinarity is that it is essentially a recognition that a plurality of disciplines address and contribute to our understanding of a particular topic. But there is no specific effort to integrate that knowledge, and there are usually no criteria to do so. Transdisciplinarity (Montuori, 2005; Morin, 2008b; Nicolescu, 2002, 2008) offers another approach that may be very useful for practitioners as well as researchers. A transdisciplinary approach can be summarized as approaching leadership through the following four dimensions (Montuori, 2005).

Inquiry-Driven vs. Discipline Driven

Transdisciplinarity is about the relationship between inquiry and action in the world. Action involves the embodiment and enaction of values in a context. It requires pertinent knowledge for those tasks and the assessment of tasks, goals, and for self-assessment. With the enormous quantity of research and literature on leadership and just about any conceivable topic, we are living in an information glut. The real challenges are the organization of knowledge so that it is pertinent to the leader's task (Morin, 2001, 2008a). This does not mean that leadership education should be narrowly defined by a specific task. There should be a balance between general knowledge and specific knowledge. In the Transformative Leadership program an attempt is made to achieve this balance by offering broad overview material in the courses, and also allowing room for students to bring in their own perspectives and issues, drawing on their own leadership context. Specific readings can then be suggested that address the contexts and issues the students are facing. An exclusive focus on specific knowledge can lead to a limited, partial, and limiting education that may not be pertinent if, as is always likely, circumstances change. An excessive focus on general knowledge means the student's experience, aspirations, and context cannot be addressed, in an effort to give an exhaustive overview of the literature without addressing its relevance to the student. We can also not assume that the student is aware of exactly what s/he needs to know now or a few years down the road. And although we should also not assume that the faculty knows exactly what is required, their task is assist students in navigating the specific and the general.

Meta-paradigmatic vs. Intra-Paradigmatic

There are many approaches to leading. In the popular literature we find everything from *Leadership Secrets of Attila the Hun* to *The Leadership Lessons of Jesus*. In academia, there are numerous different schools of thought: trait-based, psychodynamic, behavioral, relational, contingency, transformational, and more (Northouse, 2004; Western, 2008). Each of these schools is informed by an underlying set of assumptions. In the case of popular leadership works on Attila the Hun and Jesus we might have a pretty good idea of what their underlying assumptions are. In the more academic literature, some schools of thought emphasize the traits of the leader, others the behaviors, psychological, organizational, and historical dimensions and so on. We do not assume that students should develop an exhaustive knowledge of this literature: they are not leadership *researchers*. They are here to be leaders. The program's focus therefore is on having students understand the underlying assumptions that inform the various theoretical perspectives, as well as their own underlying assumptions about leadership and how they inform their thinking and action.

Whether we are aware of it or not, we all have "implicit theories" of leadership (Betts, Morgan, & Castiglia, 2008; Epitropaki & Martin, 2004). These are the theories we hold, often unconsciously, about what a leader is and should "really" be like. Growing up in a world where the vast majority of leaders are men and there are still many increasingly obsolete and dysfunctional assumptions about leaders (the "heroic," strong man image also promoted by the media), it's essential for aspiring leaders to understand the extent to which the popular images of leadership have shaped their own beliefs and assumptions. Most often we find that the implicit theories of leadership are quite limiting, because there is a certain media-supported mythology about the characteristics of leaders that still draws on a "charismatic" view, where charismatic is understood in the etymological sense of being a gift. In the same way that creativity is often thought of as a gift, we often speak of leaders being born not made, by which we mean that they exhibit the characteristics Modernity has associated with leadership. This view precludes the possibility of self-creation and learning for individuals who do not identify themselves as "born" leaders.

Meta-paradigmatic is therefore an admittedly cumbersome word to indicate that the student is not operating exclusively from within one particular paradigm, one school of thought (intra-paradigmatic), and a particular set of implicit theories of leadership, but understands the plurality of ways in which the topic can be shaped by theory, and the importance of understanding the key assumptions underlying those theories. They can range from assumptions about the nature of human nature, the way humans relate, and human possibilities (Theory X and Theory Y in the management literature are a very clear example) to assumptions about the nature of knowledge, the role of the leader, and so on. Students explore their own assumptions and dialogue with the literature and their own experience to challenge the assumptions, and in the process articulate a more coherent and well thought-out leadership philosophy.

Complex/Cybernetic vs. Reductive/Disjunctive Thought

There is little doubt that in the 20th century, the world has become dramatically interconnected and networked. The emergence of systems/cybernetic approach, and later chaos and complexity theories (Capra, 1996), reflects an awareness both in the natural and social sciences that analytic/reductionist ways of thinking must be supplemented with ways to understand processes, interaction, wholes and connect the information that has been generated in different disciplines. A way of knowing that is premised on simplicity and breaking a system down into its component parts cannot effectively address the complexities of 21st century networked society (Castells, 2000). A complex/cybernetic approach also proposes, in brief, that what we call knowledge is not a mirror of the world, but always a creative construction. The stress is on knowing as a creative process, one that can generate a number of (almost endless) different interpretations of a situation, and recognizes the nature of circular, recursive processes and the process-relational nature of systems. Approaching our very understanding of the world as a creation itself puts creativity center stage in life and leadership.

Embedded and Embodied Inquirer vs. External Observer

In recent years the concept of Emotional Intelligence has made substantial inroads into the discourse and practices of leadership (Goleman, 2000; Goleman, McKee, & Boyatzis, 2002). A transdisciplinary approach puts the experience of the leader center stage, stressing the importance of self-creation and inquiry for leaders. Developing Emotional Intelligence is one dimension of this process of self-creation. The leader/inquirer is an active participant in the process of knowledge-creation, and in action in the world. Every aspect of the person's experience plays a part in the processes of leadership and inquiry, and becomes an avenue for self-inquiry, self-understanding, and self-creation: in other words, Transformative Leadership cannot be separated from a journey of personal growth.

Self-Creation: Being/Knowing/Relating/Doing

There are four central dimensions of self-creation in the Transformative Leadership curriculum: Ways of Being, Ways of Knowing, Ways of Relating, and Ways of Doing. These dimensions are used to highlight key areas of potential self-creation, and also learning and unlearning.

1) *Ways of Being*. We begin with the overall view of the person as capable of self-re-creating as a Transformative Leader. Leadership is not viewed as something one either has or not, and in a larger sense human beings are viewed not as things with fixed essences but as ongoing relational creative process (Barron, 1999; Fay, 1996). This recognition of the processual nature of being can be amplified and embodied through the cultivation of a creative attitude. This includes, among other things, overcoming personal limiting beliefs and societal myths about creativity (Montuori & Purser, 1995; Montuori & Purser, 1999), as well as the development of the skills and competencies drawn from creativity research and articulated above for personal self-creation. A central assumption of the Transformative Leadership program is that human beings are fundamentally creative. Indeed, there is mounting research suggesting that the universe itself is an ongoing creative process (Kauffman, 2008). For our purposes, suffice it to say that we see Trans-

formative Leadership as involving creative persons, processes, products and environments. Creativity in the world involves means creating something new, making an original contribution to one's community or society, and taking a leadership role in the articulation, promotion, and implementation of this contribution.

Students come to the program to engage in a 2 year exploration of their values, beliefs, assumptions, of their very identity, and of the way they act in the world. The program offers them an opportunity to self-re-create, to apply their own creativity to themselves, and create the person and leader they want to be in the context(s) they have chosen. The program's capstone also makes their culminating project a contribution in the world—not a business plan or a case study, not a statement of leadership philosophy, but a leadership project in the world.

2) *Ways of Knowing*. How do we know what we know? It's no mystery that different people see the world differently, depending on such factors as their

us: in other words, we don't think of it as "a way of thinking," but just as thinking—or more broadly, "knowing." In order to understand something we break it down into its component parts, and we have a dominant logic of either/or. The key to this way of thinking is simplicity, clarity, and certainty. Unfortunately, life is not like that. Most of the things about life that are interesting are neither simple, certain nor particularly clear. Whether it's an election, a love affair, a ball game, a movie, or leadership in any way, shape, or form, complexity, ambiguity, and uncertainty are central.

The Transformative Leadership program focuses on the development of a way of knowing grounded in complex thought. This way of thinking is designed to face the challenges of leadership. These include at times overwhelming complexity, the inescapable uncertainty of life, and the importance of understanding every issue in its context and network of relationships.

Transformative Leaders need to understand complex, interconnected

Self-creation as a leader offers an opportunity for self-reflection, a deep exploration of our values and goals, at the personal, local, and global level, an awareness and articulation of the context in which we are creating ourselves, and the practices through which we can make this possible.

education, background, interest, gender, age, and so on. A trained musician hears a piece of music differently from a person without training, and this can actually be reflected in the person's brain: the trained musician uses both hemispheres, the lay person only the right or non-dominant hemisphere (Springer & Deutsch, 1985).

The reductive/disjunctive way of thinking is so widely accepted that it has become almost entirely transparent to

phenomena, and also generate visions of alternative, desirable futures. This means drawing more broadly on the imagination, a sense of what could be as well as an assessment of what is. Education for creativity involves the cultivation of such characteristics as independence of judgment, tolerance of ambiguity, and problem-finding as well as problem-solving (Barron, 1988; Springer & Deutsch, 1985). It also involves "metacognition," or the ability to reflect on one's thinking and one's framing of any particular situation.

In their study of Ways of Knowing Transformative Leaders explore systemic/cybernetic epistemology and creative thinking, in the context of leading in a digital, networked society. There are many ways of knowing beyond the traditional rational/analytical style that are typically (and erroneously thought of as exclusively) associated w/academia and with organizational life (Quinn, 1988). At the same time it is important not to polarize between rational and other ways of knowing, or to dismiss traditional approaches and romanticize intuition and creativity (Montuori, 2006). Transformative leaders need to integrate a plurality of ways of knowing and learn how to utilize them synergetically rather than hold them oppositionally.

3) One of the most central and constitutive assumptions informing leaders and leadership choices today pertains to the fundamental way human beings relate to each other. This is a question with deep philosophical roots, and highly practical implications. As we saw in Pfeffer's research, for instance, "perverse norms" still thrive in many organizations, based on the assumption that one must be tough, and control others. This is what Eisler calls a paradigm of domination (Eisler, 1987; Eisler & Montuori, 2001). Traditionally the underlying assumption of most of humanity's ways of relating is that we live in a world of domination or submission. These represent the two alternatives in any relationship. Leadership has traditionally been viewed through this "dominator" lens. The leader is the dominant (and often domineering) figure, and followers are submissive. Increasingly, leadership is not about domination any more, but about partnership. Not about having power *over* others, but power *with* others, in order to achieve mutually agreed on goals. Leadership these days is very much a process of collaborative creativity. Rather than having centralized, top-down leadership, transformative leadership offers a plurality of possibilities, and information flow that does not only go from the top down. Transformative leadership involves creating contexts in which people can be creative and draw on all their talents, in the context of the

task at hand. Google founder Sergey Brin tracked the success rate of ideas that came from them versus ideas that had come up through the ranks, and found that the latter had a higher success rate. Leadership therefore is about fostering this creativity, and aligning the aims of the larger mission and task with the capacities and passions of the individuals.

Eisler's work differentiating between domination and partnership systems provides one useful framework to expand both the discourse and practices of ways of relating (Eisler, 1987; Eisler & Montuori, 2001). It also presents a challenge, because new ways of relating must be *created* to counteract the prevailing ways of relating based on domination. Developing alternatives to domination systems is not easy. If the idea of "partnership" or other approaches that reject the assumption that human relations must be based on domination or submission is appealing, putting it into practice is a very dif-

and praxis. By this we also mean the exploration of the *implicit* theories of what the students already do and believe. One's actions are a reflections of beliefs, whether explicit or implicit. In a transitional era such as ours, many of the old images of "heroic" leadership are patently out of date. And yet we find in our work with students that in popular culture, in our imagination and belief systems, in the basic choices and modalities of leadership and in the behaviors displayed that these images of heroic leadership have not died. In these early stages, lacking a wide range of alternative models and constant reinforcement that leadership can be different, it is no surprise that the old images persist. Our students are therefore invited to explore their implicit assumptions about leadership, and these often come out most clearly when they are asked to do a project. The extremes range from the falling back to the heroic model, the "OK, I'm in charge now" boss-model,

Transformative leadership involves creating contexts in which people can be creative and draw on all their talents

ferent thing. The tendency is to fall into dualistic, oppositional thinking, much like in the case of the exploration of alternative ways of knowing. Anything associated with domination systems is rejected in favor of its opposite: If domination systems have strong leadership, the assumption is partnership systems will be leaderless, and likewise, free of disagreement, conflict, and competition (Montuori & Conti, 1995). This of course is a recipe for inaction, as well as a profound "error in thinking" that prevents the development of alternatives. This leads us back to the importance of developing capacious—and cybernetic—ways of thinking that can account for processes, and navigation between oppositions. It also shows how Ways of Being, Knowing, and Relating are fundamentally interconnected.

4) Leaders *act*. They do not just reflect or ponder or relate. Integral to the Transformative leadership program is the constant interrelationship between theory

to the tendency not to be at all directive, assuming that the alternative to the heroic model is the exact opposite, a complete laissez-faire, "non-leadership leadership," which of course tends to lead to chaos and confusion. The challenge of self-creation is to create not only one's Way of Being but also a Way of Doing that reflects the Transformative Leader's values and beliefs. The culminating capstone project is the most obvious way in which the program addresses this "Doing" dimension, but it should be noted that throughout the program students are always "doing"—there's simply no escaping from it. Whether it's working in class, collaborating with classmates, applying their learning in the workplace, or developing a new project, the interrelationship between theory and practice is always there. Most obviously when there's an attempt to implement a new idea or perspective, and most subtly and perhaps imperceptibly when our every action reveals a theoretical foundation which may well be implicit: we may act on beliefs we did not consciously know we had, and the excavation and exposure of these implicit assumptions and beliefs offers a tremendous opportunity for learning about ourselves.

In academic contexts "Doing" is all too often associated exclusively with academic output. As valid as the latter can be, in an educational program designed for leaders, we have felt it essential to incorporate an ongoing process of integrating the students' learning in the context of their workplace or action site. Central to this is the development of a culminating project, an action capstone where the fundamental requirement is the creation of a project in the world. The first part of the capstone, in the third semester, is a course in which students articulate their leadership philosophy, and then give and receive a 360 feedback process. The 360 feedback gives them a reality check and allows them to assess the extent to which others perceive their actions as matching their stated leadership philosophy. In the second part of the capstone, in the final semester, one of the ways the action capstone is judged is by the way the students have taken to heart the feedback from the 360, applied it in a way that is reflect in their handling of the capstone, and also thereby the extent to which they have been true to the leadership philosophy they articulated. It could be argued that the ultimate goal here is to develop wisdom-in-action.

Today, leadership is not a role confined to a few chosen individuals. Every one of us can be a leader, and increasingly individuals who want to contribute to creating a new world built on the ashes of Modernity feel they must take action. In Modernity many of our students would not have dared to consider themselves leaders, or belonged to a group that was simply not permitted to take leadership roles. Today the very concept of leadership is being transformed by a broader participation, and a wider definition of the who, what, where, and how of leadership. The Transformative Leadership MA at the California Institute of Integral Studies has accepted the challenge to prepare these leaders as they engage the new world, shedding the prejudices of the old world while incorporating the

best of what has come before us. The challenge is considerable, but the power of human collective creativity is even greater.

References

Attali, J. (1985). *Noise: The political economy of music.* Minneapolis: University of Minnesota Press.

Barron, F. (1988). Putting creativity to work. In R. Sternberg (Ed.), *The nature of creativity.* Cambridge: Cambridge University Press.

Barron, F. (1995). *No rootless flower: towards an ecology of creativity.* Cresskill, NJ: Hampton Press.

Barron, F. (1999). All creation is a collaboration. In A. Montuori & R. Purser (Eds.), *Social Creativity* (Vol. 1, pp. 49-60). Cresskill, NJ: Hampton.

Bauman, Z. (2001). *The individualized society.* Malden, MA: Polity Press.

Bennis, W., & Nanus, B. (1985). *Leaders: The strategies for taking charge.* New York: Harper.

Berliner, P. F. (1994). *Thinking in jazz: The infinite art of improvisation.* Chicago: University of Chicago Press.

Betts, S. C., Morgan, W., & Castiglia, B. (2008). Paper presented at the Proceedings of the Academy of Organizational Culture, Communications and Conflict.

Borgo, D. (2006). *Sync or Swarm: Improvising Music in a Complex Age.* London: Continuum.

Capra, F. (1996). *The web of life.* New York: Anchor.

Castells, M. (2000). *The Rise of the Network Society (New Edition) (The Information Age: Economy, Society and Culture Volume 1).* New York: Wiley-Blackwell.

Chambers, J. (1998). *Milestones: The Music And Times Of Miles Davis.* Cambridge, MA: Da Capo.

Crouch, S. (2007). *Considering Genius: Writings on Jazz.* New York: Basic Civitas Books.

Eisler, R. (1987). *The chalice and the blade.* San Francisco: Harper Collins.

Eisler, R., & Montuori, A. (2001). The partnership organization. *OD Practitioner, 33*(1), 11-17.

Epitropaki, O., & Martin, R. (2004). Implicit leadership theories in applied settings: Factor structure, generalizability, and stability over time. *Journal of Applied Psychology, 89*(2), 293-310.

Fay, B. (1996). *Contemporary philosophy of social science.* New York: Blackwell Publishers.

Godin, S. (2009). *Tribes. We need you to lead us.* New York: Portfolio.

Goethals, G. R., & Sorenson, G. L. J. (Eds.). (2006). *The quest for a general theory of leadership.* Northhampton, MA: Edward Elgar.

Goleman, D. (2000). Leadership that gets results. *Harvard Business Review.*

Goleman, D., McKee, A., & Boyatzis, R. E. (2002). *Primal leadership: Realizing the power of emotional intelligence.* New York: Harvard University Business Press.

Hampden-Turner, C. (1999). Control, chaos, control: A cybernetic view of creativity. In R. Purser & A. Montuori (Eds.), *Social Creativity, Volume 2* (Vol. 2). Cresskill, NJ: Hampton Press.

Hampden-Turner, C., & Trompenaars, A. (2001).

Building cross-cultural competence: How to create wealth from conflicting values. New Haven, CT: Wiley.

Handy, C. (1994). *The age of paradox.* Boston: Harvard Business School Press.

Kauffman, S. A. (2008). *Reinventing the sacred. A new view of science, reason, and the sacred.* New York: Basic Books.

Low, A. (2008). *Conflict and creativity at work. Human roots of corporate life.* Brighton and Portland: Sussex Academic.

Lyotard, J.-F. (1984). *The postmodern condition: A report on knowledge.* Manchester: Manchester University Press.

Maccoby, M. (2001). Making sense of the leadership literature. *Research-Technology Management, 44*(5), 58-60.

Montuori, A. (1989). *Evolutionary competence: Creating the future.* Amsterdam: Gieben.

Montuori, A. (2003). The complexity of improvisation and the improvisation of complexity. Social science, art, and creativity. *Human Relations, 56*(2), 237-255.

Montuori, A. (2005). Gregory Bateson and the challenge of transdisciplinarity. *Cybernetics and Human Knowing, 12*(1-2), 147-158(112).

Montuori, A. (2006). The quest for a new education: From oppositional identities to creative inquiry. *ReVision, 28*(3), 4-20.

Montuori, A., & Conti, I. (1993). *From power to partnership. Creating the future of love, work, and community.* San Francisco: Harper San Francisco.

Montuori, A., & Conti, I. (1995). The meaning of Partnership. *Vision/Action*(Winter), 7-10.

Montuori, A., & Purser, R. (1995). Deconstructing the lone genius myth: Towards a contextual view of creativity. *Journal of Humanistic Psychology, 35*(3), 69-112.

Montuori, A., & Purser, R. E. (Eds.). (1999). *Social Creativity* (Vol. 1). Cresskill, NJ: Hampton Press.

Morin, E. (2001). *Seven complex lessons in education for the future.* Paris: UNESCO.

Morin, E. (2008a). *On complexity.* Cresskill, NJ: Hampton Press.

Morin, E. (2008b). The reform of thought, transdisciplinarity, and the reform of the university. In B. Nicolescu (Ed.), *Transdisciplinarity. Theory and practice* (pp. 23-32). Cresskill, NJ: Hampton Press.

Morin, E., & Kern, B. (1999). *Homeland Earth: A manifesto for the new millennium.* Cresskill, NJ: Hampton Press.

Nicolescu, B. (2002). *Manifesto of transdisciplinarity.* Albany: SUNY Press.

Nicolescu, B. (Ed.). (2008). *Transdisciplinarity. Theory and practice.* Cresskill, NJ: Hampton Press.

Nisbett, R. E. (2003). *The geography of thought: How Asians and Westerners think differently... and why.* New York: Simon and Schuster.

Northouse, P. G. (2004). *Leadership. Theory and practice.* Thousand Oaks Sage.

Nye, J. S. (2008). *The powers to lead.* New York: Oxford University Press.

Obama, B. (2005, June 26). What I see in Lincoln's eyes. *Time.*

Ogilvy, J. (1989). This postmodern business. *The Deeper News, 1*(5), 3-23.

Ospina, S., & Sorenson, G. L. J. (2006). A constructionist lens on leadership: charting new territory. In G. R. Goethals & G. L. J. Sorenson (Eds.), (pp. 188-204). Northampton, MA: Edward Elgar.

Pfeffer, J., & Vega, J. F. (1999). Putting people first for organizational success. *Academy of Management Executive, 13*(2), 37-45.

Quinn, R. (1988). *Beyond rational management*. San Francisco: Jossey-Bass.

Rost, J. C. (1993). *Leadership for the twenty-first century*. Westport, CT: Praeger.

Slater, P. (2008). *The chrysalis effect*. Brighton & Portland: Sussex Academic.

Springer, S. P., & Deutsch, G. (1985). *Left brain, right brain*. New York: W.H. Freeman.

Stewart, E. C., & Bennett, M. J. (1991). *American cultural patterns*. Dartmouth: Intercultural Press.

Taylor, M. (2003). *The moment of complexity. Emerging network culture*. Chicago: University of Chicago Press.

Western, S. (2008). *Leadership. A critical text*. Thousand Oaks: Sage.

Wren, J. T. (2006). A quest for a grand theory of leadership. In G. R. Goethals & G. L. J. Sorenson (Eds.), *The quest for a general theory of leadership* (pp. 1-38). Northampton, MA: Edward Elgar.

Wren, J. T. (2007). *Inventing leadership. The challenge of democracy*. Northampton, MA: Edward Elgar.

Appendix: Sample Transformative Leadership Capstones, 2007

Philip McAdoo
The Road to Shanghai
Philip McAdoo created an opportunity for six students from East Side Community High School in New York City and led them on a China Student Exchange project, traveling to Shanghai for a 10-day trip. Philip, a Broadway actor, raised the funds for the students' trip by enlisting the support of some of his fellow Broadway performers and putting on a benefit in New York that successfully financed the major expenses for the trip.

Jennie Falco
Family Cooperative
Jennie Falco organized a childcare cooperative in Longmont, Colorado, for her Capstone Action Project. She collaborated with five interracial families to create a family-support program that focused on sharing resources and childcare responsibilities, educating parents on topics such as nonviolent communication and positive touch, creating conditions for families to grow their own organic food and become less dependent on petroleum-based products and industry, and initiating activities for children

that raised awareness in the areas of foreign language, arts and culture study, body-mind centering, health and nutrition, and the power of play.

Leanne Calandrella
Incarcerated/Formerly Incarcerated Individuals Leading Community Service Projects
Leanne Calandrella, who worked with the BEST (Being Empowered and Safe Together) Reintegration Program on Maui, Hawaii, chose to motivate incarcerated/formerly incarcerated individuals to lead volunteer service projects within their community. Interest came from her idea that engaging with community and helping people is empowering and creates strength in leadership of both self and others. Her goal was to help others learn how to help others.

Erika Bjune
Action Through Education in Virtual Worlds
Erika Bjune led the creation of a virtual nonprofit organization dedicated to raising awareness around sustainability issues through classes, interactive displays, discussions, events, and games. The organization, Avatar Action Center, was founded inside a virtual world called Second Life, an immersive 3D environment in which people are represented digitally by "avatars."

Miguel Chavez
Hispanic Leadership Development
Miguel Chavez, a TLD graduate and current TSD student, designed and implemented a Hispanic Leadership Development Training Program in the Federal Prison System.

Sierra Webb
Apple Valley, Building an Inclusive Community
Through an initiative by the National League of Cities, Sierra Webb, a Town of Apple Valley employee, worked with municipal government staff, the town council, school teachers, students and community leaders to build a coalition and enact the "Inclusive Communities Partnership" in their community.

Eric Matheny
Appreciating What Is: An Appreciative Inquiry in a Large County-Level Government Organization
Eric Matheny led an Appreciative Inquiry to discover the positive core of a 40-member community services department situated in a large, county-level government organization charged with providing a range of services to individuals with mental retardation and developmental disabilities. All members of the department were interviewed with inquiry focused on personal stories of when participants felt best about themselves, the work that they were doing, and the agency that they worked for. The group interviewed brought to the project a combined experience of more than 550 years with the agency . The project's aim was to build collective resonance within the department during a period of anxiety, precipitated by an organizational restructuring. The results of the inquiry were compiled, and the themes, quotable quotes, and great stories will be shared with the organization as a whole.

April Howenstine
Public School Showcase
April Howenstine , at brand new Whitney High School she works at in Rocklin, California, organized an event designed to foster ongoing outreach opportunities and the building of bridges between the school and community. She collaborated with teachers, students, parents, administrators, and community members in order to introduce the community to the sports, clubs, and programs offered at the school. It was an opportunity for the students to showcase their talents and skills, and raise funds for the following year.

Mark Austin Thomas
TheMiddleWayRadio.com
Mark Austin Thomas created a website titled TheMiddleWayRadio.com. The site contains podcasts that focus on broadening the political conversation by framing discussions of different issues within a Buddhist perspective, but without making explicit references to Buddhism. This was part of an effort to create a novel way to blend politics and spirituality.

Why Democracy is Taking Over Global Culture

Philip Slater

W tend to think of democracy as something invented by the Greeks, or 18th century theorists, but it's as old as humanity and the basis of our survival as a species. Democracy is part of our genetic heritage.

For most of our existence on earth we lived in small bands, gathering what food grew wild in nature, fishing, and hunting. We lived cooperatively of necessity--we knew we couldn't survive alone. Our lives were characterized by:

> personal independence, general equality among group members, including women, consensus-based decision-making achieved through open and protracted discussion, and freedom of movement, particularly as a means of conflict resolution (O'Connell, 1995, p. 6).

Surviving hunter-gatherer cultures are also egalitarian:

> There was a confusing, seductive informality about everything [the Pygmies] did...Everyone took part in everything... There were no chiefs, no formal councils. In each aspect of Pygmy life there might be one or two men or women who were more prominent than others, but usu-

Philip Slater has an A.B. and Ph. D. from Harvard, taught sociology at Harvard, Brandeis, and UCSC, and is currently teaching at California Institute for Integral Studies. He is the author of *The Pursuit of Loneliness* and, more recently, *The Chysalis Effect: The Metamorphosis of Global Culture*, from which this article is largely drawn.

ally for good practical reasons (Turnbull, 1961, p. 110).

Among the Bushmen, too, there was neither sign nor memory of chiefs. Respect for those older and wiser was the closest they ever came (van der Post, 1961, p. 210). The Teduray of the Mindanao rainforest also had no chiefs or rankings. People were esteemed for special skills, but only in context (Schlegel, 1998, p. 111).

This democratic lifestyle of hunter-gatherers simply echoed the world around them. Janine Benyus has this to say about ecological systems:

> What makes a mature community run is not one universal message being broadcast from above, but numerous, even redundant, messages coming from the grass roots, dispersed throughout the community structure. A rich feedback system allows changes in one component of the community to reverberate through the whole, allowing for adaptation when the environment changes (Benyus, 2002, p. 274).

Democracy, in other words, is the most natural form of social organization, mimicking Nature.

The Ladder That War Made

Formal leadership--what we call authority--was an invention that arose six to eight thousand years ago, with the advent of war—that is, socially-orga-

nized, premeditated group fighting for economic or political gain (O'Connell, 1995, p. 5). Two special needs created by standing armies made formal leadership necessary.

First, conquerors had to control their conquered slaves and peasants. Although the ruling class had the advantage of owning weapons, and although they were stronger and better fed, a peasant or slave might still have leadership skills, or be a talented fighter despite all these disadvantages. A line had to be drawn.

Second, men were (and often still are, rather irrelevantly) being brought up and trained to be competitive and belligerent. How could order be kept among such men? Who could such men accept as a leader? Would he have to fight constantly to maintain his position? And if so, how would the group ever have the energy or manpower to fight anyone else?

This was the origin of formal hierarchy, or the abolishing of equal opportunity. People now held fixed status positions in society. Formal rankings and levels of authority created order and consistency. Those at the top of the pyramid conferred titles, positions, and benefits on those below. You could improve your position only by gaining the approval of those 'above' you.

Obedience to those 'above' and domination over those 'below' became virtues. 'Cooperation' was merely a euphemism for obedience, as it still is in authoritarian settings.

Over time legitimacy was established through birth, with fathers passing their status down to their sons. The entire known world became redefined as a pyramid, with God, kings and nobles at the top and slaves and peasants at the bottom.

Scapegoating

Hierarchical institutions are unnatural for human beings and arouse frustration and anger. O'Connell (1995, p. 232) observes that authoritarian systems were "fundamentally dissonant to human nature as it had evolved during the millions of years we spent as wanderers, hunters, and collectors." The frustration aroused by hierarchy is usually discharged by scapegoating--that is, blaming a powerless outsider or low-status person for abuses by powerful insiders and high-status persons. People in the middle of a hierarchy can take out their frustrations on those further down the ladder, but those at the bottom are forced to look abroad.

Heads of government regularly whip up hatred of foreigners or minorities to maintain their popularity. Hitler used the Jews, Stalin the bourgeoisie, American Cold Warriors the "red menace", Saddam Hussein the Kurds, Milosevich the Muslims and Croats, and so on. For a leader to maintain despotic power he need only hint that some group is dangerous or unworthy and those members of the populace who tend to grovel before authority will feel emboldened to attack and kill.

For everyday frustrations the preferred scapegoats were women.

Bureaucracy

Long after political democracy had begun to take hold, hierarchies remained the norm for all institutions, even those--like schools, universities, corporations, and churches--that had nothing to do with fighting. The system worked fairly well for centuries but contained two flaws that have ultimately proved crippling.

The first flaw was the poor fit between status and ability. Authority means you get to exercise leadership whether you're any good at it or not.

In informal groups leaders emerge spontaneously. They may be the best liked, the wisest, the most fun, or the ones with the best ideas. Often leadership will circulate, depending on the group's activity. But leaders that emerge spontaneously tend to share certain traits. Successful leaders have a clear vision of where they want to go, an ability to communicate this to others, and a realistic and positive sense of self. They're trustworthy, pay attention to people, and induce self-esteem in others, often by challenging them (Bennis and Nanus,1985). These are qualities possessed by emergent leaders that often are not possessed by formal ones.

The second flaw in authoritarian systems is their inability to adapt quickly to change. Once the industrial era began, the days of authoritarianism were numbered. As Jeffrey Sachs points out, the reason the British were the first to enter the industrial age and able to establish global economic supremacy was that their society was the most open and democratic at that time (Sachs, 2005, p. 33). It lost that supremacy to an even more democratic nation, and it's no coincidence that the United States has begun to lose its position in the world precisely as it has begun to retreat from democracy.

Responding to Change

Authoritarianism can survive in places where conditions remain static for decades or even centuries at a time, but falters under conditions of rapid change. For a system to respond well to unforeseen situations it must be able to utilize all its resources, which in turn requires rapid communication among all parts of that system. But hierarchies require that all communication be routed through managers at the top.

Duncan Watts (2003, pp. 254-260) tells the story of what happened when a disaster threatened to shut down Toyota production for months--an event that would have had massive international economic repercussions.

Toyotas are actually manufactured by over 200 separate companies, all of which exchange personnel, assistance, and intellectual property--in other words, a network. In 1997 a plant that was the exclusive manufacturer of a crucial brake valve burned to the ground, leaving Toyota with only a two days supply of the valves and no way to make any more until the plant was rebuilt. Car production ground to a halt. Yet within three days 62 of the other companies--none of whom had any previous experience with the valves--had become emergency valve producers, with 150 other companies indirectly involved as suppliers. Two weeks after the disaster struck car production was back to normal levels.

The Toyota experience exemplifies what Benyus says about mature ecological systems: grass-roots communication throughout the system ensures that changes in one part of the community will quickly travel everywhere, enabling rapid adaptation when environmental change occurs.

Toyota's amazing recovery would not have been possible without a rich tradition of lateral communication at the ground level and cooperative daily problem solving. This flexibility is what makes networks so successful in an age of chronic change. And what makes it so easy for groups like Al-Qaida to evade conventional military bureaucracies.

Hierarchies, says Watts (2003, p. 145), "respond poorly to ambiguity", and ambiguity is the essence of the age we live in. When change is chronic, "intense communication becomes an ongoing necessity". James Surowiecki (2005, pp 174 ff.). points out that the hierarchical, top-down nature of NASA caused the Columbia disaster, since the information that would have prevented it was available at lower levels of the Agency. And the authoritarian bureaucracies of the American auto industry were a major factor in its rapid decline.

The Decline of Authoritarianism

When Warren Bennis and I predicted, in 1964, the demise of the Soviet Union and other autocracies, and maintained that democracy would be universal in fifty years (Slater, P. and Bennis, W., 1964), our prediction had nothing to do with the Cold War or idealistic values. We argued that global democracy was inevitable in our modern world because it was more efficient. Right-wingers credited Ronald Reagan with the USSR collapse, Osama bin Laden claimed he himself was responsible, while the Russians blame exposure to rock and roll. But in fact, Russian authoritarianism made it inevitable.

Authoritarian systems are too cumbersome and inflexible to survive long under the conditions of chronic change that prevail today. Bennis and I were saying that Communist and other authoritarian governments could not long survive as they were whether we did anything about them or not. Unlike government policy makers at the time we believed both in the value of democracy and in its inevitability. Time has proven us right, although Republican policy makers in Washington still complain that democracy 'handicaps' them, still believe that America enjoys a 'weak' political system sustainable only by brute force and by circumventing it as much as possible. Military dictators installed by, or supported by, the United States are referred to wistfully as "strongman Suharto" or "strongman Pinochet". Democracy is so poorly understood in Washington (as opposed to the private sector) that the government's first response to every national crisis has been to create, or enlarge, an unwieldy, over-centralized, authoritarian bureaucracy, and appoint a 'czar' to run it--the precise opposite of the successful Toyota response to disaster.

Malcolm Gladwell tells of Paul Van Riper, who commanded the Red Team (enemy) in 'Millennium Challenge'--the war games in 2000 that served as a rehearsal for the Iraq invasion. The Blue Team had at its disposal the most modern equipment, computing system, and analytic tools the world had ever known. But in the games they were utterly routed by the Red Team, even though the latter were using archaic equipment and communication methods. The secret of Van Riper's success was no secret at all: a completely decentralized, democratic, management structure, in which subordinates were told the overall intent but "were to use their own initiative and be innovative". It's a 'messy' system, but "allowing people to operate without having to explain themselves constantly...enables rapid cognition." (Gladwell, 2005, pp. 102-111).

The Pentagon handled the defeat characteristically: after a couple of days in shock they rewrote the rules so the game was completely re-scripted in the Blue Team's favor, and declared victory.

Why Democracy Prevails

In a laboratory at M.I.T. several decades ago, two types of groups were compared on their ability to solve problems. One type had a centralized leader through whom all communication had to be funneled. The other was completely egalitarian.

Given simple tasks and unchanging rules the autocratic groups were more efficient, but when the experimenters gave the groups tasks that were more complex, and introduced changes in the middle of the experiment, the autocratic groups unraveled. The democratic groups solved the complex problems more quickly and made fewer errors. They were more adaptable, corrected their mistakes more quickly, and were more open to new ideas (Bennis, 1962).

One reason for the failure of the autocratic groups was that the 'bosses' were too busy to pay attention to crucial new information. This is compounded in real-life autocracies by the tendency of dictatorial leaders to be protected by their subordinates from information they don't want to hear. The messenger who brings the bad news that the boss needs to change his policy is seen as disloyal, and is ignored, fired, or shot. But the leader who manages to eliminate all opposition usually finds that far from solving his problems, he's amputated the solution to them.

The First Casualty

Mao Zedong was at the top of his gigantic pyramid only a few years before the rigidity of his system began to destroy what he was trying to build. He refused to believe that the Great Leap Forward was a failure, and his unwillingness to face facts was nourished by his subordinates, who were afraid to report any news that would challenge his optimistic view of the matter. The only one who told him the truth, Liu Shaoki, was ever after considered an enemy (MacFarquhar, 1998).

Top-down corporations, says Surowiecki, "give people an incentive to hide information and dissemble" (2005, p. 209). In top-down governments this incentive is magnified, since the lust for power is more intense, and the lag time between error and catastrophe far longer.

The results are familiar. Unchallenged generals following outdated military principles send their troops to be slaughtered by guerillas. The unchallenged ship captain plows confidently into an iceberg. Hitler exhausts his armies in Russia. Corporate heads, thriving on past successes, ignore the invention that puts them out of business.

The WMD fiasco is a case in point, with the White House walling itself off from inconvenient data. Unwilling to rely on existing information sources, Bush Administration officials set up their own mini-agency inside the Pentagon whose 'loyal' personnel "'cherry-picked' the intelligence they passed on, selecting reports that supported the administration's pre-existing ideology and ignoring all the rest" (Pollack, 2004, p. 88).

In the Bush administration personal loyalty and ideological commitment outweighed all other values.

> The President was caught in an echo chamber of his own making, cut off from everyone other than a circle around him ...that conceals him from public view and keeps him away from the one thing he needs most: honest, disinterested perspectives about what's real (Suskind, 2004, p. 263).

Carefully prepared reports by the CIA, the State Department, the Army War College, and non-governmental

Successful leaders have a clear vision of where they want to go, an ability to communicate this to others, and a realistic and positive sense of self.

groups all agreed that the welcome of United States troops in Iraq would be short-lived, that a large and extended commitment of personnel and money top-down basis, and young officers found that

> the information often seems stale or, having been processed in the maw of Army

Authoritarianism can survive in places where conditions remain static for decades or even centuries at a time, but falters under conditions of rapid change.

would be necessary to rebuild Iraq; and warned of the inevitability of the serious dangers that would be incurred if the Iraqi army was disbanded. But the inner circle of the administration regarded any consideration of what it might take to rebuild Iraq as disloyal and anti-war. Those who publicly made what turned out to be realistic and even overly conservative assessments of the cost of the war and reconstruction were fired (Chief White House economic adviser Lawrence Lindsay) or humiliated (Army Chief of Staff General Eric Shinseki). The inner White House didn't want anyone raining on their fantasy (Fallows, 2004, pp. 53 ff.).

As a result of this triumph of ideology over truth, junior officers in Iraq found themselves totally unprepared to deal with what they encountered there. Much of their military training was useless, and with no knowledge of the language or culture they were entirely unprepared to cope with the complex problems they were facing every day.

Lateral Communication

But when the war actually came, democratic culture triumphed over military training. Junior officers came up with ingenious solutions to crises, and created unauthorized web sites where they could exchange what they were learning with other young officers, without going through channels.

> Gen X officers are markedly more self-reliant and confident of their abilities than their baby-boomer superiors. ... Instead of looking up to the Army for instructions they are teaching themselves how to fight the war (Baum, 2005, p. 44).

In time the Army set up its own web site, CALL, but it was run on the usual

doctrine, irrelevant. The war in Iraq is so confusing and it changes so fast that there's often no time to wait for carefully vetted and spoon-fed advice (Ibid., p. 45)

Just as we saw in the Toyota example, lateral communication of this kind is essential for coping with rapidly changing situations. Which is why authoritarian systems are on the decline throughout the world.

Collapsing Hierarchies, Decentralized Networks

A survey of a thousand major corporations found that 80% practice some form of participatory management, where decisions are made and implemented by teams of co-workers rather than handed down by the boss (Lawler, 1996). Workers in the field can then make decisions on their own rather than referring them to higher authority. Things happen too fast today for that. One reason the FBI failed to anticipate the 9/11 attacks, despite ample warning, was the incredible number of levels its quaint hierarchy still maintains.

> In today's...globalization system, most of the information needed to answer most of the problems now rests in the hands of people on the outer edges of organizations, not at the center (Friedman, 1999, pp. 70-71).

Eighty-five percent of the firms involved in Hollywood movies employ 10 people or less. Hollywood films today are no longer made by big studios but by "loose entrepreneurial networks of small firms" that "convene as one financial organization for the duration of the movie project" and then disperse (Kelly, 1998, p. 111).

Times of change demand creativity. Although large pyramidal corporations

pour massive amounts of money into research and development, very small firms produce twenty-four times as many new inventions per dollar (Adams and Brock. 1986).

The threat to corporate behemoths from small entrepreneurs has never been more persistent. You don't need a huge capital investment to start a new company today--especially when the product is an idea, a system, or information, rather than a thing.

> Entrepreneurs without capital can...build businesses with just ideas. They no longer have to own the tools of production to have access to them...In the United States, a third of all new capital equipment is acquired through leasing (Knoke, 1996, p. 85)

Decentralizing bureaucracies and creating ad hoc teams and networks is a trend throughout the economy and in state and local government.

The Internet

Markoff shows how the development of the computer and the Internet sprang from members of the 1960s and 1970s counterculture. Prior to their influence, computer research had been centralized, military, and secret. The idea of giving the average person access to computers was anathema to authoritarian men, who were busy computing how many mega-deaths would occur under varying nuclear war situations. The younger programmers were loose-knit networks of men and women who felt information should be free and accessible to all (Markoff, 2005).

The Internet has created a generation of people accustomed to finding their own answers, creating their own systems, forming their own new communities. And this despite constant efforts by governments and corporations to control and limit it.

The web's underlying culture of sharing, decentralisation and democracy, makes it an ideal platform for groups to self-organise, combining their ideas and know how, to create together games, encyclopaedias, software, social networks, video sharing sites or entire parallel universes. That culture of sharing also makes the web difficult for governments to control and hard for corporations to make money from. (Leadbeater, 2008).

Clots

Our planet is a bio-system of constant mutual adaptation. Every unit in that system receives information and normally reacts to it adaptively and transmits its learning to its neighbors. But when power is concentrated those transmissions are often blocked by the felt necessity of exercising control. Information is not transmitted on its merits but in terms of the power position of the person transmitting. Therefore information necessary for successful adaptation to changing conditions is lost. Information coming from the periphery of the system—invariably the source of new information about changing conditions—is ignored precisely because it comes from the periphery, from a low-power position. This is why empires always collapse in time, why small firms out-invent big corporations, why networks outperform bureaucracies.

All forms of concentrated power, public or private, are blood clots in the circulatory system of society. When an artery becomes clogged, blood doesn't get to the brain or the heart and people have strokes and heart attacks. Concentrations of power and wealth have a similar effect on the body politic--the circulation of wealth, resources, and, especially, ideas, is blocked. In a healthy system, information flows are unimpeded by clots of power or the sclerosis of hierarchy.

References

Adams, W. and Brock, J. W. (1986) *The bigness complex*. New York: Pantheon.

Baum, D. (2005). *Battle lessons*. The New Yorker, 1/17/05.

Bennis, W. and Nanus, B. (1985). *Leaders*. New York: Harper & Row.

Bennis, W. G. (1962). Toward a 'truly' scientific management: The concept of organizational health. *General Systems Yearbook, 7,* 273.

Bennis, W. G. and Slater, P. E. (1968) *The temporary society*. New York: Harper & Row.

Benyus, J.M. (2002). *Biomimicry: Innovation inspired by nature*. New York: HarperCollins.

Fallows, J. (2004). Blind into Baghdad." *Atlantic, 293*(1), 53ff.

Friedman, T. L. (1999). *The Lexus and the olive tree*. New York: Farrar, Straus, and Giroux.

Gladwell, M. (2005). *Blink*. New York: Little, Brown.

Kelly, K. (1998). *New rules for the new economy*. New York: Viking.

Knoke, W. (1996). *Bold new world*. Tokyo: Kodansha International.

Lawler, E. E., (1996). *From the ground up*. San Francisco:Jossey-Bass.

Leadbeater, C. (2008). *We-think*. London: Profile books.

MacFarquhar, R. (1998). *The origins of the cultural revolution. Vol. III: The coming of the cataclysm, 1961-66*. New York: Columbia University Press.

Markoff, J. (2005). *What the doormouse said*. New York: Viking.

O'Connell, R. L. (1995). *Ride of the second horseman: The birth and death of war*. New York: Oxford University Press.

Pollack, K. M. (2004) Spies, lies, and weapons: what went wrong. *Atlantic, 293*(1), 88.

Sachs, J. D. (2005). *The end of poverty*. New York: Penguin.

Schlegel, S. A. (1998). *Wisdom from a rainforest*. Athens, GA: Univ. of Georgia Press.

Slater, P. and Bennis, W. G. (1964). Democracy is inevitable. *Harvard Business Review, 42*(2), 51-59.

Surowiecki, J. (2005). *The wisdom of crowds*. New York: Anchor Books.

Suskind, R. *The price of loyalty*. New York: Simon & Schuster.

Turnbull, C. M. (1961). *The forest people*. New York: Simon and Schuster.

Van der Post, L. (1961). *The heart of the hunter*. New York: Morrow.

Watts, D. J. (2003). *Six degrees:The science of a connected age*. New York: Norton.

Order Past *ReVision* Issues Online
Go to www.revisionpublishing.org

What is Leadership?

Albert Low

During the last months of the Second World War Adolph Hitler was virtually entombed in his bunker. By that time he was a badly shaken man, physically shattered by a bombing attempt on his life as well as, some say, insipient Parkinson's disease. He was furthermore a nervous wreck from the blows that the allied armies had inflicted upon the German troops and from the incessant bombing raids that the allied aircraft had delivered to the German cities. As early as Dec. 26 1944, the deterioration in his condition was evident. At this time Martin Bormann, a very close aide to Hitler, had written in a letter, "The Fuhrer takes a short walk each day and this seems to do him good. I wish he could overcome these attacks of trembling – they began in his leg and have now spread to his left

arm and hand" (in Joachimsthaler, 2000, p.75).

About the same time his adjutant said, "The impression Hitler made upon me was one of complete despair. Never before or afterwards did I see him in such a state" (in Joachimsthaler, 2000, p. 76.) Another report said,

> Physically he presented a dreadful sight. He dragged himself about painfully and clumsily, throwing his torso forward and dragging his legs after him from his living room to the conference room of the bunker. He had lost his sense of balance; if he were detained on the brief journey (seventyfive to a hundred feet), he had to sit down on one of the benches that had been placed along either wall for this purpose, or else cling to the person he was talking to . . .His eyes were bloodshot....Saliva frequently dripped from the corners of his mouth. (In Joachimsthaler, 2000, p. 39)

And yet Bormann in the same letter to his wife just quoted said, "Everything depends on his health! The future of the whole nation" (in Joachimsthaler 2000, p. 132). Furthermore, during the following five-months ferocious battles were fought and under the impetus of the leadership of this stricken man. Even as late as April 25th the Wehrmacht was reporting, "Fanatical house to house fighting in the city center of Berlin is raging day and night. On the 30th April it reported, "The heroic struggle for the center of the capital continues with

unabated fury" (p. 132). Yet it was on that very day, at 13.30 to be precise, that Hitler committed suicide. Eight days later the war was over.

The question is: what made it possible for one man, -- the *Führer*, or leader -- even though he was a physical, psychological and spiritual wreck to wield such power right up to the last moment? This question is important: not simply from a historical point of view, but because some answer to it would shed much needed light on the question, "What is a leader?"

The Qualities of a Leader?

Eliot Jaquesn (1989), who wrote a great deal about management says unequivocally, "I know of no evidence that there are any particular kinds of personality traits or makeup that are specific to leadership." (p. 95). Even so, if one looks into the literature on leadership, and there's plenty of it to look into these days, one will find a plethora of traits, or personal characteristics, that the author feels that a leader should have. For example Warren Bennin's "Basic Ingredients" of leadership are "Guiding vision," "Passion," " Integrity," "Trust," "Curiosity," and "Daring," James O'Toole's characteristics of leadership are "Integrity," "Trust," "Listening," and "Respect for followers." Yet,

Albert Low was a business executive for the first half of his life employed as a senior human resource executive in South Africa and later in Canada. He has a degree in Psychology and Philosophy and an honorary Doctorate degree from Queen's University, Ontario. He has practiced Zen Buddhism intensely for 40 years. In 1976 he retired from the business world to study and teach Zen Buddhism on a full time basis. He is an internationally known author of a number of books, has given many TV and radio broadcasts, has written numerous articles for magazines and, because of this, is well known in Europe, Australia and throughout North America. His latest book is *Conflict and Creativity at work: the human roots of corporate life*.

of these ten characteristics, Hitler had at best just two: "Guiding vision" and "Passion." One could also say that he had daring, but it was the reckless daring of a gambler.

In their book, *The Guru Guide*, from which I have taken these two examples, the authors, Joseph Boyett and Jimmie Boyett (2002), give another 12 exhibits of leadership profiles provided by other writers on leadership. Hitler would have rated poorly on all of them. Of the 72 characteristics of leadership potential given in exhibit 18 of this same book, Hitler in his prime, would have had, at best, 11. During the last terrible months he displayed just one or two. Let us not doubt that, even during these last terrible months, he was still in charge. SS-Gruppenfuhrer Monke states, "Shortly after *15.00 on April 30th* I received an order signed, by Hitler personally, that I should break out of Berlin" (in Joachimsthaler, 2000, p. 727). I have put in the italics to bring to your attention the fact that this order was received an hour and a half after Hitler had committed suicide. The Commander of the Defence of Berlin received a similar directive. Right up to the end Hitler was dismissing, appointing, commanding personnel of the highest military and Governmental rank. As the historian Joachim Fest (1975) points out, "In spite of all the lies, mistakes and misconceptions, his authority remained entirely unchallenged until literally the last hour" (p. 729).

I hold no brief for Hitler. The man was a savage demon but, even so, in his prime 90% of the German population were willing to follow him as their leader, many adored him, and some even had spiritual experiences in his presence. So his example, and his failure to score higher on these leadership profiles, must prompt us to try to find some basis for understanding leadership other than simply listing a random set of characteristics.

The Center

The mythologist, Mircea Eliade (1957) tells of a tribe, the Achilpa tribe, which had a sacred pole. During their wanderings the tribe always carried it with them and would choose the direction they were to take by the direction in which it bent. Eliade says, "For the pole to be broken denotes catastrophe; it is like 'the end of the world,' reversion to Chaos. Once, according to some anthropologists who observed this tribe, when the pole was broken, the entire clan was in consternation; 'they wandered about aimlessly for a time and finally lay down on the earth together and waited for death to overtake them.'" (Eliade, 1957, p. 33).

In case someone should think this is simply an aberration of a single primitive people we must remember that throughout history, and among many different kinds of societies, it was the practice to carry a banner into battle. This banner is but an ornate sacred pole. If the banner were to be captured by the enemy, the army would collapse and panic and chaos follow. Even in our sophisticated and cynical culture the flag is still sacred to many people for whom it is the Centre of power of the group.

To give an example of the importance of the Center that is closer to home, suppose you have to make your way through a dense forest so overgrown that one cannot see the sun. You know that if you continue north you will be able to travel through the forest in a few days. You have sufficient food supplies for the journey and a compass. All that you need do is to follow the direction that the compass is pointing. Suppose now, after a day's travel, you lose confidence in the compass. You wonder if it is really pointing north. Every tree is similar to every other tree, and no central or stable point can be found. If one were not an

> # Even in our sophisticated and cynical culture the flag is still sacred to many people for whom it is the Centre of power of the group.

experienced woodsman this could well create panic. Indeed, not a few people have died from panic because they were lost in this way. Incidentally, in the book Apollo 13, (Lovell and Kluger, 1995) which tells the story of that ill-fated space capsule, the authors talk of the eight ball, "a guidance system containing a stationary component, which contained a stable element that was inertially fixed in space relative to the stars." (p. 127). What is called a 'gimbal lock,' that is a loss of this stable element in a spacecraft, would be tantamount to having no stable point in a forest of stars and galaxies, which would result in a complete loss of orientation.

We need to be oriented. At first the rising sun was the center of orientation: the word orientation comes from orient, which also means east. The discovery of the North Star was a major discovery for travelers. The North Star, the flag, the sacred pole, the leader are all dynamic centers, they all give orientation. The Pole Star and the sun orient us in physical space. The flag and the gimbal lock orient us in psychological or behavior as well as in physical space. The sacred pole and the leader orient us in spiritual space as well as in these other two. Someone said that mankind has always resisted being no-where for no reason at all. This means that a dynamic center has always been physically, psychology and spiritually necessary.

Transference

We can see that a close connection exists between what I am calling the dynamic center and what Freud called transference, and I think, provides a better explanation for the phenomenon. Transference is said to occur when one person unconsciously redirects feelings he, or she, has for one person to another person. Psychoanalysts often relate leadership to the father figure. According to psychoanalysis one transfers the feelings of power and authority that one attributed to one's father to the leader. This means that to some extent at least transference is a pathological phenomenon that is best avoided.

On the other hand, according to what I am saying, one 'transfers' to the father the power and authority inherent in the dynamic center, and then later redirects those attributes of the center to the leader. I put inverted commas around the word 'transfers' because, more precisely, the father is the child's dynamic center; later the leader is the dynamic center. One does not adopt a center consciously although, for reasons that I have given elsewhere, I feel that it is a mistake to say that it is done unconsciously.

What does "dynamic" center mean?

One would expect that such a simple question would elicit an equally simple response. But alas! This is not the case. If I was asked what is the center of a sheet of paper I would have no difficulty in replying. It is the point in the middle of the page, and by drawing lines diagonally from corner to corner of the page one can easily fix the center. One can just as easily find the center to a dinner plate or football field or any two or three-dimensional figure. But this center is the geographical center, not the dynamic center.

A dynamic center is the dominant center of power and attraction in a field of force. The field of force is made up of a number of competing centers of power and attraction. There can only be one such dynamic centre. If there is more than one, conflict will break out to determine which of the competing centers is the real one. This is quite evident when we consider human societies and groups. It is axiomatic there can only be one leader in a group; for example a company has only one CEO. Even in space vehicles in which there might be only two crewmembers, one is appointed the leader. As the dominant center, the dynamic center is the center of power and attraction. As a center of power, it is a center of centrifugal forces; as a center of attraction it is the center of centripetal forces. A leader is the centre. As the center of power, he or she is the source of initiative; as the center of attraction, he or she is at the centre of the lines of communication of the group.

The role of the leader is most often implicit during times when there is no apparent conflict; but during times of stress and confusion this role becomes very active. Revolts happen when, in addition to an existing leader, another leader arises to challenge him or her. When this happens, and until the dispute is settled, there will be confusion and even chaos in the group.

The Ambiguity of the Center

As I have said, we have no difficulty in determining what and where is the geographical Center. In the human group however we cannot so easily designate what and where the dynamic center is. At the time of writing George W. Bush is the center, but the center is not necessarily George W. Bush. If I say that slightly differently you will see what I mean. George W. Bush is the President of the USA; the President of the USA is not necessarily George W. Bush. This will be quite evident when Barack Obama is inaugurated as President. The

forces a focus from which forces issue and toward which forces converge. The interplay between various visual objects as centers of forces is the basis of composition" (p. 2).

Every visual field, according to Arnheim, " comprises a number of centers each of which tries to draw the others into subservience. The self of the viewer is just one of those centers. The overall balance of all these competing aspirations determines the structure of the whole and that total structure is organized around what I will call the balancing center" (1982, p. 2). This is as true of the field generated by human centers of power as it is of visual centers of power. This means that before we start listing the characteristics of the leader we should first understand the characteristics, the charisma, of the dynamic center of which the leader is the incarnation. Charisma means, according to the

According to psychoanalysis one transfers the feelings of power and authority that one attributed to one's father to the leader. This means that to some extent at least transference is a pathological phenomenon that is best avoided.

center is independent of the person who is its incarnation. "The king is dead! Long love the king!" expresses the point well. This means that the dynamic center has its own charisma irrespective of the charisma of the incumbent.

Rudolph Arnheim, the celebrated art critic, in his book *The Power of the Center* (1982), also made the distinction between the geographical center and the dynamic center. He said, "In geometrical space, centricity can be defined by location alone. It is the most important point of every regular figure" (p.1). But he also recognized the existence of a dynamic center as the dominant center of power and attraction in a field of competing centers of power and attraction. He said, "When we speak of a center we shall mean mostly the center of a field of

Encarta World Dictionary, "the ability to inspire enthusiasm, interest, or affection in others by means of personal charm or influence." But, it also means, according to the same dictionary, "a gift or power believed to be divinely bestowed" I am suggesting that the divinity that bestows the charisma is the dynamic center.

Not a Psychological Phenomenon.

The dynamic center is not a psychological phenomenon; it does not arise from a conscious intention. Yet on the other hand, even though in the case of the Achilpa tribe it took the form of the wood of the pole, the center is not a physical phenomenon either. Eliade tells us that this pole was fashioned by their Ancestor from a gum tree. The Ancestor, "after anointing the pole with blood, climbed it and disappeared into the sky. The pole represents a cosmic axis, for it is around the sacred pole, that territory becomes habitable" (Eliade, 1957, p. 33). It was the ancestor who gave it supra human sanction." The charisma of the pole was "a gift or power believed to be divinely bestowed." The divine power was provided by the Ancestor. In other words it was not any old pole that the tribesmen happened to pick up on the way. The pole incarnates the Cosmic Axis, or World Centre. Furthermore the World Center must have supra human sanction and it can only be discovered through the help of secret signs: "When no sign manifests itself it is provoked. A sign is asked to put an end to the tension and anxiety caused by relativity and disorientation, in short to reveal an absolute point of support" (Eliade, 1957, p. 35).

The supra human quality of the center is emphasized in the coronation of the British monarch, the dynamic center of the kingdom. The Crown, the Scepter and the Orb are all cosmic symbols bestowed on the person crowned King or Queen. That the crowning ceremony is performed by the Archbishop of Canterbury also attests to supra human origins also. In China, in the days of the emperors, the emperor was called the Son of Heaven. The symbols and the crowning ceremony all attest the to semi divine power of the king: the divine aspect was contributed by the dynamic center, the human aspect by the incumbent.

The flag is a magic center; its magic -- its supra human power -- is bestowed on it by the leader when it is brought into his or her presence. Each year in Britain a ceremony is performed in which the flags of the British regiments are brought within the presence of the monarch. The ceremony is called "Trooping the Colors." A similar ceremony was held in Nazi Germany at Nuremburg when Hitler would "consecrate" new party colors. He would touch them with one hand while his other hand clutched the cloth of the bullet-riddled *Blutfahne* (the "blood banner" allegedly drenched in the gore of Nazi martyrs killed in the abortive Putsch of November '23).

According to Eliade, the establishment of a dynamic centre for the ancients was a matter of deep concern because "nothing can begin, nothing can be done, without a previous orientation and any orientation implies getting a fixed point. This is why religious man has always sought to fix his abode at the centre of the world" (Eliade, 1969, p. 52).

These quotations help us to understand the importance of the centre, not only for primitive people, but also for all human kind. Without it there is no 'world,' everything falls into chaos, and life, as we know it, is impossible. However, as these quotations point out also, not anything can be the centre. The

The role of the leader is most often implicit during times when there is no apparent conflict; but during times of stress and confusion this role becomes very active.

centre gives the importance to things; therefore things cannot create a centre. This is why the centre has to appear, or, using Eliade's words it has to have supra human sanction.

We would use the word 'unconscious,' and say that the origin of the center, lies in the unconscious, or is even 'in' the unconscious. However, the word 'unconscious' is unfortunate for several reasons. On the one hand it suggests that the source is less than, inferior to, the conscious mind when, in fact, the conscious mind cannot operate without a dynamic center. On the hand Freudian mythology has more or less defined the meaning of the word 'unconscious,' for us and this definition includes the connotation of something murky, undesirable, primitive, and irrational. Even the Jungian notion of archetype is quite unsatisfactory suggesting as it does that the center is some kind of idea or psychic product, that is a product of a 'collective unconscious.' I have suggested elsewhere that the origin of the center is the emissary of the dynamic unity, or

will, that lies upstream of the conscious mind

The Divine Half of Leadership.

If we are to consider leadership, we have to first consider its 'divine' half, which has its origins up-stream of the conscious mind, and which I have called the dynamic center. This center is the emissary of will, which is not conscious. That will is not conscious is evident if we consider walking, talking, eating or of any other physical activity all of which are the outcome of will or intention. Although we may be conscious of performing these activities, they are not the result of, that is caused by, the conscious mind. In other books I have used the word Dynamic Unity in place of the word 'will.' I have done this for several reasons. We tend to confuse will with 'self will,' which is simply willfulness that produces no result. On occasion other words such as intention, commitment, and attention can be used instead of dynamic unity. However, dynamic unity pervades the whole of existence manifesting as unified gestalts or wholes on the one hand or as physical units and organisms on the other. The dynamic center is the force by which unity and unification are attained and maintained both within the mind and throughout the universe.

As the emissary of dynamic unity, the dynamic center is unique. This means that it bestows a quality of being distinct, special, and apart, on whatever incarnates it. It also bestows the quality of being superior, which means to occupy a higher rank. To go to the center is to go up. Referring to Eliade once more, the "symbol of a Mountain, a tree, or a Column situated at the Center of the World is extremely widely distributed" (p. 42). Later he said, "The summit of the Cosmic Mountain is not only the highest point on earth; it is the navel of the earth, the point at which creation began." Pyramids are built with a full appreciation of the power of the center and that as one goes up one goes to the center. As Arnheim puts it, "Any pyramid, taken by itself, rises from the broad base of the ground and condenses its energy to a maximum of force at the point."

Because God has always considered to be the source of all power and the destination of all worship He is always thought of as being on high. The practice, in many societies of bowing to the monarch, to the chief, of prostrating before the altar, indeed of bowing before anything felt worthy of veneration, is a way by which the centre is reciprocally raised. In Thailand it is against the law to look down on a Buddha figure. The Buddha figure incarnates the dynamic center for the Buddhist. In the film Macbeth, when Macbeth was proclaimed king, this proclamation was made by Macbeth standing in the center of a round shield and the shield then being raised by his warriors until his feet were at the height of the shoulders of those bearing the shield.

It is for this reason that one will almost always find the CEO's office, as well as the offices of 'top' management, high in the building. Furthermore the building in which the office of the CEO is located is called the Head office. If the company moves its head office into a new building, the move may well be preceded by considerable infighting among the 'higher' levels of management to determine whose office will be closest to that of the CEO. The nearer to the center that one is the more one shares in the power that emanates from the dynamic center, because, as Arnheim says, "A center, in the dynamic sense of the term, acts as a focus from which energy radiates out into the environment." We call this energy charisma; members of other civilizations have called mana, or Baraka, ki, and joriki.

In a large group of people only a few will be able to have proximity to the center. This means that most of the others will be out of touch with it and so virtually leaderless. The Romans realized this and so organized their armies by creating semi-autonomous, subordinate wholes. This has been a paradigm for organization ever since. Each of these new wholes had its own center, which nevertheless recognized the chief as the ultimate center. These sub-wholes were in their turn subdivided until every man in the army had immediate proximity to a dynamic center. Thus a hierarchy

grew naturally in which each subordinate dynamic center received its power from a higher source. The highest source received its power from heaven. The Roman Catholic Church recognized the value of this kind of organization and copied it for its own organization of archbishops, bishops, monsignors, priests and so on all having allegiance to the dynamic center called the Pope. The modern day tendency to reject hierarchies comes from a mis-guided belief that they arise from a conscious decision and so can equally well be rejected by a conscious decision. On the contrary they arise partly from the need that we have for a stable, dynamic center.

The question of the center and proximity to it, as well as its being the 'head,' came into prominence during the peace negotiations between the USA and Viet Nam. Even before the talks could get started the design of the table at which the conference would be held had to be decided. After considerable discussion it was finally decided to adopt a round table, the point being that with such a table there is no head, and so no one is the focal point or dynamic center. A similar sort of reasoning no doubt influenced King Arthur in his choice of a round table at which his knights used to sit.

For human beings a dynamic center is a vital need. In times of relative calm this need is attenuated, but in periods of stress, of uncertainty and anxiety we turn to the center which can help us find security, assurance hope. Unquestionably the rise of Hitler to power was helped by the economic stress and chaos experienced in Germany after the First World War and the stringent economic demands for the payment of reparations. The Weimar Republic, which preceded his rise to power, came to be known as the Republic with a hole in the heart, a graphic way of describing the situation of a virtually leaderless nation.

We can now appreciate the importance of making a distinction between the center and the incumbent. The center has its own characteristics regardless of the one who incarnates it. It comes from on high and is charismatic; it is the repository of power and is that which has the greatest attraction. It is the source of value and importance. It is unique and has the

power to unify and provide security and stability in potentially chaotic situations.

The Importance of the Incumbent.

A question that is often raised by historians is whether history makes world leaders or whether world leaders make history. This kind of question is based of the logic of dichotomy, the logic of either/or. One cannot separate history from people or people from the history. In the same way one cannot separate the incumbent from the dynamic center, nor the dynamic center from the incumbent. George Bush-as-president does not exist until Bush is elected. After he is elected something entirely new comes into existence.

Some people say, for example, that, at the time of writing, George Bush is the most powerful man in the world. However, it is George Bush-as-President in which such awesome power resides; problems arise when Bush begins to believe that he as a man, not as a president, is all-powerful. Winston Churchill was undoubtedly one of the Britain's greatest leaders. In May of 1940 a number of the senior statesmen in Britain, including Lord Halifax and the Prince of Wales, were ready to make a deal with Hitler. France had fallen and overnight all the cities of Britain were in easy striking distance of the German Air Force. The British Expeditionary Force had been routed and had left their armaments in France in the evacuation from Dunkirk. The German armed forces seemed invincible now that they had crushed French resistance in a matter of weeks. For a few perilous days it looked as though Britain were going to collapse into chaos. Churchill did not agree with the idea of capitulation and he became prime minister. Under his inspiring leadership Britain held on until Hitler made one fatal mistake by invading Russia and another fatal mistake by later declaring war on the USA.

Churchill received many accolades and all kinds of praise and honors were bestowed upon him. Yet in 1945, when the war was finally over, he was thrown out of office after the Labor Party gained power with a massive majority. Moreover, before the war Churchill had been a political outcast, on occasions even literally begging for some position of power in the British government. Thus it was the history that made Churchill, although it is undoubted that Churchill, in his own way, made history.

I have said that the 'human situation'– a country, a company, a club, a hospital – "comprises a number of centers each of which tries to draw the others into subservience … The overall balance of all these competing aspirations determines the structure of the whole and that total structure is organized around what I will call the balancing center." This situation is not necessarily a stable field but could, at times, be like the ocean in a storm with waves rising and subsiding, the waves being centers of power. The art of politics is to bring the greatest number of these peaks of power under the sway of the dominating center. In a company these peaks of power include the trade unions, the various stockholder interests, the centers of power in the market, the Governmental departments, public interest groups and many others. With the end of the 1939/45 war the situation changed radically and entirely new peaks of power emerged in Britain and Churchill was unable to adapt swiftly enough to accommodate this radical shift. He was out of sync with the requirements of a new dynamic center.

However a leader is not just a puppet animated by the dynamic center. In the book, *Conflict and Creativity at Work*, I have said that to do work commitment, capacity and ability are required. A person who acts in the role of a leader must have these three so the leader is not qualitatively different from the members of the group that he or she leads. It is the unique, dynamic center makes the qualitative difference. The seventy-two qualities of leadership potential given in *The Guru Guide* are the qualities that one will find to a greater or lesser degree in human beings anywhere. Yet there is a mystique that accrues to a leader, a mystique that accrues, not because of the charismatic qualities of the person, but because of the charismatic qualities of the person/dynamic center.

On commitment, capacity and ability

In the book *Conflict and Creativity at Work* I also said that all jobs have two aspects: a managerial and a technical aspect. The managerial aspects are those

aspects that require someone to make creative decisions. The technical aspects require the person to follow given procedures or to solve problems that have a right or wrong answer. The difference between these two is the following. When doing the technical aspects of a job one relies on rules and procedures that can be learned, and the results of the work can in principle be verified as being correct or incorrect. The 'managerial aspect' has no such rules and procedures, and the results of this work will be judged, not on whether the results are correct or incorrect, but on whether they are appropriate or inappropriate. The qualities required to do the managerial aspect of a role are commitment, level of perception, level of stress tolerance and level of empathy. Those required to do the technical aspects of a role are level of skill, level of education or training, and level of fit-in-ability

I can now add a third aspect, the aspect of leadership. Whereas the manager balances the competing forces within the group with a view to producing a product, the leader balances the competing forces within the group, and within the environment in which the group is situated, in such a way that the potential of the dynamic center is realized. The dynamic center is, until incarnated by someone, a dynamic center of potential. Thus leadership is not simply someone at the dynamic center, but someone realizing the potential of the dynamic center. Whenever a there is a group of two or more people, who have a mutual interest in staying together for a while, a dynamic center of potential arises. When someone is able to realize that potential, that person becomes the leader of that group.

On Commitment

Dynamic unity is always going towards unity, a 'towards' that is translated in human terms as 'a towards' in time. Time's arrow, the asymmetry of time, comes from dynamic unity 'going towards unity.' Thus it is understandable that for Christians, heaven, which presumably would be the state of complete unity, complete harmony, peace and love, is attainable only in a future life. The dynamic centre, the emissary of dynamic unity, likewise is 'in the

future' so to say. It could be likened to the center of gravity of a little boy running down hill. To realize the potential of the dynamic center would therefore require commitment, a word that I said could be used as a synonym for dynamic unity. The etymology of the word 'commitment' comes from two words com which means 'together,' and mit, which means 'put.' (as in French mettre 'to put') Commit therefore means to put one's own dynamic center together with the dynamic center of the group, to make it one's own. Hitler was famous for proclaiming, "I am Germany; Germany is me."

Level of Perception

The level of the idea of the product that his department is required to produce determines the level of perception required of a manager. In *Conflict and Creativity at Work* I have defined a product as an idea in a form with a demand. The idea reveals relations that exist in a field of phenomena. The more complex the field, the higher the level of idea required to reveal all the relations and so allow them to be taken into account when producing the product.

Leadership also requires level of perception, which some people might call 'vision.' Drawing on the work of Rudolph Arnheim I said earlier that a 'human situation'-- a country, a company, a club, a hospital – "comprises a number of centers each of which tries to draw the others into subservience … The overall balance of all these competing aspirations determines the structure of the whole and that total structure is organized around what I will call the balancing center" (1982, p. 2) The full potential of the dynamic center can only be realized if the leader can perceive the idea that can bring together the different needs, goals and aspirations of the various power groups and their centers in a single grasp. For example some of the power groups within a company are the board of directors, the trades union, the various consumer protection agencies, the government, and the suppliers. A CEO must balance the demands that each of these has in a way that maintains the viability of the company. The way that he or she does this will come from the company idea that he or she perceives. This idea in turn will determine the ethos of the company. Gestalt psychology has shown us that such perception is not a passive reception of stimuli but active creativity. The level of perception will be a function of the number, power and independence of these competing centers.

The Level of Stress Tolerance

The idea thus perceived, because it must embrace a field of conflicting forces, is not harmonious but, on the contrary, ambiguous -- or even a set of nested ambiguities -- and so is full of potential and actual conflict. To perceive and hold the idea in such a way that the potential of the dynamic center can be realized will require considerable commitment, and this in turn will generate corresponding stress. The degree of commitment and the extent of the stress will be a function of the number, power and independence of the conflicting centers of power within the group and within the environment in which the groups is situated. The ability to tolerate that stress over time is thus the second aspect of leadership.

However, to perceive the idea that will integrate the group the leader must be sensitive to the feelings, mood and interests of the group and of the power centers within the group. These are not static but will change over time. A level of empathy is therefore required.

Empathy

Empathy is the ability to identify with the situation, condition, thoughts or feelings of others. It is different to having compassion or sympathy "for" another person; empathy puts you in their shoes to feel "with" them or "as one" with them. As a leader this is important because with it one can anticipate how others are likely to react to one's leadership. It is also important because it enables one to address the various power centers in a way that they can understand and accept.

Human situations are essentially unstable and constantly tending towards chaos. To perceive, hold and modify an idea according to the changes that occur, and that will likely, occur requires commitment. Thus as a leader one must constantly reaffirm one's commitment,

one must be ready to modify the way one perceives the situation and be ready for a constant fluctuation in the level of stress. In order to be able to anticipate the changes one must have "one's ear to the ground," which is possible depending on one's level of empathy.

The Dynamic Center and Commitment and Capacity

The dynamic center is the emissary of dynamic unity. The dynamic center focuses dynamic unity. An analogy would be holding a magnifying glass to focus the rays of the sun. The intensity with which dynamic unity is focused is again the function of the number, strength and independence of the competing centers. Through his or her level of perception, level of stress and level of empathy, a leader realizes the potential of the dynamic center to focus dynamic unity and so realize the creative potential of the center. In this way the leader incarnates the dynamic center and so acquires the power of the center.

This incarnation is marked by the tendency of the leader to be given, in addition to his or her own name, a special designation such as "your Majesty" or your Highness, or Mr. President, Prime minister, Fuhrer, or El Duce. Transference of power of the Center from one incarnation to another is performed by some ritual or by decree of an authority empowered to make that transference.

That Hitler was able to rule even when his capacity and ability had been reduced almost to nil bears out what I have to say. As long as he was alive, and as long as the political structure, and by that I mean the balance of competing centers, remained relatively unchanged, Hitler continued to incarnate the dynamic center and was protected by the mystique that surrounds it.

I have brought together three dominant theories of leadership.

Leadership has often been looked upon as a quality or the sum of a collection of qualities that a man or a woman possesses. Often this "leadership" is considered to be a property that someone has independently of the circumstances. I spoke earlier of the book by Joseph Boyett and Jimmie Boyett their book, The Guru Guide, who give various lists of qualities provided by other authors

that a leader should have. One hears the expression: leaders are born not made. As I have shown, we can only speak of a leader-in-a-situation. Furthermore, many of the attributes, such a charisma, power, center of attraction, cohesive power are not attributes of the person but of the dynamic center whose potential the leader is able to realize. A leader must, however, have the necessary commitment and capacity to be able to realize the potential of the dynamic center.

Another explanation for the power and authority of the leader is that these qualities are not inherent in the leader but are projected on to the leader through what is called transference. I would surmise that, in what I have said about the importance of the dynamic center, we have the true foundation this so-called transference. Some writers, Elliott Jaques being chief among them deny altogether the value of talking about leadership within the context of a business organization, claiming that it is pointless to ask whether 'management' or 'leadership' is more important as the two words mean more or less the same thing. However, Jaques looks upon management as a rational activity capable of being reduced to exact procedures that can be spelled out in vary clearly defined terms. Leadership is not a rational activity

The last theory of leadership is that a leader is made by the circumstances of the situation. In other words it is claimed that history makes a leader; the leader does not make history. This seems to be the case with Winston Churchill, in that at the end of the Second World War he was ejected from office. Times had change; the power centers in Britain had shifted and he could no longer fill the role of leader. Yet, at the same time, he has been called the greatest British leader since Cromwell, and received accolades from all over the world for his great powers of leadership thorough the darkest days of British history and truly of European history as well. Thus although the situation brings about a certain distribution of centers of power within a group and so makes a potential dynamic center possible a person in the must realize that that potential, and in this way makes leadership active.

References

Arnheim, R. (1982). *The Power of the Center*. Berkeley, CA: University of California Press.

Boyett, J. & Boyett, J. (2000). *The guru guide: The best ideas of the top management thinkers*. New York, NY: John Wiley and Sons

Eliade, M. (1957). *The sacred and the profane*. New York: Harcourt Brace Jovanovich.

Eliade, M. (1969). *Images and symbols*. London: Harvill Press.

Fest, J. (1975). *Hitler*. New York: Vintage Books.

Jaques, E. (1989). *Requisite organization*. Arlington, VA: Cason Hall

Joachimsthaler, A. (2000). *The last days of Hitler: The legends, the evidence, the truth*. London: Cassell Military Paperbacks.

Low, A. (2002) *Consciousness*. Ashland, OR: White Cloud Press.

Lovell, J., & Kluger, J. (1995). *Apollo 13*. New York: Pocket Books.

Schopenhauer, A. (trans. 1969). *The world as will and representation*. New York: Dover Edition:

Wegener, M. (2002) *The illusion of the conscious mind*. Cambridge, MA: MIT Press.

THE 27TH INTERNATIONAL CONFERENCE
OF THE SOCIETY FOR THE STUDY OF SHAMANISM, HEALING, AND TRANSFORMATION

WISDOM OF OUR ANCESTORS

BRIDGE TO THE FUTURE

SEPTEMBER 4-6, 2010
LABOR DAY WEEKEND
SANTA SABINA RETREAT CENTER, SAN RAFAEL, CA

An opportunity to engage with shamans, healers, scientists, anthropologists, medical doctors, psychologists, and artists and to explore new directions of cross-cultural healing in the 21st century.

For more information and to register, visit our webpage:
www.shamanismconference.org

Leadership Among Spiritual Teachers

Constance A. Jones and Wendy Mason

T his conversation between Constance A. Jones, Ph.D., Professor in the Transformative Studies Doctoral Program at the California Institute of Integral Studies and Wendy Mason, MSN, ARNP, and graduate student in the Transformative Studies Doctoral Program at the California Institute of Integral Studies, offers insight into spiritual leadership in both Eastern and Western contexts. Professor Jones has been interested in the religious traditions of south Asia for over thirty years and has documented in her research how south Asian religions that have some basis in Hinduism and Buddhism have been disseminated in the West, particularly through new religious movements in the United States and Europe. During residence in India she met spiritual teachers of many different types,

Constance A. Jones, Ph.D., is Professor in the Transformative Studies Doctoral Program at the California Institute of Integral Studies in San Francisco. Her research centers around Eastern religious practice in Western contexts. Her most recent publications include *The Heritage of G.I. Gurdjieff* and *Encyclopedia of Hinduism*.

Wendy Mason, MSN, ARNP, and graduate student in the Transformative Studies Doctoral Program at the California Institute of Integral Studies has over ten years of working in mental health and wellness. She has published articles related to policy and decision making, mental health and wellness, and is currently exploring transdisciplinarity as an approach to living in open inquiry.

traced lineages of spiritual schools, and returned to the United States to visit centers set up by these teachers, as well as American teachers who have adopted Eastern paths of spirituality. Living in a variety of ashrams in both East and West has helped her understand how spiritual teachers in Hinduism and Buddhism hold definitions of what is real, how they relate to their devotees, and how their practices are adopted in different cultural contexts. Her work appreciates the diversity of leadership and spiritual expression in Hinduism itself and the ways in which Hinduism is pervasive in many quasi-Hindu movements in ways that are not always apparent.

Professor Jones recently collaborated with James Ryan, a Sanskrit scholar and colleague at the California Institute of Integral Studies, to publish the *Encyclopedia of Hinduism*, a unique volume that provides understanding of a number of spiritual teachers, Hindu movements both inside and outside India, a pre-history and history of Hinduism in many places around the world, and several theoretical essays that situate Hindu spirituality and practice in the larger context of religious experience. Working on the volume demonstrated with expanded clarity the diversity, complexity, and appeal of Eastern spirituality.

Wendy Mason: The topic of leadership in religions is complex and often contro-

versial as scholars, devotees, and casual observers identify personal characteristics, styles of leadership, and examples of successful as well as unsuccessful communities. The first element in identifying salient characteristics of successful spiritual leaders and communities must include, it seems to me, consideration of the worldview or worldviews that Hindu teachers hold and how these worldviews differ from Western worldviews. How would you describe the major differences between Eastern (particularly Hindu and Buddhist) spirituality and Western (primarily Abrahamic) spirituality?

Connie Jones: Although exceptions exist, Hinduism and Buddhism generally encourage personal inquiry into the relationship between self and cosmos as a central practice and foundation to spiritual experience. In contrast, Western religions encourage and value belief. Hence, in the West, we identify a person's adherence to a religious tradition by inquiring into what ontological and theological beliefs one holds. Theological beliefs and adherence to dogma can be inconsequential in many Eastern traditions.

Mason: Is this difference reflected in the ways in which Eastern masters teach and tutor their disciples?

Jones: Yes, very much so. In the West, we find that spiritual teachers in institutionalized religions are educated in a religious tradition and uphold that tradition through didactic methods such as discourses, sermons, lessons, and tutorials. In the East, other types of teaching are often used. Some spiritual masters transmit energy through a glance or touch and disciples find that their consciousness is transformed instantly. This is the meaning of the word darshan, which means "to see" (Jones & Ryan, 2007, p. 119). Other teachers sit in silence their entire lives and disciples receive some degree of "awakening" by being in proximity to the silent master. There is a long tradition of placing silence as the supreme mode of communication in the practice of Advaita Vedanta, which goes back as far as the Upanishads. In a hymn to Dakshinamurti, one of the forms of Shiva, attributed to the great Advaitan sage Shankaracharya, seventh century CE, this tradition is described: "A young master is sitting with aged disciples under a banyan tree. The master teaches in silence and the doubts of the students are dispelled" (Sharma, 2006, p. 134).

Ramana Maharshi, a great saint of the 20th century regarded silence as the preferable mode of teaching, even after he became accustomed to answering questions verbally. Shakyamuni Buddha was said to hold up a flower when asked by a disciple to explain the meaning of his teaching. One assumes from this gesture that the Buddha was demonstrating that meaning need not always be conveyed linguistically.

Other teachers, often women such as Mother Meera and Amritananda Ma, are said to embody the goddess, so that their love and compassion is said to transmute the consciousness of those in attendance. Still others teach by example, constructing the walls of buildings, stone by stone, and demonstrating how directed awareness can become a laser that transforms material reality and consciousness simultaneously. Underlying each of these methods of teaching is the assumption that the teaching must be appropriate for the student and that the teacher/guru must know the student well in order to create conditions for teaching the student. That is why the guru-chela relationship depends upon an in-depth knowledge of the student by the teacher and why the guru takes on each person

as an individual. This situation is quite different from delivering a sermon to an audience of a thousand people.

Mason: Also, there appears to be a difference among the perspectives of spiritual leaders in the West and the East in terms of authority. Do different worldviews operate in East and West, so that spiritual authority and the legitimation of that authority have different ontological bases?

Jones: Yes, the sociologist Max Weber offers a useful dichotomy to distinguish two types of teacher or prophet. An exemplary or emissary prophet provides a model for a way of life that others can practice. As an "exemplar", such a teacher embodies a higher level of "being" than others. Any number of Hindu teachers are examples of this category of exemplary teacher, such as Ramana Maharshi, Nisargadatta Maharaj, Meher Baba, Anandamayi Ma, Mother Meera, and Amritananda Ma.

The ethical prophet on the other hand teaches precepts of an impersonally defined normative order. Followers are not exhorted to emulate the ethical prophet, but to follow the directives that the ethical prophet brings, the following of which is a moral obligation. Any Christian preacher, Jewish rabbi, or Muslim imam would fall into this category.

The two types of prophet or teacher rest on very different conceptualizations of their sources of legitimation. The exemplary prophet sees herself or himself in some personal relationship to, in identification with, or even as an embodiment of the divine. The ethical prophet, by contrast, defines herself or himself as an instrument of a divine will, with a mission to promulgate norms and obligations that express that will, yet not necessarily a person of greater "being" than followers.

Mason: These appear to be two very different approaches to spiritual leadership. When we contemplate the contrast between the two, it can be quite challenging to comprehend such ontological differences. How do two such contrasting approaches emerge?

Jones: Behind these differences in assumptions of leadership are differences in conceptions of divinity. Exemplary prophecy is associated with an imma-

nent, pantheistic principle of divinity, in which the prophet participates. Others who follow an exemplary prophet can aspire to participate in the same identification with the divine. Ethical prophecy is associated with legitimation of authority by reference to a transcendental conception of divinity, with one god or multiple gods who exist outside and above the world in which humans participate and who legislate moral obligations for that world. The religious philosophy of India represents a clear example of the exemplary form of teaching, while the Abrahamic religions of Judaism, Christianity, and Islam are for the most part examples of the ethical form. I note that elements in this Weberian dichotomy are what he termed "ideal types" and are not universally the case in East and West. Yet, they are useful for understanding major differences between East and West.

Mason: I am sure that you have met many spiritual teachers. Who are some of the gurus you've met?

Jones: I've met a variety of teachers in India and the West. They vary widely in their pedagogies and practices. Satya Sai Baba, Swami Muktananda, and Swami Chidvilasananda relate to disciples through a glance or a touch. J. Krishnamurti, Swami Krishnananda, Ramesh Balsekar, and Prem Rawat give discourses. Mother Meera, Amritananda, and Baba Hari Das teach in silence.

Mason: Many people seek spiritual leaders or gurus in pursuit of spiritual growth. Obviously, problems can occur when seekers and teachers hold varying, perhaps conflicting conceptions of divinity and spiritual leadership, especially when those seeking leadership are unaware of these differences in perspective. And there are, of course, multiple challenges in selecting a spiritual leader. How does one know how to choose a good spiritual leader? Are there any similarities you can identify amongst the tremendous range of gurus you've met personally? And have you seen these characteristics in spiritual leaders in the West?

Jones: Similarities exist, yes, along with considerable differences. In the East, spiritual teachers, as compared to ordinary people, are usually assumed to have greater awareness, expanded consciousness, and an integration of realization into their selves. This attribution is often spoken of as a "higher level of being." Westerners might say that these teachers have "evolved". Even though it is axiomatic in the East that disciples cannot comprehend the extent of realization of a spiritual teacher, somehow disciples can recognize the authority of a teacher and can be touched in some way. For example, I visited one teacher in India often and every time I would see him I would cry, and the minute I left, I would stop crying. I asked, him, "Tell me what's going on here?" and he said to me, "Well... maybe you see something about love" and that is exactly what it was. I was in the presence of objective love. This person seemed to love everyone and see divinity in every person. I could not rise to his level or comprehend him, but I could taste or feel or sense something that is higher than my level of development. It is this personal connection or touch that opens a disciple to what the guru offers. One could say that this is a portal to compassion.

So, in the guru tradition the assumption is that spiritual leaders somehow live at a different level than followers and embody a different level of being, yet they are not assumed to have achieved something that others cannot achieve. In fact, they promise that if followers awaken or become enlightened, followers can achieve the level of leaders or even higher. If followers see who teachers are and follow the path offered by the teachers, followers can become like the teachers. This goes back to the idea of exemplary prophecy—that these leaders are, in their very core, different from others. And they are different in their level of spiritual development, not because they are "trained" or "educated" in a theological system or belief structure. By the way, this ideal of an emissary prophet is also at the center of Western esoteric traditions as well, including esoteric Christianity, Judaism, and Sufism, so that we see similarities between Eastern spiritual teachers and Western esoteric teachers. Often this quality of teachers operates as charisma, so that spiritual teachers can exercise inordinate sway over others, as do all people with charisma, whether religious or not.

Mason: Is it possible that Western people who have had experience with only the methods of pastors, preachers, and priests might miss the import of these other teaching methods, even when they are direct observers of these methods? It would seem that Westerners could miss even what is before their eyes if they were not aware of other dimensions of teaching and learning.

Jones: Most definitely. I have had such experiences of seeing a person radically changed even though I could not

Some spiritual masters transmit energy through a glance or touch and disciples find that their consciousness is transformed instantly.

perceive how the guru or teacher was guiding the transformation. Once in Rishikesh, I studied with Swami Krishnananda of the Divine Life Society, a teacher who was known as a jivan-mukta, an enlightened person. I saw him give an assignment to a disciple who reported the next day that the assignment had been done. When Krishnananda examined the work, some masonry, he derided the disciple, ridiculing him publicly. My response was to criticize (in my own mind of course) the guru. Yet, the next day I saw the disciple with a glowing countenance. He appeared to be transformed. I simply did not understand the method or the exchange of energy that took place between the guru and the disciple.

Mason: In the West, our focus is on individuality, individual rights, and self-determination. And we tend not to see divinity as pervasive in all of manifestation. Holding these perspectives must surely limit our understanding and appreciation of the various teaching styles and methods in the East. This is particularly true considering the fact that Buddhist and Hindu teachers have very different ways of teaching than the teaching styles employed in the West. What are some of the teaching methods

used by spiritual leaders in Hinduism and Buddhism?

Jones: A number of teaching methods rare in the West are found in India. For example, some teachers in India use silence as a method for instructing disciples, a method we know little about here. It is difficult for us in the West to understand how a disciple will sit with a teacher who is not going to say a single word and learn about a teaching by simply being in the presence of a guru. When we observe Ammachi (Amritananda Ma), we see that she does not give discourses, per se. Yes, her sayings are printed in books, but when one goes to her darshan, she does not speak to an audience, but rather hugs each person, one by one. At the darshan of Mother Meera, one sits in silence in her presence. She doesn't deliver a discourse, a sermon, or a lecture. Ramana Maharshi did not speak to most people who came to learn from him. Even when disciples honed their questions in advance of meeting Ramana, they would often forget their prepared remarks once in his presence. They would be mute. That is what happened to Paul Brunton. He said "I could not remember my question because I was in the presence of Ramana Maharshi." The more austere practice of continual silence, practiced by Meher Baba and even today by Baba Hari Dass, is also a teaching in itself that we understand little about in the West. Meher Baba's words summarize this method of teaching and communicating, "Things that are real are given and received in silence." Unaccustomed as we are to this method of communicating, we can be perplexed by students' reports of radical transformation from sitting in silence with their teachers. Another method of teaching that is rare in the West is direct transmission of energy from a teacher to a disciple. Swami Muktananda and his successor Swami Chidvilasananda touch disciples with a peacock feather or a fingertip and the disciples report radical changes in their lives. This transmission of energy-- literally from body to body, from one person to another—is another form of teaching with which we are quite unfamiliar. The notion that a person can be radically transformed in the moment by the touch or the glance of a teacher is not commonly understood in the West. So to be seen by a guru, to be transformed by the very sight of a guru, is a method of teaching that is common in Indian spirituality, but occurs rarely in the West. Even when gurus in India deliver discourses, being in their presence carries a weight that exceeds the import of hearing a sermon in Western situations.

Mason: How does the notion of meditation come in here? I often hear individuals discuss their meditation practices and their subsequent frustration in not gaining clarity or achieving peace of mind. They feel restless and their minds won't slow down-- rather they grow increasingly agitated instead. Sometimes I wonder if we really understand what meditation is.

Jones: You point to another difference between East and West in this question. In the East, each person is assumed to be an enlightened person in the making. Eastern traditions teach that discipline and awareness lead to transformation. And central to this transformation is a recognition on the part of each person that one's life is sacred and worthy of respect. After discipline is established, one begins to see a sacred nature in all existence— in one's own person and in the world around one. Further, once the sacred nature of one's existence is appreciated, one begins to find a higher place in self, a teacher within oneself, often referred to as the "guru within." The assumption is that one knows more than one is able to access consciously and by going into meditation, one can still the everyday mind and can come to greater realization. To have a taste of the sacred requires stilling the mind so that a higher wisdom can be accessed. A quiet mind, absent the gyrations of everyday

life, is a requirement for realizing the higher Self.

Mason: Well, maybe that's my problem!

Jones: That is everyone's problem! In the West we are conditioned to act, to do, to manipulate the world around us. Yet, we also need to stop and practice awareness of our being in the moment. Being is quite different from doing and we are conditioned to remain in the doing mode incessantly.

Mason: Earlier, you discussed how spiritual leaders need to know their disciples. Understanding each disciple and how each navigates in the world is a critical component for the spiritual leader, and, I suspect, for those who are in the process of choosing a guru. For example, there are various kinds of yogic paths. How can we develop a better understanding of these various paths and the role these play in spiritual leadership and discipleship?

Jones: Eastern traditions are quite clear in recognizing that people are different in the ways in which they perceive and act in the world. One spiritual

Obviously, problems can occur when seekers and teachers hold varying, perhaps conflicting conceptions of divinity and spiritual leadership, especially when those seeking leadership are unaware of these differences in perspective.

path will not be suitable for all people. Some people perceive the world primarily through their minds, some through their emotions, and some through their bodies. In a parallel way, some require a spiritual path that revolves around intellectual study, some around devotion, and some around action and service. These are the three central yogas described in the *Bhagavad Gita*, along with the path of the integration of all of those three. Individuals inclined to devotion find that the path of bhakti is more congenial to

their abilities than the paths of jnana (knowledge) or karma (action). And of course, concentration on one path to the neglect of the other paths leads to imbalance, not spiritual growth.

There are examples in the East, as in the West, of people who are imbalanced in their spiritual pursuits. For example, fakirs subject their bodies to extreme austerities, such as lying on a bed of nails or puncturing the body or standing on one foot for years or being buried with little oxygen for days. These people overcome certain limitations of the body as we define them, with the goal of achieving Self-realization. Yet, even these masters of physical austerities can also find themselves in states of imbalance.

Disciples who are devoted to a lifetime of spiritual searching will often work with a series of gurus, each chosen for tutelage in specific teachings and practices.

Mason: And, as you have mentioned before, in traditional Hindu or Buddhist thinking, a guru need not be the most accomplished spiritual adept to serve as a teacher for a disciple. The operative principle in the guru-disciple relationship seems to be the obedience and service that the disciple offers the guru. This principle is quite different from Western notions of how one learns from a spiritual teacher. Learning from an emissary or exemplary prophet, essentially a spiritual teacher who recognizes that the higher Self is within each person and assists in pursuit of realization of this higher Self, is quite different from learning from an ethical prophet, who is believed to be a conduit for some other spiritual entity outside oneself.

Jones: Study with a guru from the emissary perspective in the Hindu tradition requires that disciples question how they might understand the teaching of the guru and adapt their lives to the requirements of the guru. In the West, we critique the teacher's perspective and method in terms of our own worldviews.

We think to ourselves, "Do I agree with what this person said?" So we subject Western spiritual teachers to our personal critiques based on who we are, whereas in India disciples are required to attempt to fit into the guru's worldview. This difference between East and West is the source of much misunderstanding and conflict, as the two worldviews collide when Western disciples choose to study under Eastern teachers. The usual complaints against Eastern teachers, which revolve around money, sex, or psychological control, are indictments made from a Western individualistic paradigm. These indictments are rarely observed in Eastern venues, where the guru-disciple relationship is firmly entrenched in the worldview of all adherents. And so, to a considerable extent, the complaints against Eastern teachers revolve around Western notions of what constitutes legitimate authority on a spiritual path and reflect how we in the West attempt to judge Eastern teachers according to a Western worldview.

Mason: This distinction between Eastern and Western worldviews includes radically different notions of "self" and what constitutes "death to self." In the Western psychological perspective, we are very centered on the value of the individual self and the development of self throughout life. Our psychology stresses the value of the individual self, the rights of that self, and the lifelong commitment to maturation and actualization of that self. Yet in India, the concern isn't about a psychologically constructed self, but rather it's about releasing this egoic constructed self while seeking a higher Self. And one finds this Self through seeking enlightenment with the assistance of one's spiritual leader.

Jones: Yes, there's a paradox here, which is central to all major religions. By giving up oneself—one's individual self—one finds a new self, a higher self that participates more fully in the divine.

Mason: And underlying this paradox a distinct contrast between conceptions of self in East and West appears. A central focus in the West is the value of indi-

viduality and the rights of each individual self. So, there is a difference between East and West in the ways in which the self is supported. When we look at Western philosophical assumptions about the self, and the history of ideas relating to self, we find much research, for example, models from psychology such as Maslow's self-actualization, Kohlberg's ideas on moral development, Gilligan's explanation of gender differences in moral conceptualizations, and others. In the West, the self is assumed to be a flexible and dynamic construct that is ever evolving. Yet, when we consider the *Bhagavad Gita*, this self is essentially superfluous. In the West, we spend considerable time modeling the self, studying its maturation, and describing its

> One spiritual path will not be suitable for all people. Some people perceive the world primarily through their minds, some through their emotions, and some through their bodies.

"ideal" development. Yet, in Eastern traditions, the self is in many ways irrelevant because what must be pursued is the higher Self, which emanates from and participates in a divine source.

Jones: Here we have two different conceptions of self: in the West, we spend our time building up the self, gratifying self, looking into all the elements of the self, strengthening the self, working toward an undivided self. While in the East, the self is something to be identified with the larger Self, the Atman of Hinduism. In Buddhist terms, there is no persistent self that exists over time. The main difference between East and West is the assiduous study of the nature of the self on the part of Eastern philosophies, while in the West, we are only beginning to analyze the nature of the self, and unfortunately often in very reductionist ways.

Mason: We hear often about a "higher self," a "higher mind," an "enlightened mind," and an awakened heart. It is difficult to see how the higher is connected to the lower, considering that the lower is the consciousness that we all participate in every day.

Jones: The East and West also differ in directionality of development. In the East there is a higher mind that we can touch and that can be incorporated and integrated into everyday life. Development involves the drawing down of something or the opening to something higher, as opposed to building up from the bottom, from nothing. The distinction is between involution and evolution. The West tends to be engrossed in the evolution paradigm, with little regard for involution. The evolutionary paradigm posits building from simpler forms to more complex forms, until a higher spirituality emerges. Perhaps we should consider how both evolution and involution are required for spiritual growth, so that we understand how there is both a building up from the bottom and a drawing down from above. Sri Aurobindo describes the integration of the two processes quite eloquently.

Mason: In the West, there is the idea that there is a goal to be achieved, a cut off point, for example, self-actualization. Our philosophy asserts that when one becomes self actualized, one has attained the goal, as opposed to the notion of seeking enlightenment in Buddhism or Hinduism where there really is no end to growth. In essence, we have an individualistic end goal, an achievement to be attained.

Jones: In some ways, Western inquiry into the nature of spirituality and self is only beginning. In the East, thousands of years have been devoted to the exploration, refinement, and documentation of inner states. India has a long history of acute observation and exposition of nuanced differences among spiritual experiences. Our language is largely devoid of these terms. We are only beginning to understand the depth with which Indian philosophy describes human spiritual experience. The image of the carriage, with driver, horse, reins, and master is an excellent example of how relationships among the various parts of a human must be studied and understood for a higher consciousness to emerge. In this image, the driver must control the horse by using the reins, but he must listen to the master, seated behind him, to pursue a purposeful path. It is that master that we are trying to get in touch with. This is the classical image described in the Katha Upanishad to illustrate the notion that there is a higher wisdom, a master. The path to enlightenment is to provide a way to come in touch with the master. For example, when we hear people say "Everyone is Buddha", they are not referring to the persons here today, but rather they are talking about a higher self that one can be touch with or have the potential to be in touch with.

Mason: Looking at this from the perspective that we are such a young country, we can see how we are trying to usurp some of these ideas without comprehending the actual concepts we are attempting to employ and apply. We are missing the overarching picture.

Jones: This discussion brings us to the whole element of time. In the East, there are no assurances that one will be enlightened in the next two years. One makes a commitment to search for enlightenment or an evolution of consciousness. It may take many lifetimes or only a few days. Indian stories explain, again and again, the tedious life of giving oneself to the spiritual search, even when everyone in the world persecutes the aspirant.

Mason: When I look at Western authors on spirituality, growth, and enlightenment, I find much of the writing is often focused on individual growth. Earlier, you mentioned Weber's classification. I find that the role of the ethical prophet in the West is part of a reification of patriarchal values and a patriarchal paradigm. Instead of a shared collective, composite view that explores the relationship between self and the cosmos, which depicts the exemplary or emissary prophet, we hold the notion that we are instruments, conduits of a Divine will from something that is other than ourselves, something "out there."

Jones: On the whole, East and West include different world views and different notions of the nature of divinity. Divinity is immanent in the East in contrast to a totally transcendent divinity who creates a moral code and obligatory system.

Mason: In terms of differences in ontologies, disciples who reside in a Western paradigm may find the idea of immanence to be threatening, because it challenges a codified structure, which is also usually patriarchal. This considerable discrepancy, which could also be a major conflict in meaning systems, could play a role in the problematic nature of spiritual teachers in the West

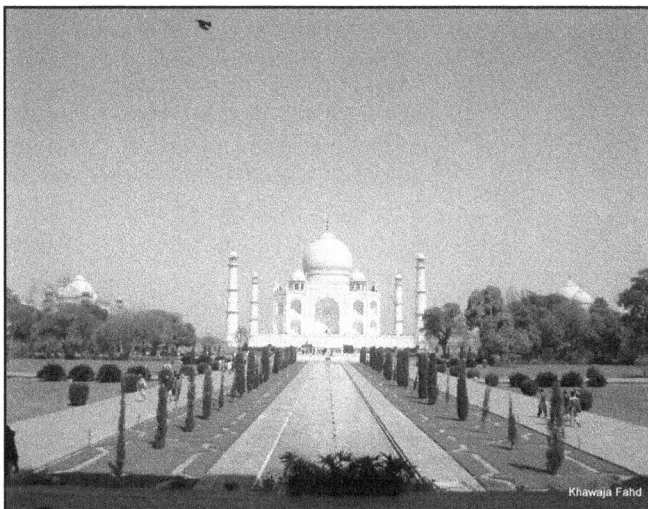

Photo: Khawaja M. Fahd

who use the philosophy and the methods of Eastern teachings. How might this discrepancy affect those who follow a particular leader?

Jones: In Eastern ontologies, the assumption is that one's real guru resides within. The phrases "Jivan is Atman" in Hinduism and "You are Buddha" in Buddhism reflect the assumption that one's highest nature is one's real teacher. These phrases are difficult to understand from a Western perspective, which views God as elsewhere, transcendent to the human world. When divinity is immanent, as in most Eastern ontologies, the quest to follow an embodied guru is the quest to find eventually the guru within oneself. Even during the phase that one studies with an embodied guru, the practices and assumptions are quite different than the practices and assumptions in the West. The guru in the East bears much responsibility for the student/disciple, to

the point of even taking on the karma of the student. This system is radically different from the relationship between a student and a pastor, priest, or spiritual teacher in the West. Western teachers are not assumed to be able to touch the state of an individual's soul.

Mason: How does one achieve the kind of legitimation or authority necessary to become a spiritual leader in India?

Jones: One sees that spiritual leaders in India are often considered as having a decidedly different consciousness from ordinary people; their authority rests on social recognition or social ratification of this difference. For example, Ramana Maharshi, certainly one of the most famous saints of the last century, at age 16 had a life changing experience and, from that moment on, even though sitting in rags with ants and vermin crawling on him, was recognized as a spiritual being and as a teacher. People would come to be in his presence, even though he wasn't giving any kind of verbal teachings. In his very existence he was the teaching. He was said to "rest" in the awareness of his union with the divine. The teaching is the person; the person is the embodiment of the teaching.

Mason: Is avatar the appropriate term for this?

Jones: There are many kinds of spiritual teachers in the East. An avatar is assumed to be a person that is sent from another dimension, from a higher level, who comes as a manifestation of God on earth. Some believe that there is one avatar per age, which is roughly 2100 years. For example, many believe that Meher Baba is the avatar of the Aquarian Age. Interestingly, there are many claims to avatarship in the 20th century, so the concept is a bit overused, and the term has come to be synonymous with enlightened teacher. Traditionally an avatar has a much more important role in the cosmic process than a spiritual teacher. In the *Bhagavad Gita,* the Lord Krishna says essentially that when things get very bad, he will come to manifestation. The coming of an avatar in the East is comparable to the coming of Jesus

Christ in the West. Similarly Buddha is considered an avatar.

The major difference between most Christian beliefs about the coming of Jesus and beliefs in avatars is that in the avataric scheme each individual is expected to become, over many lifetimes, like Krishna and Buddha, while in the West few believe that all Christians are to become like Jesus. Having said that, we need to recognize that many Christians do see the task of every person to become like Jesus.

Another important distinction is that, in the East, the goal is Self realization,

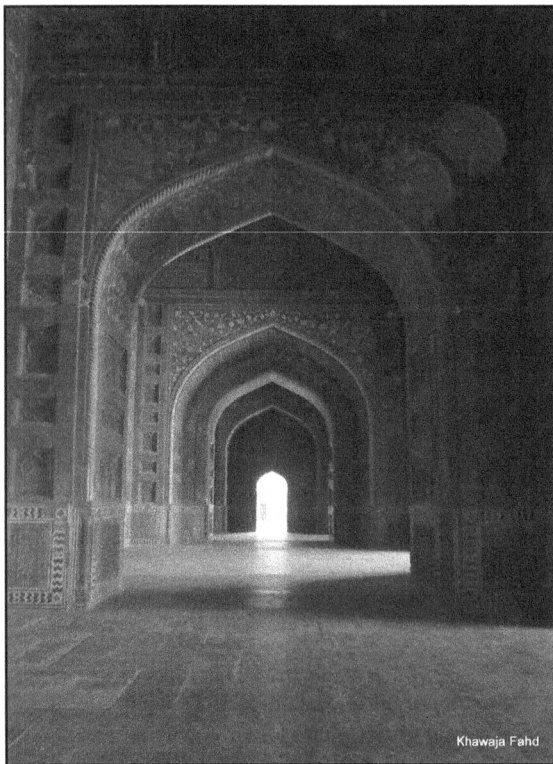
Photo: Khawaja M. Fahd

meaning that one undergoes a cognitive and spiritual shift to realize who one's real self is, which is part of the highest divinity, the Self with a capital S. In the West, salvation, described as transition from a state of no grace to a state of grace, is usually defined as the goal of life.

Mason: That goes back to our conversation earlier about the contrast between the definitions of the concept of "self". As I understand it, in Hinduism or Buddhism, when one achieves this knowledge or realization of the higher

Self, one actually finds the guru within. As opposed to our perspective in the West where finding one's self would be grounded on the idea of finding one's self from a psychological perspective,

Legitimate authority seems to be defined quite differently in East and West.

more like achieving individuation (in the Jungian sense) or self-actualization (in Maslow's scheme). So, from this perspective, exploring spiritual leadership based on an Eastern philosophy that is introduced into the West, we can see how spiritual teachers can be misinterpreted and misunderstood because of significant differences in ontology and epistemology between teacher and student.

Jones: Right, not only misinterpretation of teachings, but also misunderstanding of the motives and practices of the teachers themselves when they appear in a Western context. In the West, we ask spiritual teachers from any tradition to fit into the Western mold; we critique them from our perspective, which in the last analysis is all that we can do. For example, we might ask, "Is this guru good enough for me", whereas in India and Western esoteric schools, the notion is that an appropriate teacher need not be an avatar or God on earth to be a legitimate teacher. Someone who knows more than one knows can be one's teacher.

We are again reminded of assumptions about divinity and, derived from these assumptions, the creation and use of a normative order. In the West we believe that living by a moral and ethical code will increase the likelihood that grace will be achieved. The whole notion is that we think we can judge ourselves and spiritual teachers according to this code.

We apply this code when we assume that we can know how and why spiritual teachers whose actions have been judged improper (such as Jim Jones, Rajneesh, Adi Da Samraj, Swami Rama, Swami Muktananta, Amrit Desai, and many others) went awry in failing their followers. In contrast, the spiritual goal in the East is transformation of a person and reliance on an embodied guru to facilitate that transformation. Negative judgment of a guru by followers is rare, as followers assume that they cannot judge a person who participates in a higher level of consciousness. In fact, it is often said that the guru is beyond duality, beyond good and evil.

Mason: From our gaze through a Western paradigm, we often judge harshly someone who teaches from an Eastern philosophy. What can you say about Western teachers who are Western in their perspective and method, yet choose to teach Eastern traditions, particularly Hinduism and Buddhism? Is their interpretation of these philosophies from a Western standpoint problematic?

Jones: Well, that's an interesting question. Here we must recognize differences in assumptions about leadership style, legitimation of authority, authoritarianism and what we call totalism. Totalism is involved in the traditional guru-disciple relationship and involves a requirement by the guru that the disciple give the guru all allegiance, all time, and all devotion. In the old days, in the classical Hindu tradition, a young boy who became a *brahmachari* would give his life to his guru for the time spent in the guru's school, staying with the guru until he became ready to establish a household. But the whole idea of giving one's entire life to one other human being, even a spiritual teacher, is difficult when perceived from a Western perspective.

Totalism is not valued in the West and is often the source of much disparagement, even lawsuits, against Eastern teachers. The traditional guru-disciple relationship in the East exists within a well-defined system that has been worked out for thousands of years. The real problem with questions of legitimacy for Eastern spiritual leaders is that they represent a traditional system of authority that is not embedded in a Western normative structure. So, the question becomes one of adapting traditional notions of spiritual allegiance to current life in the West.

Mason: In the West, we are tenacious about individuality and autonomy, and we recognize many teachers' methods as challenges to personal self-determination. These challenges lead to charges of brainwashing or a suspicion of psychological control or even violence.

Legitimate authority seems to be defined quite differently in East and West. In Christianity, for example, a definite structure has emerged since the 16th and 17th centuries or so that involves institutionalized authority, a codified hierarchy, and patriarchal practices. In both East and West, there are power dynamics at work, but they are quite different from each other. Each involves notions of self, allegiance to authority, and normative structures, but different ontological questions appear to drive the two systems—and in different ways.

Jones: This consideration takes us back to the underlying ontology of the ethical and exemplary prophets. In the West, the dominant ontology involves the state of one's soul and salvation. These ontological assumptions become codified in a belief system, even a doctrine or catechism with a well-honed structure of belief and normative rules. One typically identifies with a religious tradition by specifying what one's belief is. In the East, by contrast, the goal is more of an ongoing inquiry, about the nature of self, the reason for existence, and one's relationship to the cosmos. Both systems search for meaning and transformation, but use different methods and practices.

Mason: Considering the existence of this deeply codified belief system and the ensuing polarity of belief versus unbelief, we see how conflicts can arise within institutionalized religious systems. An exemplar of a teaching is difficult to house within a rigid structure. How do we pursue enlightenment within a codified structure that prohibits inquiry as opposed to an open structure that supports and encourages inquiry? It seems obvious that as we critique Eastern spiritual leaders from a codified system, we can close ourselves off to potential growth. We are not open to what they can offer.

Jones: Exactly, and that's what happens when we assume that we can use the normative order and ethical system that we derive from a codified structure or catechism to judge exemplars of a living tradition. Many Eastern teachers have been criticized for a number of violations of Western ethical principles. Yet, they have devoted followers who attest repeatedly to the spiritual growth that these teachers offer in great measure. Are we dealing with legitimate or illegitimate authority when we speak of these teachers from the East? This is not an easy question to answer. We have to look at all the variables we have talked about: ontological notions of divinity, self, and the nature of the world; the goal of the spiritual life; differences in levels of development between teachers and followers; the degree to which inquiry and belief function on a spiritual path. And to these considerations, one should always be aware of an inexplicable ability to influence others that is found among many spiritual teachers—charisma. Max Weber has told us that charisma is difficult to explain and occurs without clearly observable causes. Why was Hitler charismatic and Adlai Stevenson not charismatic? Perhaps we have to look at the relationship between the charismatic person and followers. What is it that attracts us to charismatic teachers?

Bob Altemeyer, social psychologist, draws on the classic study of authoritarianism by Adorno et al. and his own research over decades to explain a personality variable called authoritarianism. He finds that right wing authoritarians, because they act mainly from fear and from a desire for conventionality, more often than not accept what others in authority dispense as knowledge. If the authoritarian personality perceives a leader as having authority, that personality will follow the leader, almost blindly and with little critical reasoning. Altemeyer has documented an extremely strong tendency toward right

wing authoritarianism in current Western venues, even among young people. So we see that the question of legitimate authority hinges on considerations of the basis of authority attributed to a leader and also the personality of the follower. When we add this complexity to the differences in ontology and epistemology, we see that there are many relationships to analyze in our effort to understand spiritual leadership. We must consider social, psychological, cultural, and even unconscious factors when we examine how authority operates in different venues.

Mason: The issues here are complicated and complex. And our well-entrenched assumptions are not always useful. Perhaps what we really need to do is side step much of what we know, or rather what and how we think we know, dust ourselves off, shed some skin and open our eyes for inquiry.

Jones: As post-modern sensibilities increase our acceptance of the validity

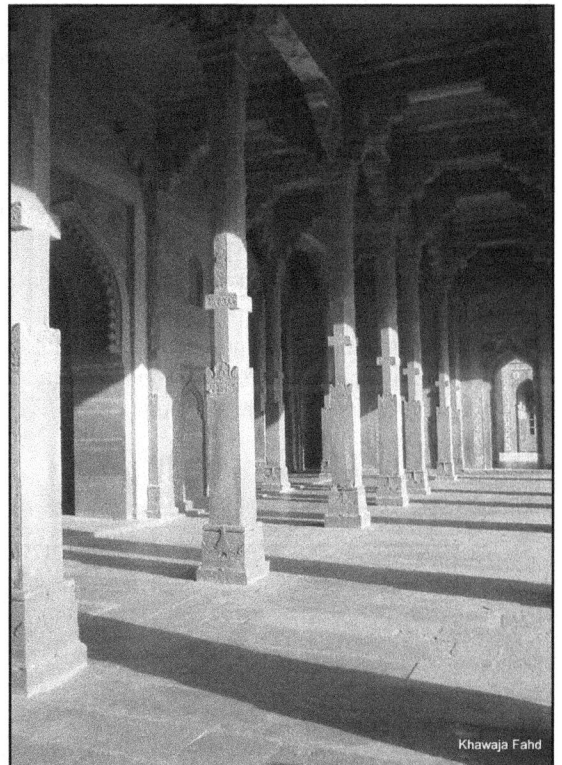

Khawaja Fahd

Photo: Khawaja M. Fahd

of multiple worldviews, methodologies and paradigms, we move consistently to value increasingly complex thinking and explanations that derive from a purview larger than any one academic discipline can offer Interestingly, Western methods of inquiry have been furthered by

Eastern influences, especially those that emphasize the necessity of a shift in consciousness.

Mason: This statement is interesting when we try to elicit exactly what we mean by the word consciousness. Many disciplines remain steadfastly beholden to the positivist paradigm and quantitative methods. For them, the study of consciousness resides within neurochemistry and exploration of neurological structures. Others use quantum analysis. In many of these cases, the study of consciousness is reductionistic, even scientistic. There is a risk of remaining entrenched in isolated models of consciousness, without finding an overarching, even transdisciplinary, perspective that will include the intricacies as well as the changes in consciousness.

Jones: We live in a multi-paradigmatic world, to be sure. As humans and as scholars, we are obliged to recognize the existence and validity of multiple ontologies and multiple epistemologies. The study of spiritual teachers makes this necessity quite clear. Reductionist analyses of consciousness, religious experience, and leadership will no longer suffice, as we encounter growing complexity in all spheres. Thus, in an effort to overcome the fragmentation that can arise from engaging multiplicity, we search for integral ways to conduct inquiry, to perform as scholars, and to live as humans.

A new appreciation of the importance of understanding consciousness is felt in the West. This appreciation includes the consciousness of the religious aspirant, the spiritual teacher, and the observer, the scholar of religion, as well. Even as reductionist approaches operationalize consciousness with EEG measures, others from a growing number of traditional academic disciplines are finding that consciousness may be the field in which we all operate, and, as such, may be the ground of being of all—the meeting place where scholars, devotees, and leaders converge.

Mason: Thus we move closer to an understanding of the traditions of India and Eastern philosophy in general. We can use the study of consciousness to share insights from East and West. The lessons of the *Bhagavad Gita*, take on a new clarity, as we see that our examination of spiritual authority and leadership requires examination of practice, consciousness, methods of teaching, and ontological assumptions of all involved, including ourselves as "objective observers." We have compared East and West and have seen that contrasts occur alongside similarities. I know that you pursue these questions in much greater depth in several of your courses in the Transformative Inquiry Department, namely "Spiritual Teachers," "Religious Innovations," and "J. Krishnamurti as Integral Philosopher."

Jones: Thank you for this exchange. We have opened up several avenues of inquiry into the pursuit of integral, and one hopes enlightened, scholarship and living.

References

Adorno, T.W., (1950). Frenkel-Brunswik, Levinson, and Sanford. *The Authoritarian personality*. New York: Norton. REFERENCE INCOMPLETE, AUTHOR FIRST INITIALS MISSING

Altemeyer, B. The authoritarians. http://members.shaw.ca/jeanaltemeyer/drbob/Introduction_links.pdf . Downloaded 1-15-09. YEAR MISSING

Amritaswarupananda (1994). *Ammachi: A biography of Mata Amritanandamayi*. San Ramon, CA: Mata Amritanandamayi Center.

Anzar, N. (ed.) (1985). *The ancient one: A disciple's memoirs of Meher Baba*. Englishtown, NJ: Beloved Books.

Aurobindo, Sri (1993). *The integral yoga*. Twin Lakes, WI: Lotus Light.

Feuerstein, G. (1990). *Holy madness: The shock tactics and radical teachings of crazy-wise adepts, holy fools, and rascal gurus*. New York: Arkana.

Goodman, M. (1998). *In search of the divine mother: Encountering Mother Meera*. London: Thorsons.

Jones, C. A. and Ryan, J. R. (2007). *Encyclopedia of Hinduism*. New York: Facts on File.

Krishna Prem. (2008). *The Bhagavad Gita*. Sand Point, Idaho: Morning Light Press.

Murphet, H. (1983). *Walking the path with Sai Baba*. York Beach, ME: Samuel Weiser.

Rawlinson, A. (1997). *The book of enlightened masters: Western teachers in eastern traditions*. Chicago, IL: Carus Publishing (Open Door Pub).

Satprem (1968). *Sri Aurobindo or the adventure of consciousness*. Pondicherry, India: Sri Aurobindo Ashram Trust.

Sharma, A. (2006). *Ramana Maharshi: The sage of Arunachala*. New York: Penguin.

Stark, R., & Bainbridge, W. (1985). *The future of religion*. Berkeley, CA: University of California.

Weber, M. (1922). *The sociology of religion*. Boston: Beacon.

Photo: Jürgen Werner Kremer

it's started
snowing more heavily
now
I add more white beans
to the soup

Linda Galloway

Tanka previously published as Editor's Choice Award in *moonset literary newspaper*, Spring/Summer 2009

Theses On Michael Murphy And Esalen

Jay Ogilvy

L eadership takes many forms, some individual, some institutional. And leadership is exhibited in many domains: not just in business or the military, but also in culture and religion. Michael Murphy, cofounder (with Richard Price) of Esalen Institute is a leader, as is Esalen. To assess the innovativeness of their contributions, we need to situate them within their time and place. In order to see how Murphy and Esalen led, we need a sense of how religion and psychology stood in California in the 1960s and 70s.

Murphy and Esalen staked out new possibilities for the human spirit. But the boundaries of the new were in part determined by the borders of the old. Murphy and Esalen ventured into outlaw country. But in order to assess the measure of their leadership, we need a sense of the order they transgressed.

My initial assessment will be purposefully rough rather than carefully crafted. The point is not to prove the real condition of religion and psychology in California in the sixties by citing statistics on

Jay Ogilvy, Ph.D., began his career teaching philosophy at Williams College and for seven years at Yale University. He then spent another seven years at SRI International (formerly Stanford Research Institute) before cofounding Global Business Network in 1987. Jay chairs the Global Potentials Program at Esalen. Preferred e-mail: j.a.ogilvy@ gmail.com, mail: 177 Moraga Way, Orinda, CA 94563.

church membership or numbers of visits to different schools of psychotherapists. Instead my aim is to state what was obvious, what was taken for granted, what "everyone knew." For it is precisely in its challenge to the commonplace that Murphy and Esalen had their greatest impact.

What was obvious in the 1960s? First, that "God transcended man." Religion was a matter of belief, not practice or action. To be a believer was to go to church and worship a deity at a distance, the Lord of lords who loved "mankind," but a Lord who dwelt at a distance, remote from the affairs of men and women; a transcendent God whose essence could be seen only through a glass darkly.

Second, psychology was mainly Freudian. It supplied a map of the human condition that was based on the pathologies most evident in Freud's Vienna, namely, the neuroses, psychoses and hysterias produced by the Victorian repression of sexuality.

Third, to the youth of the sixties, the bloom was off the rose of post-WWII economic growth as manifested in the suburbs of America. Sociologist Kenneth Keniston wrote a book about the young entitled *The Uncommitted*, and followed it up with an article in the *New York Times Sunday Magazine* entitled, "You Have to Grow Up in Scarsdale To Know How Bad It Really Is." The kids were

alienated from bourgeois America so, following the beatniks of the late fifties, they started tuning in, turning on, and dropping out.

Then along came Michael Murphy and Richard Price, two smart young men schooled in philosophy and the practice of meditation, and suddenly what seemed obvious to most of California's *haute bourgeoisie* seemed stale and in need of revolutionary reframing.

I begin with the obvious before moving on to some subtleties because the significance of subtler refinements will be lost unless the larger context is clear. To put it fairly crudely, Esalen provided a school for kids who were tired of a desiccated scholasticism that was irrelevant to their experience, and a church for those to whom mainstream religion was a dead letter. All those religious rituals, the (un)likely stories about virgin birth, crucifixion and resurrection, the miracles, the God of Abraham to whom Jews prayed, the mumbo-jumbo … it was all so patently implausible to bright young students raised on a diet of post-Enlightenment science.

The dominant paradigm in psychology was as suspect as the reigning orthodoxy in religion. The very idea that the talking cure of Freudian depth psychology represented the best we could do in cultivating the psyche … talk about a glass half empty! Abraham Maslow was already articulating a theory about a psychology of health rather than a psychology of sickness. All that remained was the practice.

The religion of the day was too 'idealistic'—too preoccupied with the divine, a distant God in whom one should believe, but never actually experience. The psychology of the day was too mechanistic—too preoccupied with drives and instincts, resistances, displacements and other processes of plumbing in the unconscious, rather than experience as experienced. And the social mores of the day seemed stilted, artificial, phony. For those too young to remember, or too eager to forget, see the movie *Far From Heaven* to get a sense of the values and the inhibitions of those decades.

Then along came a community where people walked their talk; where a ruthlessly honest gestalt psychology flourished in the work of Fritz Perls and his followers; where members of the world famous massage crew joined with visiting gurus like Ida Rolf, Charlotte Selver, George Leonard and Don Johnson. Esalen advanced the field of somatics far beyond where the likes of Wilhelm Reich last left it. As for religion, the word wasn't much used. People preferred 'spirituality.' What's the difference?

Religions have doctrines—dos and don'ts, articles of faith, dogmas, catechisms. And more often than not, religions push scientifically implausible stories about how the world came to be and where it is going. Spirituality tends to be less concerned with some sacred high society out there in the cosmos. Spirituality is all about what's in here— subjective, experienced, immanent rather than transcendent.

To scholars of religion, this recital of what was obvious in California in the sixties is less likely to sound revolutionary than all too familiar. Weren't the Gnostics more concerned with what was in here rather than out there? Can't we find precursors to a psychology of health as far back as the neo-Platonic ascent up the Great Chain of Being? Yes, we can, and Michael Murphy found himself pursuing some of that literature under the mentorship of Frederic Spiegelberg in the graduate department of philosophy at Stanford. But that department was dominated by positivists like Patrick Suppes, who vowed "to bury the

Photo: Daniel Bianchetta

metaphysicians." So in order to pursue his studies of the past, in preparation for a new future, Murphy traveled to India to study in an ashram founded by Sri Aurobindo. Like many others on a spiritual path that deviated from the western, Judeo-Christian tradition, Murphy made his journey to the East.

Returning home to California, however, Murphy did something different. Rather than simply bowing down to a new orthodoxy, eastern rather than western, he looked for a new synthesis. Still speaking crudely and simplistically before getting into subtler refinements, Murphy and his colleagues at Esalen saw the extent to which the journey to the East led up rather than down. Beyond the tremendous respect Murphy paid to the intellectual and spiritual paths of his teachers, beyond the discipline to which he dutifully and thoroughly subjected himself, beyond the hours of medita-

tion, Murphy realized that there was something missing in a tradition that paid too little attention to the body, too little attention to the psychology of the unconscious, to sex and to the sensuous realities of this world. And so Michael Murphy and Dick Price set out to found an institute where the wisdom of the world's spiritual traditions could be wed to the materiality of this-worldly, bodily existence. They would join the sacred to the mundane, at times by way of the downright profane. Esalen was outlaw country!

Here again, to students of the history of religion this taste for the mundane is not altogether new. Isn't the very essence of Christianity about the incarnation of the Holy Spirit? And as for dabbling in profanity, there is a tradition going all the way back to the Song of Songs, the *Confessions of St. Augustine*, and the erotic art gracing Hindu temples. So what's so new? Perhaps not that much. To those who are convinced that there is never anything new under the sun, it's not that hard to find precedents for what Esalen is all about. It's possible to tame the outrageousness of outlaw country by placing Esalen in traditions that go clear back to pagan rituals. It's possible to lend legitimacy to Esalen by locating and describing earlier precedents. But when you try to do so, by seeking out precedents among pagans and Gnostics for example, you find yourself quickly in the company of people and practices regarded as heretical if not scandalous. How orthodox or legitimate can you be if you're located in a tradition of heretics?

So much for the simplistic and obvious. In order to take a more refined cut at just how Esalen has wed the sacred and the mundane, the spiritual and the material, I would like to call up two voices from the past and attempt a kind of scholarly mixed-track sampler like the songs that kids create by sampling swatches from different CDs and then adding their own riffs. The songs I'll conjure up are those of Marx and Feuerbach, specifically Marx's *Eleven Theses on Feuerbach*. Why this choice? Because the more I think about the innovative leadership of Michael Murphy's Esalen Institute, the more I am reminded of both the innovative leadership of Feuerbach and of his critical appropriation by Marx. Beginning at the end, with the most famous and oft-quoted of Marx's Theses, how does this sound as a characterization of Esalen's difference from most academic institutions? "Heretofore philosophers have only interpreted the world in various ways; the point, however, is to change it." And this last of the eleven theses is only a beginning.

Feuerbach was a so-called "left Hegelian." Born in 1804, he was raised on Hegelian philosophy, and taught Hegel's system for several years. But as his thought matured he found himself critical of Hegelian idealism. Feuerbach's feet were planted firmly on the ground of this-worldly existence and he found the philosophy and theology of his day flying too quickly aloft toward the ideal and a distant divinity.

Feuerbach's main contribution to philosophy and theology consisted in redirecting attention to the importance of sensuous existence. He scandalized the theologians of his day by interpreting the main features of Christian dogma as projections from the features of material human existence. Feuerbach is the original author of that saying emblazoned on the walls of health food stores everywhere: "You are what you eat"—in German, closer to a pun, "*Man ist was er isst*."

In addition to materializing Hegel's idealism, Feuerbach also anticipated Marx in his use of the concept of alienation. In Feuerbach's philosophy, humanity was alienated from its own highest potential precisely to the extent that it projected that potential onto a distant divinity.

Marx was much taken with the way Feuerbach stood Hegel on his head, stressing the primacy of the material to the ideal. As Engels put it,

The spell was broken; the 'system' was exploded and cast aside. . . One must himself have experienced the liberating effect of this book [Feuerbach's *Essence*

of Christianity] to get an idea of it. Enthusiasm was general; we all became at once Feuerbachians (Engels, 1968, p. 602f.).

Marx was particularly influenced by Feuerbach's portrayal of human beings as alienated from their own highest potential. The concept of alienation was absolutely central to the young Marx's philosophy (Marx, 1844/1961). But Marx was not entirely happy with the rest of Feuerbach's philosophy. Nor should we be entirely happy with the rest of Marx's philosophy. The fall of communism in the Soviet Union and Eastern Europe—a chapter in history with which Esalen was influentially involved—should teach us something about the

Leadership takes many forms, some individual, some institutional. Some leaders exercise their leadership most effectively through the mediation of an institution that exercises, in turn, its leadership on a culture.

shortcomings of Marxism, even in the philosophical, humanistic form it took in Marx's early writings. So in the following variations on themes from Marx and Feuerbach, there are themes and counter-themes, dialectical dances that will allow us to find greater subtlety behind the statements of the obvious with which we began.

The strategy of this essay is similar to that described by Louis Althusser in his essays on Marx and Feuerbach. Althusser describes a "double rupture" between Marx and Hegel in which Feuerbach provides a crucial link:

What is at stake in this double rupture, first with Hegel, then with Feuerbach, is the very meaning of the word philosophy. What can Marxist 'philosophy' be in contrast to the classical models of philosophy? … The answer to this question can largely be drawn negatively from Feuerbach himself, from this last witness of Marx's early 'philosophical conscience,' the last mirror in which Marx contemplated himself before rejecting the borrowed image to

put on his own true features. (Althusser, 1970, p. 48)

Here we are looking at Murphy's double rupture with traditional psychology and religion through his break with a California culture that was itself breaking away from what was then prevalent in religion and psychology. Althusser's words may be as true of Murphy as of Marx:

If it is true that we can learn as much about a man by what he rejects as by what he adheres to, then a thinker as exacting as Marx [or Murphy] should be illuminated by his break with Feuerbach [or Murphy's break with his predecessors] as much as by his own later statements. (1970, p. 47)

But here we are entertaining not just a double, but a triple or quadruple rupture: Murphy breaking with received wisdom in 1960s California, which was breaking with traditional religion, society and psychology; but further than that, traditional religion, society and psychology breaking with Marx's break with Feuerbach's break with Hegel. If Marx was fond of describing his relationship to Hegel as one of standing Hegel on his head, then here we are contemplating a sequence of somersaults off the high dive of history.

Why such scholarly contortions? Because the body being flipped consists of many more than just one binary opposition between head and feet, right-side-up and upside-down. Both in Marx's relationships to Feuerbach and to Hegel, and in Esalen's relationships with California and Vienna and India, a whole series of binary oppositions call for sorting into a whole series of possible constellations. Consider the following binary pairs:

Theory/Practice
Subjective/Objective
Internal/External
Ideal/Material
Individual/Social
Abstract/Concrete
Mystical/Naturalistic

Esoteric/Literal
Contemplative/Engaged
Passive/Active

While it may be tempting to clump all of the elements on the left as features of a contemplative, quasi-Hegelian, philosophical pursuit of enlightenment, and all of the elements on the right as features of an engaged, concrete social practice . . . life isn't that simple. And neither is the history of philosophy, psychology or religion. So we will proceed more slowly toward a more subtle appreciation of Murphy's leadership by starting, first, with a review of Feuerbach's philosophy; then turn, second, to Marx's famous Theses on Feuerbach; and then, third, through another half gainer by way of a critique of Marx, to a set of similar-yet-different Theses on Murphy and Esalen.

Feuerbach's Break With Hegel

In his *Principles of the Philosophy of the Future* (1843), Feuerbach paid his respects to Hegel before criticizing him: "The culmination of modern philosophy is the Hegelian philosophy. The historical necessity and justification of modern philosophy attaches itself, therefore, mainly to the critique of Hegel" (Feuerbach, 1966, p. 31). In his best-known and most influential work, *The Essence of Christianity* (1841), Feuerbach had already made a case, impressive in its anticipation of both Marx and Murphy, for bringing the lofty ideas of Hegelian philosophy down into the everyday practice of embodied human beings:

> This philosophy does not rest on an Understanding per se, on an absolute nameless understanding, belonging one knows not to whom, but on the understanding of man; ... it declares that alone to be the true philosophy which is converted *in succum et sanguinem* [in flesh and blood], which is incarnate in Man. (Feuerbach, 1957, p. xxxv)

The radicalism of Feuerbach's views, and the subtlety of his thinking, are both evident in the following passage that touches on both his humanism and his understanding of how religion alienates our humanity by projecting it onto the divine:

> When religion—consciousness of God—is designated as the self-consciousness of human beings, this is not to be understood as affirming that the religious human being is directly aware of this identity; for, on the contrary, ignorance of it is fundamental to the peculiar nature of religion. To preclude this misconception, it is better to say, religion is humanity's earliest and also indirect form of self-knowledge. Hence, religion everywhere precedes philosophy, as in the history of the race, so also in that of the individual. Man first of all sees his nature as if outside of himself, before he finds it in himself. His own nature is in the first instance contemplated by him as that of another being. Religion is the childlike condition of humanity; but the child sees his nature—man—outside of himself. (Feuerbach, 1957, p. 13)

Religion, it seems, is esoteric psychology. Lacan's essay "On the Stage of the Mirror in the Formation of Consciousness" reads remarkably like this last passage. But Feuerbach uses the term 'anthropology' rather than the term, 'psychology.' He does so in a way that differentiates his reduction from a critical debunking: "While reducing theology to anthropology, I exalt anthropology into theology, very much as Christianity, while lowering God into man [in the person of Jesus], made man into God" (Feuerbach, 1957, p. xxxviii).

Feuerbach does not dismiss religion any more than Freud dismissed dreams. Instead he interprets religion as the dream-work of the human spirit. "Religion is the dream of the human mind," writes Feuerbach. "Hence I do nothing more to religion—and to speculative philosophy and theology also—than to open its eyes, or rather to turn its gaze from the internal towards the external, i.e., I change the object as it is in the imagination into the object as it is in reality"(Feuerbach, 1957, p. xxxix).

Feuerbach's view of religion is thus very different from Freud's. To say that religion is esoteric anthropology is not to say that religion is an illusion, for, quite to the contrary of a Freudian reduction of religion to wish fulfillment, Feuerbach sees in religion an esoteric reading of the human spirit that features the role of love rather than that of Oedipal envy.

> The clearest, most irrefragable proof that man in religion contemplates himself as the object of the Divine Being, as the end of the divine activity, that thus in religion he has relation only to his own nature, only to himself ... is the love of God for man ... God, for the sake of man, empties himself of his Godhead! Herein lies the elevating influence of the Incarnation; the highest, the perfect being humiliates, lowers himself for the sake of man. . . How can the worth of man be more strongly expressed than when God, for man's sake,

Along came Michael Murphy and Richard Price, two smart young men schooled in philosophy and the practice of meditation, and suddenly what seemed obvious to most of California's *haute bourgeoisie* seemed stale and in need of revolutionary reframing.

becomes a man? (Feuerbach, 1957, p. 57)

Only when this high estimation of human potential remains central to the reading of Feuerbach can we appreciate why as rigorous and orthodox a theologian as Karl Barth would say of Feuerbach, "The attitude of the anti-theologian, Feuerbach, was more theological than that of many theologians" (1957, p. x). And further, "Feuerbach wants, in the end, to help man secure his due. Therefore his philosophy begins with the sentence: 'I am a real, a sensuous, a material being; yes, the body in its totality is my Ego, my being itself.' His teaching aims to be a 'frankly sensuous philosophy'" (p. x).

Does this not begin to sound like something close to what was said, in a different idiom, at Esalen?

Marx's Break With Feuerbach

We'll have more to say about Feuerbach in the course of reversing some (but not all) of Marx's reversals of Feuerbach, but enough has been said to give traction to Marx's critique. Because Marx's theses are, for the most part, relatively succinct, I'll begin by simply quoting all eleven of them. Where the first goes on at some length, I'll mark an omission with ellipses like so ... Only after quoting all eleven theses will I go back and add some commentary, and then suggest changes that give measure to both an appreciation of Esalen's leadership and a criticism of Marxism's failures.

The essay proceeds this way for three reasons: First, because Marx's theses are remarkably dense, an understanding of the earlier theses will benefit from a reading of the later theses. They reward several readings. Second, I want to give Marx his due by letting him speak for himself before "sampling" him into a more contemporary tune. Third, given the setup thus far, the overall strategy of this essay—the series of somersaults that will land us back on an appreciation for Murphy's and Esalen's innovative leadership—I encourage the reader to add his or her own riffs before I make mine.

Like a video game, I would like to think of this essay as interactive. In addition to reviewing Marx's double rupture with Hegel, and Murphy's double rupture with traditional religion and psychology, this essay should rupture it's own boundaries by breaking with didacticism to provoke the reader's own reading of Marx on Feuerbach on Hegel, as well as the reader's own reading of Ogilvy on Murphy on California on spirituality.

From Marx and Feuerbach to Theses on Esalen

As stated earlier, these theses are

Theses on Feuerbach
by Karl Marx

(1967, pp. 400-402; translation amended)

I. The chief defect of all hitherto existing materialism—that of Feuerbach included—is that the thing [*Gegenstand*], reality, sensuousness, is conceived only in the form of the object [*Objekt*] of contemplation [*Anschauung*], but not as human sensuous activity, practice [*Praxis*], not subjectively. Hence it happened that the active side was developed by idealism rather than materialism—but only abstractly, since idealism knows nothing of real, sensuous activity as such. Feuerbach wants the sensuous object really differentiated from objects of thought, but he does not conceive human activity itself as objective [*gegenständliche*] activity.

II. The question whether objective [*gegenständliche*] truth can be attributed to human thinking is not a question of theory, but is a practical question. In practice man must prove the truth, that is, the reality and power, the this-sidedness [*Diesseitigkeit*] of his thinking. The dispute over the reality or non-reality of thinking which is isolated from practice is a purely scholastic question.

III. The materialist doctrine that men are products of circumstances and upbringing, and that, therefore, changed men are products of other circumstances and changed upbringing, forgets that it is men that change circumstances, and that the educator himself needs educating. Hence this doctrine necessarily arrives at dividing society into two parts, of which one is superior to society [as in Robert Owen, for example, Engels added].

The coincidence of the changing of circumstances and of human activity can be conceived and rationally understood only as revolutionary practice.

IV. Feuerbach starts out from the fact of religious self-alienation, the duplication of the world into a religious, imaginary world and a real one. His work consists in the dissolution of the religious world into its secular basis. He overlooks the fact that after completing this work, the chief thing still remains to be done. For the fact that the secular foundation detaches itself from itself and establishes itself in the clouds as an independent realm is really to be explained only by the self-cleavage and self-contradictoriness of this secular basis. The latter must itself, therefore, first be understood in its contradiction and then, by the removal of the contradiction, revolutionized in practice. Thus, for instance, once the earthly family is discovered to be the secret of the holy family, the former must then itself be criticized in theory and revolutionized in practice.

V. Feuerbach, not satisfied with abstract thinking, appeals to sensuous contemplation, but he does not conceive sensuousness as practical, human-sensuous activity.

VI. Feuerbach resolves the religious essence into the human essence. But the human essence is no abstraction inherent in each single individual. In its reality it is the ensemble of social relations.

Feuerbach, who does not enter upon a criticism of this real essence, is consequently compelled:

To abstract from the historical process and to fix the religious sentiment [*Gemüt*] as something by itself, and to presuppose an abstract—isolated—human individual.

Human essence, therefore, can with him be comprehended only as 'genus,' as an internal, dumb generality, which unites the many individuals naturally.

VII. Feuerbach, consequently, does not see that the 'religious sentiment'is itself a social product, and that the abstract individual whom he analyzes belongs in reality to a particular form of society.

VIII. Social life is essentially practical. All mysteries, which mislead theory to mysticism find their rational solution in human practice and in the comprehension of this practice.

IX. The highest point attained by contemplative materialism, that is materialism, which does not understand sensuousness as practical activity, is the contemplation of single individuals in 'civil society.'

X. The standpoint of the old materialism is 'civil' society; the standpoint of the new is human society, or socialized humanity.

XI. Heretofore philosophers have only interpreted the world in various ways; the point, however, is to change it.

dense. Don't hesitate to read them again, from the first to the last, and as you do so, consider how you might want to amend them to read as theses on Esalen.

Before I make my own amendments, let me clarify the transform I will use: a quasi-mathematical operator, like a rotation function that would torque everything clockwise 90 degrees. The transform derives from a critique of Marx based on the lessons of history read through a commentary on his texts. The main points are three: first, Marx placed too much emphasis on the social vis-à-vis the individual; second, Marx paid insufficient respect to the practice of contemplation. Third, Marx's theory of alienation was internally incoherent. Let me clarify these points by adding qualifiers to each:

1. Marx overemphasized the social to the expense of the individual.

Consider Kierkegaard's critique of Hegel. The unhappy Dane objected to the way the life of the concretely existing individual got swallowed up and subsumed by the over-powering influence of The System (Kierkegaard, 1941, pp. 99-113).

a. The practical expression of this theoretical shortcoming is evident in the insufficient protection of civil liberties in communist societies.

b. Creativity and innovation suffer when the rights of the individual are subordinated to the needs of the collective. As Harold Bloom argues in *The Western Canon*, "Social energies exist in every age, but they cannot compose plays, poems, and narratives. The power to originate is an individual gift, present in all eras but evidently greatly encouraged by particular contexts" (Bloom, 1994, p. 46).

2. Marx showed insufficient appreciation for the practice of contemplation.

a. Consider the testimony of tens of thousands of meditators, from ancient India to modern Esalen. From ancient Buddhism to the present, there is a tradition of centuries of inner empiricism,

an inter-subjectively validated compendium of evidence whose texts and oral teachings amount to an owner's manual for the human mind.

b. This practice of meditation is very different from the imperative to practice, practice, practice before you can perform in Carnegie Hall. The stress on the practice of meditation is actually quite close to the definition of praxis as a revolutionary activity that changes everyday reality.

c. Seen as inducing change rather than the mere contemplation of existing reality, the practice of meditation may be every bit as pragmatic and efficacious as the manning of barricades.

3. Marx's theory of alienation was incoherent.

a. In his early work, which some regard as humanistic to the point of being moralistic, Marx spoke of alienation as an estrangement (*Entfremdung*) from humanity's essence.

b. In his later work, Marx realized that morality based on an ahistorical essence violated the revolutionary historicism of his dialectical materialism.

c. The proof of his own realization of this incoherence shows up in the fact that in his later work, particularly the three volumes of Das Kapital, he says almost nothing about alienation.

So clarified, this operator called What's-wrong-with-Marx will render, when applied to Marx's Theses on Feuerbach, a series of slightly different theses that take us closer to Esalen's and Murphy's innovative leadership in religious, philosophical, social, and psychological thought. Let's have a look.

First Thesis

Take the first thesis. Once again:

I. The chief defect of all hitherto existing materialism—that of Feuerbach included—is that the thing [*Gegenstand*], reality, sensuousness, is conceived only in the form of the object [*Objekt*] of contemplation [*Anschauung*], but not as human sensuous activity, practice [*Praxis*], not subjectively. Hence it happened that the active side was developed by idealism rather than materialism—but only abstractly, since idealism knows nothing of real, sensuous activity as such. Feuerbach wants the sensuous object really differentiated from the objects of thought, but he does not conceive human activity itself as objective [*gegenständliche*] activity.

Feuerbach got the stress on materialism right, just as America surpassed India in the material realm of economics. But what Feuerbach missed was the active aspect of world-making, which idealism grasped in Kant's stress on the constitution of the object of knowledge by the activity of the human mind—Kant's so-called "Copernican revolution" according to which the object of knowledge had to correspond to the active constitution of the categories of understanding and the forms of intuition, rather than to a passively received impression of an external object. (Kant, 1961, p. 22)

What Murphy and Esalen add to the spirituality imported from India is a similar stress on American materialism—spirituality incarnate in the body of the existing individual. And just as Marx chides Feuerbach for his insufficient attention to the moment of activity that was grasped by Kantian idealism but not by Feuerbachian materialism, so we can criticize Marx and the tradition of Marxism for giving insufficient latitude and liberty to individual activity in the form of artistic creativity and individual dissent. Dissident writers like Viktor Erofeyev, a frequent guest at Esalen, paid too high a price under the strictures of Soviet Communism. The thaw at the end of the Cold War allowed a blossoming of individual expression of human potential.

> To put it fairly crudely, Esalen provided a school for kids who were tired of a desiccated scholasticism that was irrelevant to their experience, and a church for those to whom mainstream religion was a dead letter.

So let us amend Marx's first thesis to read as follows:

1. The chief defect of all hitherto existing materialism—that of Marx included—is that sensuousness is conceived only in the form of the object of political action but not as the object of meditative contemplation. Hence it happened that the active side was developed by Marxist materialism—but only politically, since Marxist materialism knows nothing of meditative practice as such. Marx wants the sensuous object really differentiated from the objects of thought, but he does not conceive meditation itself as objective activity. Murphy and Esalen brought meditation down out of the ether of pure contemplation and implemented an incarnate practice that helped change the world.

Second Thesis

Consider the second thesis:

II. The question whether objective [*gegenständliche*] truth can be attributed to human thinking is not a question of theory, but is a practical question. In practice man must prove the truth, that is, the reality and power, the this-sidedness [*Diesseitigkeit*] of his thinking. The dispute over the reality or non-reality of thinking which is isolated from practice is a purely scholastic question.

It's not enough just to think the liberation of the human spirit. You must act it out. So workshops at Esalen are not like classes in universities. How often have gestalt workshop leaders said to those in the hot seat, "Be that locomotive you dreamt about … Be that limp dish rag …"? Acting it out, speaking the part, taking the appropriate body posture, feeling the associated feelings … these constitute a practice that is altogether different from just talking about different ideas, symbols, mere words.

Through its hundreds of workshops, Esalen pioneered in the field of experiential learning. Unlike university classrooms where students listen to teachers pose scholastic questions seeking merely academic answers, Esalen's workshops called for movement, body contact, and

real confrontations with the demons of the psyche.

Marx's second thesis requires very little amendment to apply to Esalen:

2. The question whether objective truth can be attributed to human thinking is not a question of theory but of practice and experience. In practice human beings must prove the truth, that is, the reality and power, the intentionality of their thinking. At Esalen you must put up or shut up or be called for the hollowness of your intentions. The dispute over the reality or non-reality of thinking which is isolated from practice is a purely scholastic question.

Third Thesis

III. The materialist doctrine that men are products of circumstances and upbringing, and that, therefore, changed men are products of other circumstances and changed upbringing, forgets that it is men that change circumstances, and that the educator himself needs educating. Hence this doctrine necessarily arrives at dividing society into two parts, of which one is superior to society [as in Robert Owen, for example, Engels added].

The coincidence of the changing of circumstances and of human activity can be conceived and rationally understood only as revolutionary practice.

Here Marx is addressing the old nature vs. nurture dispute, and in a way

that runs contrary to facile criticisms of liberals and lefties. Against those who believe that the left places too much emphasis on social conditioning rather than human nature, Marx places a plague on both houses. Neither circumstances, nor an innate human nature determine the course of human action. Instead, autonomous human beings who take charge of their own destinies can change the circumstances that in turn change men. As is said of great architecture, our buildings shape us … but we shape our buildings, sometimes even after they have been built and occupied by their initial tenants.

Marx's famous phrase, "that the educator himself needs educating," applies especially to an education for the future—something that Feuerbach, the author of *Principles of the Philosophy of the Future*, as well as forward looking

Photo: Daniel Bianchetta

Californians care about. If Parmenides was correct in thinking that all change is illusory, if Plato was right in thinking that the true forms of things are eternal, if Aristotle was correct (contra Darwin) in claiming that the number and nature of living species remains fixed for all eternity, then society could be split into two parts: the gurus who are in contact with the eternal truths, and a vast unwashed student body awaiting the dispensing of those truths. Ever since Hegel and

Darwin, though, we know that human consciousness develops. History is real. Things change, and sometimes the kids get the news before the elders. Hence the educators themselves need perpetual re-education.

Rather than the sage on the stage, the teacher becomes the guide on the side. Group leaders in Esalen workshops must mix it up with the workshop participants and make it up as they go along in real time. Maintaining a dynamic frontier at Esalen entailed, as Michael Murphy often puts it, that no one "capture the flag." Esalen could have easily become the Fritz Perls Instititute of Gestalt psychology, or the Ida Rolf Institute of Structural Integration. Any number of very strong personalities made bids to become the reigning guru, but Murphy and Price maintained a pluralistic culture very distinct from authoritarian cults. No one gets tenure at Esalen. While there is a community that has sufficient stability to maintain institutional memory, build expertise, and get all the necessary jobs done, the Esalen community is like a living body that is perpetually sloughing off old cells, taking in new energy, and re-generating new cells.

3. The leftist idea that men are products of circumstances and upbringing, and that, therefore, changed men are products of other circumstances and changed upbringing, forgets that it is men and women that change circumstances, and that the educator himself needs educating. The old guru approach arrives at dividing society into two parts, of which one—e.g. Fritz Perls or Werner Erhard—is superior to the rest.

A truly progressive practice demands a self-reflexive cycling of changing personnel, changing circumstances, and changing human activity.

Fourth Thesis

IV. Feuerbach starts out from the fact of religious self-alienation, the duplication of the world into a religious, imaginary world and a real one. His work consists in the dissolution of the religious world into

its secular basis. He overlooks the fact that after completing this work, the chief thing still remains to be done. For the fact that the secular foundation detaches itself from itself and establishes itself in the clouds as an independent realm is really to be explained only by the self-cleavage and self-contradictoriness of this secular basis. The latter must itself, therefore, first be understood in its contradiction and then, by the removal of the contradiction, revolutionized in practice. Thus, for instance, once the earthly family is discovered to be the secret of the holy family, the former must then itself be criticized in theory and revolutionized in practice.

You can see why the Christian right

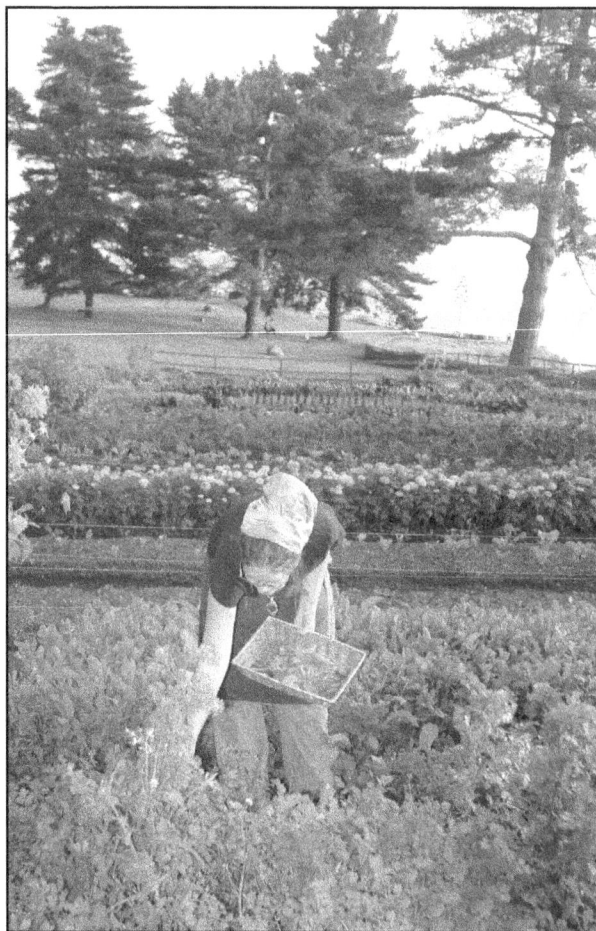
Photo: Daniel Bianchetta

went apoplectic over the threat of Communism: The Reds were against family values! "The earthly family . . . must be criticized in theory and revolutionized in practice!" Next thing you know we'll have lesbians raising kids conceived in Petri dishes.

Feuerbach saw that the holy trinity was a projection of Dad, Mom and Junior. Like Freud, Feuerbach understood the extent to which religious beliefs were scripted by secular realities.

Marx accepted Feuerbach's insight into the dynamics of projection, but Marx was not content with stopping there. Rather than deconstruct the sacred as a projection of the secular, he wants to revolutionize the secular that is the source of the sacred.

This move is not unlike the radical challenge that Esalen poses to many ordinary lives. People come to Esalen, take part in workshops, and the next thing you know they want to quit their jobs, file for divorce, and start their lives over from scratch—as if their ordinary lives need to be "criticized in theory and revolutionized in practice." Where too much of Freudian therapy was aimed at getting people to "adjust" to their circumstances, as critics like Thomas Szasz and R. D. Laing pointed out, Esalen was ready to revolutionize the circumstances.

4. Freudian therapy starts out from the fact of religious self-alienation, the duplication of the world into a religious, imaginary world and a real one. Its work consists in the dissolution of the religious world into its secular basis. But Freudian therapy overlooks the fact that after completing this work, the chief thing still remains to be done. For the fact that the "politics of the family" (Cf. R. D. Laing's book by that name) projects itself onto a sacred nuclear family is really to be explained only by the pathologies of its origin in ordinary, alienated life. The latter must itself be understood in its alienation and then, by the overcoming of alienation, revolutionized in practice.

Fifth Thesis

V. Feuerbach, not satisfied with abstract thinking, appeals to sensuous contemplation, but he does not conceive sensuousness as practical, human-sensuous activity.

5. Americans, not satisfied with the other-worldliness of Indian asceticism, find themselves pumping iron at the gym. But they do not conceive of their body-building as part of a larger context of humane, social self-construction.

They separate mind from body, and their bodywork is therefore mechanistic, like taking their cars to mechanics. They don't see, until they come to Esalen, the potentiality for an integral practice that harmonizes the development of body, mind, soul and spirit.

Sixth Thesis

VI. Feuerbach resolves the religious essence into the human essence. But the human essence is no abstraction inherent in each single individual. In its reality it is the ensemble of social relations.

Feuerbach, who does not enter upon a criticism of this real essence, is consequently compelled:

To abstract from the historical process and to fix the religious sentiment [*Gemüt*] as something by itself, and to presuppose an abstract—isolated—human individual.

Human essence, therefore, can with him be comprehended only as 'genus,' as an internal, dumb generality which unites the many individuals naturally.

Here, as I have often heard Michael Murphy say, "we are getting into the high grass." I've never been quite sure whether this expression referred to the grass on some honorifically elevated plateau ... or to grass so tall one could lose visibility and get lost in it. In any case, the plot thickens with the sixth thesis, especially with Marx's acknowledgement that human essence is not some ahistorical abstraction, but instead, "the ensemble of social relations," which are, of course, subject to historical change.

The problem is just this: If you want to make a moral case against current social conditions as somehow alienated from what they could or should be, you need a theory of human nature or essence from which we are alienated. But if you posit such a theory of human nature or essence, you deny the very historicity of humanity that was so dear to both Hegel and Marx—if not to Feuerbach, as Marx noted. In the end, Marx sided with Hegel on this point, and not with Feuerbach. Marx himself credited Hegel for acknowledging the historicity of humanity:

The outstanding thing [*die Grösse*, the greatness] in Hegel's Phenomenology and its final outcome—that is, the dialectic of negativity as the moving and generating principle—is thus first that Hegel conceives the self-genesis of man as a process, conceives objectification as loss of the object, as alienation and as transcendence of this alienation; that he thus grasps the essence of labor and comprehends objective man—true because real man—as the outcome of man's own labor. (Marx, 1961, p. 151)

This is a powerful idea, and it is one that is at the very heart of what Esalen is about. Call it the human potential movement. Rather than simply repeating over and over again some fixed and ahistorical essence, we human beings continue to make it up as we go along. We make history. We evolve toward actualizing what in earlier times was only latent or potential. Hence Michael Murphy's very well documented argument in *The Future of the Body* and his later collaboration with James Redfield, *God and Evolution*, to the effect that extraordinary human performances by athletes and mystics represent pre-figurations or presentiments of human capacities that will later become commonplace.

But there are problems, deep problems, theological and philosophical problems, with this concept of potentiality. E.g., how precisely—or dimly—is higher potential prefigured? If the pattern is as precise as that of the oak in the acorn, then we are back to the kind of ahistorical essentialism we find in a pre-Darwinian Aristotle. But if the potentiality is as broad as that of wet clay that can be shaped into any form whatever, then what sense does it make to say that higher potentials are prefigured at all? Further, if we are like wet clay, entirely plastic, then by what standard could one say that we were either alienated from our true nature, or falling short of some higher potential?

Marx wavered on these issues, as have Marxists ever since. At times, as in his honoring of the greatness of Hegel's Phenomenology, Marx seems to see alienation as a good thing—as the objectification or externalization (*Entäusserung*, or othering) of human potential through the medium of labor or constructive work in the world. This positive read of "alienation" has a long history. Nathan Rotenstreich notes the correspondence between the Latin term, *alienatio*, and the Greek term *ekstasis*.

"Just as '*ekstasis*' connotes the state of being beside oneself or transported from one's self, so '*alienatio*' means the state of being of a man who, having been beside himself, is transformed into another" (1965, p. 144).

From this "ecstatic" sense of alienation as *Entäusserung*, there derives a more positive connotation than from the negative connotations of alienation as estrangement (*Entfremdung*). Throughout the neo-Platonic tradition, alienation is a state to be sought after rather than resisted. For Plotinus the aim of contemplation is a loss of consciousness of self in order to seek unity with the One, and "like Plotinus, St. Augustine conceived of alienation as a state of ecstatic contemplation in which the human soul or spirit is elevated" (Rotenstreich, 1965, pp. 146-7). And certainly we can say that this sort of ecstatic transformation is a consummation devoutly to be wished by many who come to Esalen.

This ambivalence between the positive connotations of alienation as *Entäusserung* and the negative connotations of alienation as *Entfremdung* are noted by the translators of the official Foreign Languages Publishing House edition of Marx's *Economic and Philosophic Manuscripts of 1844*. Nicholas Lobkowicz has traced the use of both terms through the work of Fichte and Schelling. (Lobkowicz, 1967, pp. 301ff)   I believe that this very same ambivalence can be traced all the way forward to R. D. Laing's claim that sometimes so-called "breakdowns" are really breakthroughs; also to the radical criticisms of psychotherapy as forcing people to "adjust" to circumstances that should themselves be changed; and to J. D. Salinger's wonderful line, somewhere in *Franny and Zoe,* "This is the age of Kaliyuga, Buddy. If you're not schizophrenic you're part of the enemy."

High grass indeed. Sometimes real leadership requires one to be out of step, alienated from prevailing beliefs and practices. But how is one to know just which times? Certainly not by reference to some ahistorical essence. Hegel, Marx, and the evolutionary/ developmental path toward higher potential at Esalen are all united on this point. But what other point of reference, what other criterion can serve as a norm or standard if not an ahistorical essence? If not some fixed and original alpha, then perhaps some eventual omega, e.g., the "omega point" posited by Theilhard du Chardin? The trouble with that sort of teleology is that it drives one toward the denial of history just as surely as does an ahistorical alpha essence. If the goal has already been set, the die cast, then time, as Plato put it in the *Timaeus*, is just "the moving image of eternity."

Murphy understands these issues. This is why he has sponsored a series of invitational conferences at Esalen on evolutionary theory. This is why he is so eager to find a third way between "intelligent design" or the Omega Point on the one hand, and on the other those advocates of a neo-Darwinian synthesis that sees no directionality or progress whatever in evolution. According to Murphy, the realization of potential is neither completely pre-scripted, nor is it a blind game of chance going nowhere in particular. As Murphy likes to put it, "Evolution meanders."

While there is neither alpha essence nor omega telos to serve as a standard for distinguishing breakdowns from breakthroughs, or destructive alienation from constructive ecstasy, the evolving, changing human body and soul seem able to find guidance in a spiritual practice that is monitored, checked, and shared with others on the path. Hence we can say …

6. *Murphy resolves human essence into spiritual essence. But human essence is no abstraction inherent in each single individual. In its reality it is the ensemble of social relations.*

At Esalen, a community of practice makes it possible to avoid the renegade insanities of isolated ecstasies that veer into pathological alienation.

Seventh Thesis

VII. Feuerbach, consequently, does not see that the 'religious sentiment' is itself a social product, and that the abstract individual whom he analyzes belongs in reality to a particular form of society.

At Esalen, to the contrary, there is a hyper-sensitivity to the diversity of social conditions behind different religious and spiritual beliefs. Yes, it is good to make sure that no one "captures the flag" in the name of some single orthodoxy. But at the opposite extreme a community so

Photo: Daniel Bianchetta

tolerant can lapse into what Ken Wilber has called "Boomeritis": the green meme run rampant. Rather than try to footnote and explain what may sound like jargon to some readers (though well known to others), let's just say …

7. *At Esalen the degree of tolerance toward different religious and spiritual beliefs and practices runs the risk of allowing (to use a bit of distinctly Californian argot) whatevah …*

Eighth Thesis

VIII. Social life is essentially practical. All mysteries which mislead theory to mysticism find their rational solution in human practice and in the comprehension of this practice.

Here we need to grab hold of the What-is-wrong-with-Marxism operator and take issue very directly. Both Marx and Soviet Communism had a blindspot

when it came to religion and mysticism. While Feuerbach was quick to say, "While reducing theology to anthropology, I exalt anthropology into theology," Marx accepted only the first half of that equation. He saw religion as esoteric psychology, or worse, as "the opiate of the people," and nothing more.

As Michael Murphy well knows, I myself claim very little by way of religious belief or regular spiritual practice. Yet even I regard the radical secularism in Marx and his heirs as deficient. While I am reluctant to subscribe to almost any known religious orthodoxy, I still find Marx and his heirs guilty of a hyper-rationalism that violates the test of experience. Apart from the official atheism, this hyper-rationalism shows up in two other obvious errors: the denial of the unconscious in Soviet psychology until well on into the 20th century, and the arrogance of central planning, as if a few smart minds in the Kremlin could figure out how to allocate resources without feedback from the market.

Think of religion as the social unconscious, somewhat the way Carl Jung and James Hillman speak of psychological archetypes using the names of the gods and goddesses to personify dynamics at work well below the radar of rational cognition. So-called myths, the narratives of the gods and goddesses, speak truths about our human condition that cannot be captured by the hyper-rationalism of Marxists, computer programmers, or philosophers of consciousness who preach "eliminative materialism." A radical empiricism of the sort William James advocated forces us to recognize certain experiences that are best described as mystical. But rather than describe those experiences any further by clothing them in the garbs of any religious orthodoxies, I prefer to quote the famous last lines of Wittgenstein's *Tractatus*: "What we cannot speak about we must pass over in silence."

8. *At Esalen, there is a healthy suspicion of attempts to eff the ineffable. There is no common creed, no orthodoxy. Murphy likes to quote a phrase he picked up from his teacher, Frederic Spiegelberg: "The religion of no religion."*

Ninth Thesis

IX. The highest point attained by contemplative materialism, that is materialism which does not understand sensuousness as practical activity, is the contemplation of single individuals in 'civil society.'

"Civil society" is a slippery phrase with a long and diverse history. Most recently it has been raised to a fairly honorific status to the extent that it refers to all of those non-governmental organizations (NGOs) like Greenpeace, unions, Amnesty International and the PTA that mediate in the vast and growing space between shrinking governments (the public sector) and growing markets (the private sector). This is not exactly what Marx had in mind. In the Marxist tradition, 'civil society' is code for the kind of society envisaged by the social contract theorists like Rousseau for whom the collective—society—is a result of implicit and explicit contracts drawn up and agreed to by individuals who, like Robinson Crusoe, somehow come to self-consciousness prior to their entry into these social contracts. Both Hegel and Marx found this story implausible. In the collectivist creation myth, humankind comes on the scene as a herd. Only later, through the process of alienation, are individuals alienated from the herd, cut away from the herd like so many cattle in a penning contest at the rodeo.

So individuated have we Americans become, we may find it difficult to comprehend social solidarity as prior to individuality. Communal life, if not communism, can serve as an antidote to our knee-jerk individualism. So can workshops at Esalen where the process encourages a "transcending of ego" … but the fact is that much of the process at Esalen has quite the opposite effect. Depending on the method, and the convictions and techniques of the group leader, much of the group process is actually very individualistic in its assumptions and in its outcomes. Much of the rhetoric is about getting in touch with your real feelings. What do you *really* want? Can you find your inner self?

To anyone familiar with Hegel and Marx, or to anyone steeped in oriental traditions, this rhetoric of Robinson Crusoe individualism is highly suspect, whether or not one embraces the equal and opposite abstraction of extreme collectivism. Further, it invites ridicule of the sort that Tom Wolfe leveled in his essay about the 1970s entitled, "The Me Decade." I'm reminded of a friend who is fond of poking fun at those whose conversations can be glossed as, "Enough about me; now, what do you think of me?"

Marx's critical ninth thesis on Feuerbach therefore still has some bite:

9. *The highest point attained by Esalen in its first several decades, is the contemplation of single individuals in 'civil society.'*

Herbert Marcuse summarizes part of the argument of the 1844 Manuscripts as saying,

> Man is free only if all men are free and exist as 'universal beings.' When this condition is attained, life will be shaped by the potentialities of the genus, Man, which embraces the potentialities of all the individuals that comprise it. The emphasis on this universality brings nature as well into the self-development of mankind." (1960, p. 275)

So, as philosopher Peter Singer puts it, even trees have standing. Next stop, the Buddhist vow to honor and protect all living things. Again, this sounds like a great idea. But as we increase the radius of solidarity to include not only all human beings but also all living things, great and small, from whales to microbes, we find ourselves, conceptually speaking, in what Hegel called a night in which all cows are black. We lose the ability to distinguish anything from anything else. Just as an extreme individualism invites ridicule of egocentric Yuppies from the Me-Decade, so this extreme totalism invites ridicule of

To the extent that spirit is incarnate, then spiritual practice must manifest itself not only in meditation, but also in commerce, politics, praxis in all its forms.

Tenth Thesis

X. The standpoint of the old materialism is 'civil' society; the standpoint of the new is human society, or socialized humanity.

Marx may have been right to criticize Feuerbach—and Esalen—for being limited to the "contemplation of single individuals in 'civil society.'" But it does not follow that the socialism of "socialized humanity" is a preferable alternative. One of the fruits of the decline and fall of the Soviet Union has been a growing awareness of the dangers of totalizing too far and too quickly. The refrain, No one is free until we're all free, sounds nice. It is so non-parochial, so expansive, so generous in spirit. But in practice this lofty sentiment greases a one-way slide to totalitarianism.

those chanting over and over, We are all One, We are all One, We are all One … until, say, a telemarketer calls.

In an important address marking the end of Esalen's first forty years and the beginning of the next forty years, Gordon Wheeler and Keith Thompson sounded a much-needed refrain: "From Me to We." They did not say, From Me to Absolutely Everyone. Nor were they trying to set up an antagonism between Us and Them. But they were acknowledging, with due humility, the need for expanding the radius of human potential from the individual self to a larger social and natural milieu. Ecological sustainability was part of the purview. But the move toward sustainability may have to take place one acre at a time, though not one square foot at a time.

In moving away from the preoccupation with the precious self toward a larger horizon of concern, Esalen will not make the Marxist mistake of totalizing too quickly. Just how far and how fast the radius of care can usefully and practically expand is very much up for grabs. A refrain I often sound goes, "Not one, not all, but some" (Ogilvy, 1977). This is not about elitism, but humility. The point is not to protect we precious few against them, but to foster an intimacy and a community among as many living beings as can plausibly constitute a living and viable ecology. The length of the radius of concern varies depending upon the issue. Global warming is a global issue. Cultural integrity is not. Romantic love and the raising of a family may be best nested in a village, but not necessarily in an entire nation.

Part of what I find most remarkable about Esalen is its leadership as a social invention. We are all familiar with technological inventions. They happen all the time. Just look at the number of patents. But social inventions are extremely rare. If you start counting with your fingers, you may not need your toes: the nuclear family, the church, the university, democracy, the corporation ... what else? Before 1962 there was nothing on the face of the earth that looked much like Esalen. Now there are dozens of clones incorporating experiential learning, group living, bio-dynamic gardening, financial viability, and an aspiration toward expanding human potential. It could be that Esalen's leadership has less to do with any particular theory, doctrine, or –ism and more to do with its unique incarnation of many spiritual traditions in a new crucible, a new kind of social body, a new body politic—very old wines in a new wineskin.

The standpoint of Marxist socialism is equality for all: everyone will be equally poor. Esalen is neither a classless society, nor a tyranny, but an intentional community organized around principles

of mutual respect, a shared mission, the development of human potential, and sustainability.

Eleventh Thesis

XI. Heretofore philosophers have only interpreted the world in various ways; the point, however, is to change it.

Esalen has changed the world in several ways:

1. By serving as the inaugural exemplar of a new social invention

2. By changing the lives of many who have visited Esalen

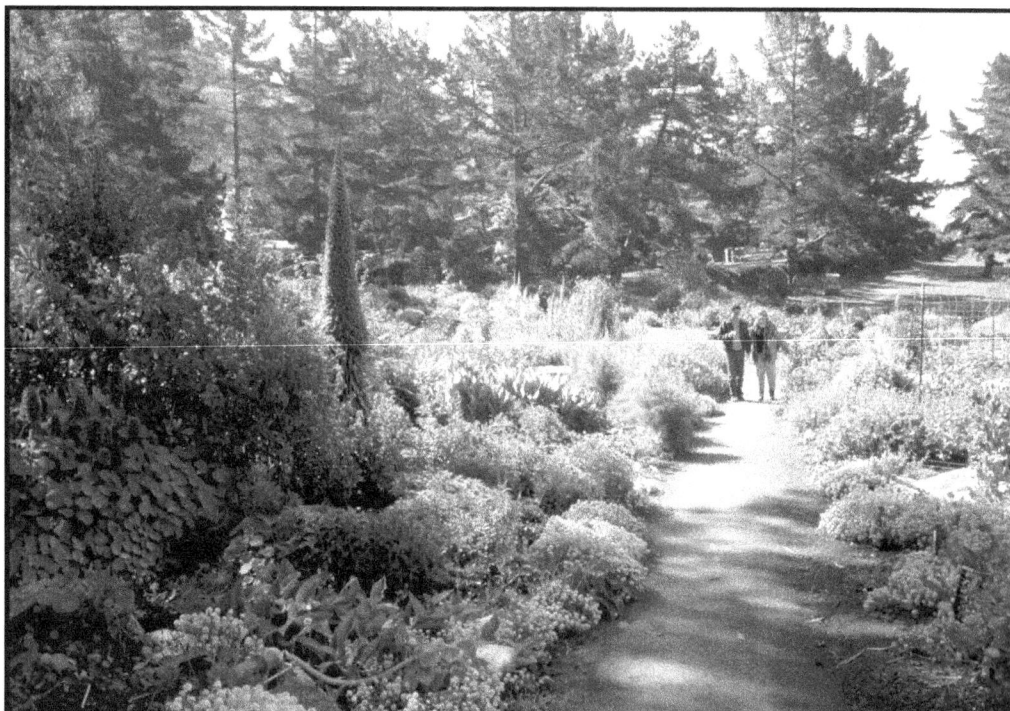

Photo: Daniel Bianchetta

3. By introducing into our discourse the new meme of "the human potential movement" and all that implies

4. By helping to bring about an end to the Cold War.

Given the fact that Esalen's involvement in citizen diplomacy with the Soviet Union is less well known than its contribution to the human potential movement—as well as the play on (and with) Marx running throughout this essay—it may be worth saying a few words about this fourth point. First the facts: After reading the book, *Psychic Discoveries Behind the Iron Curtain*, Michael and Dulce Murphy made several trips to Russia in the 1970s as part of their research on paranormal phenom-

ena. They met many people in Russia and established friendships and professional relationships. Then came the deep freeze in Russian-American relations when Russia invaded Afghanistan in 1979. Virtually all exchange programs between the U.S. and the Soviet Union came to an abrupt halt—except Esalen's.

Starting in 1980, Esalen hosted a series of annual conferences to which influential Russians were invited. These meetings, as well as a number of trips that some of us made to Russia, were part of a movement now known as "citizen diplomacy." Joe Montville, then serving in the State Department, coined the term "Second Track Diplomacy" at one of our meetings at Esalen. The idea was to identify professionals from both countries who shared similar interests—health, psychology, energy, space exploration, future studies, philosophy—and then allow them to meet one another, talk shop with one another, further their shared interests, and eventually create friendships, all below the radar of the ideological differences and mutual suspicions of the official, first track diplomats and politicians. Fruits of those meetings included the creation of the International Society of Space Explorers that joined U.S. astronauts like Rusty Schweickart with Russian cosmonauts. Another participant in those meetings, philosopher Sam Keen, wrote a book of text and pictures called *Faces of the Enemy*, whose main point was to show how the unknown, un-experienced enemy gets demonized by projections from the fears of one side onto images of the other. The best way to combat such demonizing, and halt the deadly dynamics of projecting one's own shadow onto the image of the enemy, is to meet the other face-to-face. And so the practice of Second Track Diplomacy was born at Esalen and practiced through dozens if not hundreds of human and humanizing relationships throughout the 1980s.

We will never know for sure just how influential these relationships were. Some say that Gorbachev's decision to throw in the towel was primarily motivated by the Reagan administration's evil empire rhetoric, America's immense arms build-up during the 80s, and Soviet fear of the Star Wars deployment—a new level of technology that Russia could neither master nor afford. Perhaps. But on the basis of my visits to Moscow and Tblisi in 1983 and 1985, I can bear witness to Esalen's influence on the climate of opinion and ideas in good favor in high places. When I went to the American Embassy to debrief toward the end of one visit, the officials I met were amazed at the access I'd been granted on the basis of my association with Esalen. "I've been here for four years and I haven't been able to get a meeting with those people," said one frustrated member of the diplomatic staff. This I took as a testament not to my reputation or abilities, but to the level of friendship and trust that Esalen had generated by keeping the lines of communication open in the early 80s when all other avenues of communication had been shut down.

Esalen hosted Yeltsin's first visit to the United States. During that visit, Boris Yeltsin experienced an epiphany. In a supermarket in Houston he confronted shelves containing dozens of brands of mustard and, as he put it in his tearful revelation, he suddenly understood, "what seventy years of communism had denied the Russian people."

Esalen did not cause the end of the Cold War … but it nudged the wheel on the bridge of world history. It helped to bring an end to hostilities by melting some of the suspicions of our former adversaries. It exercised leadership in a benign direction.

Returning to Marx's eleventh thesis, it's now worth pondering the lines of a great scholar, a former Marxist, Manuel Castells. Toward the very end of the third volume of his magnum opus, *The Information Age*, he writes, with explicit reference to the eleventh thesis, "In the twentieth century, philosophers have been trying to change the world. In the twenty-first century, it is time for them to interpret it differently" (Castells, 1998, p. 359). My point in invoking these lines is not simply to seek help in standing Marx on his head, but rather to temper and add measure and deliberation to the way Michael Murphy and Esalen have both changed and reinterpreted our world.

To the extent that spirit is incarnate, and not some ethereal essence at a distance from everyday life, then spiritual practice must manifest itself not only in meditation, but also in commerce, politics, praxis in all its forms. The greatness [*die Grösse*] of Esalen is thus first that Murphy conceives the self-genesis of the human being as a process, conceives breakdown as loss of an old self, as alienation and as transcendence of this alienation; that he thus grasps the essence of practice and comprehends incarnate human being—true because the real human being—as the outcome of humanity's own practice.

11. Heretofore philosophers have only interpreted the world; the point, however, is both to reinterpret it and thereby to improve it.

After flipping Marx's reading of Feuerbach on its head to get closer to Murphy's leadership in the invention of Esalen, it seems only appropriate to give Feuerbach the last word—a word that is appropriate to that sacred land where salt water meets fresh water and the mineral water of the hot springs. At the very end of *Essence of Christianity*, Feuerbach has a few paragraphs about the sacraments. Then he concludes:

Hunger and thirst destroy not only the physical but also the mental and moral powers of man; they rob him of his humanity—of understanding, of consciousness. Oh! If thou shouldst ever experience such want, how wouldst thou bless and praise the natural qualities of bread and wine, which restore to thee thy humanity, thy intellect! It needs only that the ordinary course of things be interrupted in order to vindicate to common things an uncommon significance, to life, as such, a religious import. Therefore let bread be sacred for us, let wine be   sacred, and also let water be sacred! Amen. (Feuerbach, pp. 277f.)

References

Althusser, L. (1970). *For Marx*. (B. Brewster, Tran.). New York: Vintage.

Aptheker, H. (Ed.). (1965). *Marxism and alienation: A symposium*. New York: Humanities Press.

Barth, R. (1957). Introduction. In Feuerbach, L. (G. Eliot, Trans.) *The essence of Christianity* (pp. x-xxxii). New York: Harper & Brothers.

Bellah, R. (1985). *Habits of the heart*. Berkeley, CA: University of California Press.

Blauner, R. (1964). *Alienation and freedom*. Chicago: University of Chicago Press.

Block, N., Flanagan, O., Güzeldere, G. (Eds.) (1997). *The Nature of consciousness*. MA: MIT Press.

Bloom, H. (1994). *The Western canon*. New York: Harcourt Brace.

Cassirer, H. W., (1954). *Kant's first critique*. New York: Macmillan.

Castells, M. (1998). End of Millennium. *The information age: Economy, society and culture*: Vol. 3. Oxford: Blackwell.

Churchland, P. S. (1986). *Neurophilosophy: Toward a unified science of the mind/brain*. MA: MIT Press.

Dawkins, R. (2006). *The god delusion*. Boston: Houghton-Mifflin.

de Vleeschauwer, H. J. (1962). *The development of Kantian thought* (A. R. C. Duncan, Trans.). London: Thomas Nelson & Sons Ltd.

Dennett, D. (1991). *Consciousness explained*. Boston: Little Brown & Co.

Dennett, D. (2006). *Breaking the spell: Religion as a natural phenomenon*. New York: Viking.

Harris, S. (2005). *The end of faith*. New York: W. W. Norton.

Engels, F. (1968). Feuerbach and the End of Classical German Philosophy. In *Karl Marx and Frederick Engels, selected works*. New York: International Publishers.

Ewing, A.C. (1938). *A short commentary on Kant's Critique of pure reason*. Chicago: University of Chicago Press.

Feuerbach, L. (1957). *The essence of Christianity* (G. Eliot, Trans.). New York: Harper & Brothers.

Feuerbach, L. (1966). *Principles of the philosophy of the future* (M. H. Vogel, Trans.). Indianapolis, IN: Bobbs-Merrill, Library of Liberal Arts.

Fromm, E. (1961). *Marx's concept of man*. (T. B. Bottomore, Tran.). New York: Frederick Ungar Publishing Co.

Harris, S. (2005). *The end of faith*. New York: W. W. Norton.

Harris, S. (2006). *Letter to a Christian nation*. New York: Knopf.

Hitchens, C. (2007). *God is not great: How religion poisons everything*. New York: Twelve, Hachette Book Group.

Kant, I. (1961). *Critique of pure reason* (Norman

Kemp Smith, Tran.). New York: St. Martin's Press.

Keniston, K. (1965). *The uncommitted*. New York: Harcourt Brace & World.

Keniston, K. (1969, April, 27). You have to grow up in Scarsdale to know how bad it really is. *New York Times Sunday Magazine*, pp. SM27-28.

Kierkegaard, (1941). *Concluding unscientific postscript 1*. (D. Swenson and W. Lowrie, Trans). Princeton, NJ: Princeton University Press.

Kripal, J. (2007). *Esalen: America and the religion of no religion*. Chicago: University of Chicago Press.

Kripal, J., Shuck, G. W. (Eds.). (2005). *On the edge of the future: Esalen and the evolution of American culture*. Bloomington: Indiana University Press.

Labedz, L. (Ed.) (1962). *Revisionism* New York: Praeger.

Lobkowicz, N. (Ed.). (1967). *Marx and the Western world*. Bloomington, IN: University of Notre Dame Press.

Lobkowicz, N. (1967). *Theory and practice*. Bloomington, IN: Notre Dame University Press.

Marcuse, H. (1960). *Reason and revolution*. Boston: Beacon Press.

Marx, K., (1961). *Economic and philosophic manuscripts of 1844*. Moscow: Foreign Languages Publishing House.

Marx, K. (1967). Theses on Feuerbach. In Easton, L., Guddat, K. (Eds. and Trans.), *Writings of the young Marx on philosophy and society* (pp. 400-402). New York: Doubleday Anchor.

Montouri, A. and Purser, R. (1999). *Social Creativity* (Vol. I). Cresskill, NJ: Hampton Press.

Montouri, A. and Purser, R. (2001). *Social Creativity* (Vol. II). Cresskill, NJ: Hampton Press.

Ollman, B. (1971). *Alienation: Marx's conception of man in capitalist society*. Cambridge, MA: Cambridge University Press.

Ogilvy, J. (1977). *Many dimensional man: Decentralizing self, society, and the sacred*. New York: Oxford University Press.

Ogilvy, J. (Ed.). (1991). Beyond Individualism and Collectivism. In J. Ogilvy (ed.), *Revisioning philosophy* (pp. 217-233). Albany, NY: SUNY Press.

Pappenheim, F. (1959). *The alienation of modern man*. New York: Monthly Review Press.

Petrovic, G. (1967). *Marx in the mid-twentieth century*. New York: Doubleday.

Rotenstreich, N. (1965). *Basic problems of Marx's philosophy*. New York: Bobbs-Merrill.

Rotenstreich, N. (1965). *Experience and its systematization: Studies in Kant*. The Hague: Martinus Nijhoff.

Shear, J. (Ed.). (1998). *Explaining Consciousness, the Hard Problem*. Boston, MA: MIT Press.

Smith, N.K. (1962). *A commentary to Kant's 'Critique of pure reason.'* New York: Humanities Press.

Wheeler, G. (2000). *Beyond Individualism*. Cambridge, MA: GIC Press.

soliloquy

the stars shall not be eclipsed forever
under the spell of city lights
and the moon shall rise unattainable again
fields shall sow themselves wild
no more shall the waters be parted by ships
and the wind shall blow indifferently as ever
when the earth has rid itself of men
as for myself (the mountain confides)
I like to press bones into stones
to keep as souvenirs—any volunteers?

John Thompson

Photo: Jürgen Werner Kremer

N/om and Transformative Leadership

Considering the Embodied Know-How of the Kalahari Bushman N/om-Kxaosi

Bradford Keeney

Over the last fifteen years I have conducted fieldwork with the oldest living culture on earth – the Kalahari Bushmen(1) of southern Africa (Keeney 2003, 2005). There I worked closely with their n/om-kxaosi, the women and men who help heal physical, emotional, relational, and community suffering. Not unlike other indigenous cultures, the n/om-kxaosi are regarded as natural leaders in their community. Their authority does not stem from inheritance, political influence, material wealth, or public vote. They are looked upon for guidance because of the ways in which their lives exemplify being in direct contact with what they call n/om, a concept somewhat comparable to chi, kundalini, or the universal life force. It is the n/om-kxaosi's vibrant and spirited presence in ceremonies and everyday affairs that earns the respect of their community. It arguably shows them to be occasionally "more alive" than

Bradford Keeney, Ph.D., is a social cybernetician, anthropologist of cultural healing practices, and innovator of creative therapy, he has authored over 30 books including *The Creative Therapist: The Art of Awakening a Session*. His fieldwork with the Kalahari Bushmen has been honored in a permanent installation at the Origins Centre museum in Johannesburg, South Africa. His websites are www.thecreativetherapist.com and www.

others and those moments of "aliveness" momentarily qualify them to lead.

Bushman culture provides a way of knowing, interacting, and leading that is radically distinct from cultures that are predominantly driven by words, ideas, theories, and texts. The Kalahari people have lived for thousands of years without a written language and have successfully managed to never declare war. I am not claiming that their lack of textuality breeds peace, but am hinting that their de-emphasis of the hegemony of linguistic meaning may have something to do with their long term peaceful exis-

> ## Bushmen teach us to be more careful than we have been with our authoritative use of words and theories.

tence. Their relatively harmless way of life, though interspersed with inevitable human conflict and relational difficulty, is kept in check by the way in which they relate to n/om, both privately and in community. Yet n/om remains outside their domain of understanding and little interest is given to explaining it - they do not make laborious efforts to understand n/om, they simply want to own n/om

("own" to them means "own the feeling for it"). As anthropologists have found, Bushman culture has no clear explanation of n/om, yet they revere it as the most important aspect of life.

N/om is valued over any belief or understanding. With it, they believe they have no need for high priests of explanation or enforcers of textually prescribed law. Not only does Bushman culture give no exaggerated importance to written texts, it isn't concerned with stabilized oral narratives. Spoken stories are encouraged to constantly change and talking is principally valued as a means of teasing one another and bringing forth laughter. Their playful and improvisational use of language has confounded scholars over the years, leading them to believe that Bushman culture was largely "mulitifarious, inchoate, and amorphous" (Guenther, 1999, p. 126).

Leadership among Bushmen is established by the social experience of n/om. A song or dance that is performed with great emotional intensity and authenticity is said to have n/om. In the same way that we might say that a musical performance has "soul," they differentiate heart-felt and soulful impact over technical virtuosity. The Bushmen are moved and led by what touches their hearts. They lead through n/om, that is, bringing forth heightened inspiration that stirs them to action.

Maslow's "Theory-Z" of management (1965, 1971) proposed that as people grow toward self-actualization, they begin to change the dynamics of their motivation. For instance, opportunities for being creative and autonomous become as important as salary and benefits. The switch to what Maslow called "metapay," driven by "being-values," characterized a "good souled" form of management and leadership. Bushmen culture arguably comes close to exemplifying Maslow's "eupsychian management" in that it skews aside dominance-subordination hierarchies, utilizes trust and sharing, enacts synergistic relations, and values mystical and peak experiences.

Bushmen also naturally demonstrate what Maslow called "dichotomy transcendence." They can easily hold both sides of dichotomies, polarities, opposites, and contradictions. This takes place effortlessly because they believe that everything in life is constantly shape-shifting and morphing, including their emotional climate and the understandings that are voiced in words. One of their most important words is no!'an-kal'ae which refers to the force that changes everything. They see n/om as indistinguishable from this force. N/om, however, is not an intellectual abstraction, but a reference to the most heightened feelings one can experience. Feeling n/om requires ecstatic experience that makes the body tremble, quake, and shake. Body shaking is a felt and visible sign of constant movement and changing – indication of an entry into the realm of no!'an-kal'ae.

Keep in mind that the ever-changing experiential universe of the Bushman has overlaps with the phenomenal world

that textually driven cultures know. Our emotions, thoughts, descriptions, and understandings also readily change. However, unlike the Bushmen, we tend to underscore and stabilize one side of our conceptual distinctions, maximizing what we frame as the "good" variables such as happiness, health, well-being, and prosperity, while minimizing what we frame as the "bad" variables like suffering, sickness, disease, and poverty. In the Bushman universe, everything is supposed to constantly change. When it doesn't, problems and illness arise. The n/om-kxaosi address stuck issues by shaking and loosening the contextual matrix of experience, encouraging more freedom of movement, whether of ideas or the body, both regarded as intertwined and embodied. Shaking is done through shape-shifting stories and through ecstatic dances, where the shaking hands, voices, and bodies of the n/om-kxaosi help shake all participants of a village.

The Bushman's key to transcending dichotomies, to use Maslow's phrase, involves a willingness to allow shape-shifting, morphing, and continuous transformation of experience, feelings, body sensations, physical movement, ideas, understandings, strategies, and over-arching paradigms. Such an epistemological universe is circular and recursively dynamic rather than lineal and fixed. This is not to say that it is circular

versus lineal or dynamic versus fixed. Remember that it transcends dichotomies. It will shape shift from being lineal and monadic, when appropriate, and then morph toward circularity and processual complexity, and then shape-shift again to something that is neither one nor both of the before mentioned.

The Bushman's shape-shifting universe enables us to recognize the limitation of the way in which Maslow presented his arguments – showing management/leadership orientations as progressing in an assumed developmental way from Theory X (based on power) to Theory Y (based on cooperation) to Theory Z (based on Being values). He did recognize that Theory Z (and self-actualizers)

Photo: Bradford Keeney

held onto contradictions and that a person or social system could be simultaneously selfish and altruistic, among other dualities. What he theoretically needed was a model of circularity and recursion to account for shape-shifting and never-ending morphing without getting caught in the paradoxes brought forth by lineal developmental assumptions.

I suggest that the Bushmen teach us to be more careful than we have been with our authoritative use of words and theories. They might advise caution when stringing language out over a linear time line, warning that it too easily leads us to uncritically assuming that the phenomenal world can be categorized, sorted, and then linked in various forms of developmental progressions. What a contrast to modernist efforts depicting developmental stages of spirituality, typically categorizing Bushman knowing as the lowest level of spiritual knowing. Though the over-simplicity and naively hierarchical implications of such a mapped progression may be denied and obscured by claims of inclusiveness, references to dynamic processes, and other rhetorical maneuvers, these models too easily project and evoke images, forms, and metaphors that depict the world of spirituality as moving from the African primitives to the enlightened ones from the East (e.g., Beck and Cowan, 1996).

The problem arises from typologizing the world of experience into categories and then trying to sort them into some logical scheme, box, quadrant, hierarchy, network, lattice, spiral, or hyperform. Theorists who model the universe always find themselves in quicksand, trying to subsequently say, "yes, it may look that way, but it is not what I mean." The cover-up continues with more rhetorical sleight of hand: "the 'whole' can be seen as the 'parts' and the 'parts' are also the 'wholes'" and "everything is true" (possibly including the assertion that the particular model is not true). Critics characterize these efforts, often citing Ken Wilber as the prime example of naïve modeling, as "compulsive mappings and textbook categorizations" (William Irwin Thompson, 1996)

From the Bushman perspective of the world, the n/om-kxaosi would most likely see the mapmakers as lost in trickster's mind games which are most often organized by tactics of power and oneupsmanship rather than the play and humility (no theories of everything!) that characterize a "risen heart." Bushmen do not trust any language created model, theory, or explanation to have any special importance other than to serve as amusement or inspiration for improvisation. They would be equally entertained by the managerial theories called X, Y, and Z. This is not to say that they would be aggressively critical of these created forms of expression. They would just see them as impotent and irrelevant to owning n/om unless they are used as grist for the improvisational mill. Furthermore, they would see little difference in people's spiritual development or management effectiveness that could be attributed to their espoused theories or models.

Transformative leadership is arguably an alternative to psychological theory with the latter's over-emphasis upon categorization, pathology, and evaluation. It instead focuses more on what Bugental (1965) called "ontogogy" referring to the process of helping people and social systems grow to their fullest potential. What we need is an alternative way of knowing and talking about transformation that is free of the static renderings that block the primacy of its heraclitean, shape-shifting, and recursive nature. In other words, our understanding (or theories) of transformation must themselves be transformative, that is, evoke ongoing changes of understanding.

The Bushman n/om-kxaosis have something to contribute to our conversations about transformational leadership. At the least, they bring new questions and considerations beginning with the challenge that totalizing theoretical models may be the least important contribution to bringing forth both transformation and transformative leadership.

Photo: Kern Nickerson

Some of the considerations their way of knowing evokes will now be presented, with the hope that they help shake up new creative possibilities for the performance of transformative leadership:

1. Emphasis upon the ownership of n/om (or the universal life force) as the key ingredient of transformative leadership. The transformative leader should seek ownership of n/om – what folk traditions simply call "good spirit" and "soulful" presence. This requires an open heart, a willingness to feel and express heightened emotions, and a commitment to the presence of mystery rather than understanding. An article in the business section of the New York Times (Nov. 28, 1995) entitled, "The Life Force in the Briefcase" described how Japanese executives seek the life force to make them more effective leaders and business practitioners. The Kalahari Bushmen also "hunt" the life force or n/om as the key to living and leading.

With the "force," one's whole being (mind/heart/body/soul) is tuned and made ready for effective Being-presence and Taoistic natural management. In the tuned state, one does not take theories and models too rigidly or over-seriously. They are given the same importance and relevance as a musical lyric or a funny line from a standup comic. This is not to deflate their importance, but to lift them onto the more important ground of evocative art rather than representational accounting. The flow of n/om insures that all things will be kept in their appropriate place – on the ever-changing stage of transforming performances.

With this orientation, a transformative leader is always considering the most appropriate and effective ways of arousing and circulating n/om as the best preparation for being an agent of transformation. Like the Bushman n/om-kxaosi, leadership is determined by the presence of n/om, not by any adherence to a particular belief, understanding, theory, or model. This constitutes an alternative way of specifying "leadership with soul" (differentiated from leadership based on psychological theories about an abstract "soul"). In other words, soul is that which awakens and inspires what is present in the moment, mobilizing what everyone brings to the table so as to bring about creative and revitalizing performance and interaction.

2. Theories, models, ideas, and understandings should be used to evoke possibilities for performance rather than objectively represent or explain generalized accounts. The Bushmen turn the relationship of hermeneutics and praxis upside down. They do not first diagnose a situation like a conventional psychotherapist or organizational consultant, and then proceed to design a strategy for action. Knowing does not precede acting. It is the opposite and involves a more circular view paraphrased by the cybernetician Heinz von Foerster (1981) as follows: "If you want to know, then first act." In the field of systemic and cybernetic family therapy (Keeney, 1983), this orientation was characterized as "diagnose a system by seeing what it does in response to your efforts to change it."

Bushman and cybernetic knowing are clearly differentiated from mainstream psycho-social approaches. For the Bushman and cybernetician, one first intervenes, that is, acts, in order to know. This invites an openness to the idea that a unique theory may be created for each situation that is encountered. The transformational leader should not primarily be driven by a particular theory or meta-theory, but be open to forming particular theories, maps, and models for each situation.

3. "Shaking" – whether of structures, ideas, habits, bodies, relationships, interactional patterns, or organizational cultures – is regarded as an appropriate metaphor for the process of transformation. Bushman n/om-kxaosi emphasize that the expression of n/om takes place in the ecstatic performance of "shaking." In their transformative healing dances, music and rhythm inspire them to shake their bodies and bring forth ecstatic forms of consciousness. In this shaking, transformation takes place (see Keeney 2007).

Shaking is not limited to the spontaneous movements of the human body. It also refers to shaking assumptions,

ideas, theories, and philosophies. Here we celebrate the presence of trickster, coyote, and crazy wisdom voices that turn our most cherished beliefs and understandings inside out. A theory of transformative leadership can be said to have n/om if it is playful and full of contradictions. If it has n/om, it will not take itself too seriously – even when it is being serious.

Shaking also refers to shaking up

Photo: Grant Lessard

everyday routines, whether at home or in the professional workplace. Here patterns of interaction are altered so as to bring forth more possibilities and creative influence. This applies to both routines that are regarded as trivial (e.g., taking out the trash, filing papers, and answering the phone) as well as to those scenarios that are regarded as more serious (e.g., business transactions, legal issues, and employment counseling). Finally, the whole organizational culture can be shaken. Imagine the presence of a corporate trickster or clown, someone who might influence things in the way that the clown physician Dr. Patch Adams (1998) has shown in medical hospitals.

4. More absurdity and less seriousness are required in the workplace. Over-seriousness is potentially toxic to creativity

and healthy social interaction. When n/om is fully present in the organization, any totalizing grand theory or rules of conduct will lose their authoritative grip. In their place will be a more caring presence for the concerns of the whole group and how each person's needs can be appropriately addressed. As the Bushman n/om-kxaosi say, "n/om makes the strings of relationship strong."

Shake up an organization in a good way and people will get closer and provide a synergistic whole that empowers the organization's presence in the world. Existential therapist Carl Whitaker (1982) proposed that absurdity provides an anesthesia that enables serious issues to be more effectively addressed and handled. The serious work of an organization arguably cannot be actualized without an absurd foundation that enables transformational process to take place. Another way of saying this is that difficult work must also feel like play and that the challenges of an organization, as serious and sometimes impossible as they may seem, also need to be felt as absurd so as to lighten the emotional climate of the workplace, enabling action to proceed without the unnecessary heaviness that can make people feel overwhelmed.

5. Leadership is momentary rather than fixed. The Bushman n/om-kxaosi believe that they are leaders only when they are shaking in a ceremony. When they aren't in ecstatic states, they are not regarded as any different than anyone else. This suggests that a transformative leader is only a leader in the moment in which they are facilitating transformational process. This idea helps keep the organization free of any inappropriate maintenance of social hierarchy, while maintaining an appropriate respect of hierarchical moments.

For example, when a talented singer is performing, the audience respectfully maintains a hierarchical relationship, quietly listening and enjoying the voice of another. However, after the show, the singer is no different than anyone else and the hierarchy is flattened. The Bushmen have a practice they call "insulting the meat." Clearly there are hunters who have superior skills. When they bring home the meat, everyone rejoices, but to make sure that the hunter doesn't get inflated, the community insults the meat. They might tease the hunter, saying that he is successful because he sings courtship songs to the animals and seduces them to come near him. Organizations need to find ways to do the same – maintaining both equality and difference, shifting as the occasion calls for it.

6. Space must be allowed for both the presence and transcendence of dichotomies and difference. I propose modifying Maslow's Theory Z management to say that self-actualizers are able to both maintain and transcend dichotomies. What is important is that anything – whether an idea or a social role – is able to shift if the situation calls for it. In the same way that a healthy family requires shape-shifting roles (where sometimes the children can playfully act as parents, and other times the adults can momentarily be children, while the roles of "white knight" and "scapegoat" constantly shift), a healthy organization also needs role shifting. All aspects of organizational life should respect and cultivate the different sides of dichotomies as well as allow them to change positions and morph into other forms of distinction. This dynamic underlies all humor, the absurd, and creativity. Without difference, nothing can make a difference. Transformative leaders, like Bushman shakers, must be able to juggle the differences, dance among the dichotomies, and promote differentiation and integration alternately or at the same time.

Any integral approach to transformative leadership is not possible without its sidekick – a differential approach. Bushman n/om-kxaosis handle distinctions in a manner that is similar to Francisco Varela's (1971) "star cybernetics" which transforms Hegelian dualistic pairs into being part of a more encompassing cybernetic complementarity. For instance, the dualism of "predator/prey" becomes part of "ecosystem/species interaction." In transformational leadership, the dualism of "Theory X/Theory Y" becomes part of the more encompassing context specified as "conversation about leadership/interaction of theories" or more generally "understanding/dialogue," which is subsumed by "mystery/experience."

7. The transformative leader is a master of improvisation and creativity.

Improvisation is another metaphor for the self-corrective circuit of cybernetics. Namely, the outcome of a particular action is utilized to shape the course of subsequent interaction. When self-correction is employed in music, there is a discipline that aesthetically brings melodic lines, harmonic principles, and rhythm sequences into account. It is not simply a "doing your own thing," but a dance between the known form and the unknown, order and chaos, the familiar and the wild (see Montuori 2003).

Creativity is the way in which a dance or interaction brings surprise to both rigor and imagination. When the performer is aesthetically pleased and surprised by the outcome, then it may be said that creativity rather than the performer had the upper hand in the delivery of the performance. Similarly, all the shaking of the Bushman n/om-kxaosi is a disciplined way of trying to get beyond the clichéd, routinized, spiritless, and unimaginative condition of a stuck moment, and awakening the presence of newborn vitality and creativity.

Bushman shamans and transformative leaders are both engaged in jazz - utilizing the elements at hand and shaking them through a process that neither fully surrenders to the familiar or to the wild. In doing so, they serve the gods of transformation, creativity, and improvisation.

In this mix, the leader surrenders control to become led by the circular, recursive processes that can never be fully known.

The transformative leader and the Bushman shaman are not leaders in any static sense. They are servants to the callings of creative imagination, though it involves more than the mind that is limited by the boundaries of self. There is an obedience and submission to the greater minds of relationship, organization, culture, and even the whole ecology that constrains and frees them to be midwives for the higher order processes of transformation and growth (Bateson, 1972; 1979). Transformational leaders are lighting rods for attracting the presence of the life force into the social situations that are in need of revitalization, inspiration, and leadership. Transformational leaders are also tricksters, shape-shifters, performers of the absurd, improvisers, and facilitators of interactional jazz.

Again, leadership only takes place for a moment. After the work has been done,

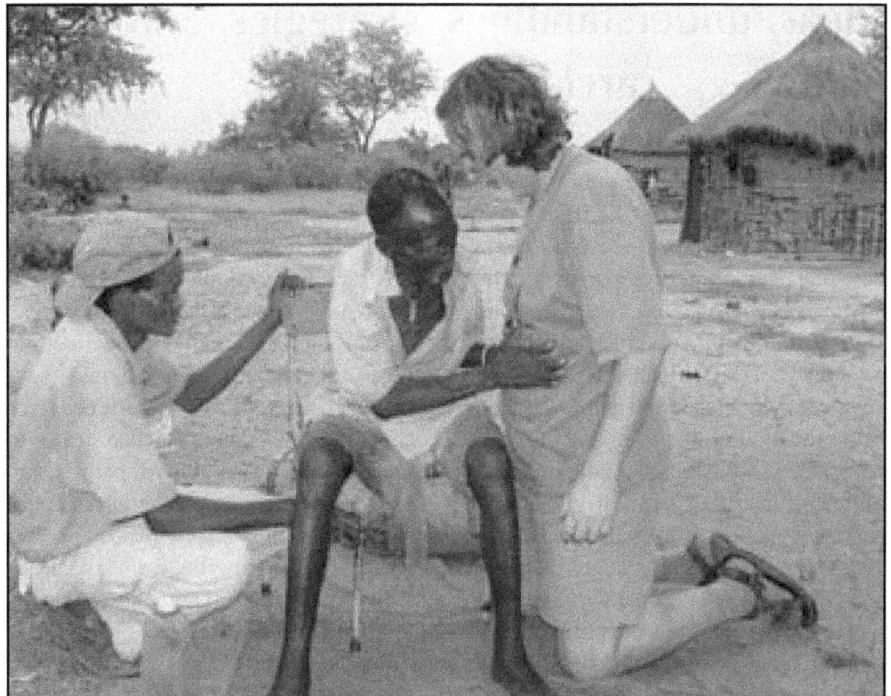

Photo: Grant Lessard

the so-called leaders find themselves no different that those they are supposed to lead. This return to being fully human is necessary in order for the circular recursion of leader-follower, teacher-student, therapist-client, shaman-spiritual seeker to play itself out. The hierarchy must be exercised so as to extinguish itself and then be followed by an unpredictable rebirth of a never-ending birth and death of transformational process.

As Maslow (cited in Hoffman 1988) found, Theory-Z does not work if the participants are not dedicated to the truth, whether it be about their relations or their product. As he said it, "If the product they turn out is not good, then [enlightened management] will destroy the whole enterprise, as truth will generally destroy untruth and fakery . . . [Enlightened] management only works for virtuous situations . . . If the product is not good and must be concealed and

Theories X, Y, and Z. They would ridicule all totalizing maps and models produced by theorists and have fun with the quadrants, diagrams, and models that aren't shape-shifting. All overly serious debates about such matters would be lightened. The Bushman shaking leaders would enter the scene with the intent of shaking things up.

Rather than seeing the Bushmen as "primitive" (whether implied or literally called that), let us regard the Bushmen n/om-kxaosi as holding some relevance for our becoming transformative leaders. They would invite us to have more heart,

calls it forth. All of this is to say that we must reach toward evoking contexts of transformative leadership and lessen our quest for transformative leaders.

Footnote

(1) The name "Bushman" is used to refer to the people discussed in this paper because it seems to be the preferred term by most of the people interviewed over the years. "San" has a pejorative connotation in Nama, the language from which it comes, though "Bushman" also has limitations and historical disqualifications. I use the latter term with the hope that it be "gradually 'ennobled'" (Biesele, 1993). The Bushman n/om-kxaosi referred to in this paper are all members of the Ju/hoansi Bushmen of the Nyae Nyae Conservancy, Namibia.

The Bushman's key to transcending dichotomies involves a willingness to allow shape-shifting, morphing, and continuous transformation of experience, feelings, body sensations, physical movement, ideas, understandings, strategies, and over-arching paradigms.

faked and lied about, then only Theory-X managers, customers, and sales people are possible." Maslow wasn't happy with the way some companies applied his ideas because he felt they abandoned B-values in the process, instead favoring an overly narcissistic "New Age management style" (see Hoffman). I assume he would also cringe at the more recent "prosperity" business ideologies that mix spiritual metaphors with material success, whether propagandized by conservative or New Age evangelists.

Transformational leadership does not cower away from the truths of the world that include poverty, sickness, social corruption, greed, and suffering in all its forms. It embraces the whole that includes suffering and bliss, knowing that each is inseparable from the other. The truth is found in the marriage of heaven and hell. In contraries, lies true progression and transformation.

I believe the Bushman n/om-kxaosi would have a good laugh at how seriously we take our theories, including

but with no less mind. In this more relational holding, we become freer to tease one another about our ideas and theories, resulting in more play, improvisation and creative advancement.

From the Bushman perspective, no one is a leader, though we may pass through momentary experiences of occupying that role. We can learn to make ourselves available for being ready to lead in situations that require such a presence. In this way, we become servants to the "bringing forth" of leadership, something that resides outside the boundaries of our psychological and sociological self.

Perhaps the next stage of leadership will involve more shaking of ideas and roles, along with less piety surrounding the creation of texts and authoritative voices. If so, we can expect all sorts of surprises: politicians dressed as clowns, leaders sucking helium before they talk, meetings that aim to shake things up, and a recognition that we are X, Y, and Z people depending upon the context that

References

Bateson, G. (1972). *Steps to an ecology of mind.* New York: Ballantine Books.

Bateson, G. (1979). *Mind and nature: A necessary unity.* New York: E. P. Dutton.

Beck, D., & C. Cowen. (1996). *Spiral dynamics: Mastering values, leadership, and change.* Oxford: Blackwell Publishing.

Biesele, M. (1993). *Women like meat: The folklore and foraging ideology of the Kalahari Ju/'hoansi.* Johannesburg: Witwatersrand University Press.

Bugental, J. F. T. (1965). *The search for authenticity.* New York: Holt, Rinehart, & Winston.

Guenther, M. (1999). *Tricksters and trancers.* Bloomington: Indiana University Press.

Hoffman, E. (1988). Abraham Maslow: Father of enlightened management. Alfred Adler Institute of San Francisco and Northwestern Washington: *Training Magazine,* September issue: 79-82.

Keeney, B. (1983). *Aesthetics of change.* New York: The Guilford Press.

Keeney, B. (2003). *Ropes to god: Experiencing the Bushman spiritual universe.* Philadelphia: Ringing Rocks Press.

Keeney, B. (2005). *Bushman shaman: Awakening the spirit through ecstatic dance.* Rochester, Vt.: Destiny Books.

Keeney, B. (2007). *Shaking medicine: The healing power of ecstatic movement.* Rochester, Vt.: Destiny Books.

Maslow, A. (1971). *The farther reaches of human nature.* New York: The Viking Press.

Maslow, A. (1965). *Eupsychian management: A journal.* Homewood, IL: Richard D. Irwin.

Montuori, A. (2003). The complexity of improvisation and the improvisation of complexity. *Human Relations,* 56: 237-255.

Thompson, W. I. (1996). *Coming into ceing: Texts and artifacts in the evolution of consciousness.* New York: St. Martin's Press.

Varela, F. (1971). Not one, not two. *CoEvolution Quarterly 11*: 62-67.

Von Foerster, H. (1981). *Observing systems.* Seaside, Calif.: Intersystems Publications.

Whitaker, C. (1982). *From psyche to system: The evolving therapy of Carl Whitaker.* New York: The Guilford Press.

Leading from Within the Whole of Time

Jack Petranker

There are those who question whether a body of knowledge or set of methods capable of molding transformative leaders truly exists (e.g., Gronn, 1995). In this article I suggest that it does. But it does not depend on new theories or plans, new models or organizational structures. Instead, it operates at a pre-theoretical level, the level where individuals engage the world around them. At this level of lived reality—a level I hope to invoke in writing this article—a valuable starting point for transformation is a new way of relating to time.

If linking time to transformation seems surprising, consider that transformative leadership is all about change: anticipating change, adapting to change, and bringing change about (cf. Kotter, 1990). The leader who wishes to transform the organization, those within it, or those with whom it interacts must be a master of change, and this in turn means cultivating a special kind of temporal competence. I do not wish to claim that all transformative leaders are 'in' time in the same way, but I do maintain that different ways of engaging time make the knowledge that leads to transformation more accessible, and that transformative leaders are those ready to engage time at a fundamental level.

Knowing the Whole of What's Happening Now

Successful leaders, we like to imagine, know what to do, whether this 'knowing' has to do with precise sensitivity to particular situations or with visionary insight. But which comes first? Do I know and then act, or do I come to know only as I set out on a course of action? Perhaps both alternatives are too limited. A more encompassing view might be that knowledge and action arise together, each shaping the other. When this interaction flows smoothly, action is 'timely'. It responds to the needs of the situation as a whole, taking into account all that is happening and effortlessly shaping the prevailing temporal momentum toward the goal at hand.

We are living at a time when this need to shape the temporal momentum is very much on our minds. In the recently concluded American presidential election, both candidates competed to be the candidate of change. Now, the election over and the new administration operating at full speed, we face an economic downturn more severe than any in recent memory. There is widespread agreement that change at a fundamental level is needed, that timely action is essential, and indeed, that the time for effective action has almost passed.

The natural question in such circumstances is how a leader can meet the needs of the times, can engage in timely action. Lacking the expertise to prescribe particular policies or approaches, I want to go to a more basic level. In the most general terms (terms I will refine below), the leader leads by being open to what time presents, refusing to stop at what is known. The leader turns away from pre-established identities, including that fundamental self-identity of 'me' and 'mine' that gathers up, coordinates, and makes sense of all other identities (Tulku,

> **There is a tide in the affairs of men Which, taken at the flood, leads on to fortune.**
>
> **Shakespeare,** *Julius Caesar*

Jack Petranker, MA, JD, is the director of the Center for Creative Inquiry and the past dean of the Tibetan Nyingma Institute and sits on the boards of several non-profit organizations. An author and teacher, he is also a member of the California State Bar.

1987). The transformative leader acts 'into' the unfolding situation, accepting what time has to offer as a challenge and opportunity. Moving forward into the emerging situation, with *all* its knowns and unknowns, the leader responds to what is happening and makes adjustments accordingly. Always improvising ('improving' on what has gone before), the leader turns from the image of what has been toward the immediacy of what time presently presents, gathering the whole of the moment into an active response, shaped by a vision of what might be possible.

The Extended Present of Transformative Leadership

A story is told by Margaret Stevens (quoted in Fields, et. al., 1994, 85) about three men at work on a construction project. A visitor asks what they are doing. The first says, "I am laying bricks." He is bitter. The second says, "I am building a wall." He is disengaged. The third says, "I am building a church!" He is filled with pride and joy.

In the story as it is told, only the workman who is building a church is engaging timely action. He knows what he is doing and why, and that knowledge informs his action, just as his action gives body to his knowledge. In contrast, the first worker, the bricklayer, can hardly be said to be acting at all; certainly not in the sense that Hannah Arendt (1957) has in mind when she contrasts 'action' to making or doing. He may know (to flesh out the story a bit) that he is working because he needs the wages to support his family, that this is a dead end job, that after this wall there will be another and then another, year after year, until the day his back gives out. Perhaps he knows also that he has a mortgage to pay and a young boy who is hyperactive, on medication, and in trouble at school. But he does not know that he is laying bricks, at least not in the sense that he is engaging fully what he is doing. And because this is true, we can say that he is not acting in time. He is not there in the present, he sees no future, and he finds no inspiration in the past.

Of course, it would not have to be this way. The bricklayer involved in the immediate act of laying bricks has available the feel of the bricks and the mortar, the wish to perform to a level of excellence, the pride in working efficiently and producing a superior result. Taking on these intentions, these meanings, would be one way to be present to what is happening, one way of acting in time. But it is not yet a way of acting that can provide leadership. That is why we must stay focused on the third bricklayer, the one inspired by the vision of building a church. Like that worker, the leader unites her intention with her activity to create an extended and dynamic time.

> **What is needed is a different way of being open to the future, a course of action attuned to time that can leave the future open and make of that openness the heart of transformation.**

She brings herself fully into the moment, collecting past and present and future as one. And that unified way of being in time, that marriage of past and future with the present, leads quite naturally to a concern with the purposes of the organization, the institutions within which the leader acts. To act in time means to act with others in mind, whether those others inhabit the past ("our forebearers"), the present ("our people"), or the future ("generations yet to come").

Communicating the Temporal Dynamic

I am invoking here what is often called the visionary aspect of leadership and noting its temporal dimension: a way of seeing that unites past and present and future. But leadership requires more than vision. It requires that the vision be communicated. What this means in practice is that the leader instills in others a shared and unitary vision of past, present, and future that allows them to see beyond the moment and beyond immediate concerns.

Our present social and political situation brings this temporal dimension of leadership to the fore. A great change is surging through our society and through the countries of the world. Wherever we turn, we hear predictions that there has been a fundamental shift, and that things will never be the same again. The leader will be the one who naturally responds to these circumstances. She will do so by engaging unitary time, communicating the temporal dynamic.

It is natural to look here to the example of President Obama, for the hallmark of his rise to the presidency was his ability to present the American people with a grand vision of change that brought past and future together in a way that transformed the present. During the course of the recently concluded presidential campaign, Obama consistently identified his presidential ambitions with the need for change, inviting others to join with him through his rallying cry, "Yes we can!"

One of the signal moments of the Obama campaign provides a remarkably clear example of what it means to engage a unitary temporal vision. In March of 2008, the campaign was reeling from charges that Obama had failed to distance himself sufficiently from his ex-pastor, Jeremiah Wright, who had repeatedly denounced whites for their treatment of African-Americans in incendiary and (to many) racist and offensive terms. On March 18, Obama delivered a speech intended to address these concerns (http://www.huffingtonpost.com/2008/03/18/obama-race-speech-read-th_n_92077.html). He began with a historical perspective, invoking the early history of the country and the adoption of the American constitution, and noting that the resolution of the question of slavery, though debated at length at that convention, was left to future generations. Thus, the speech begins by invoking an open temporal dynamic, bringing past and present together. The question unresolved at the outset of this nation remains unresolved today. It is this very same dynamic that Obama now evokes. He place his own campaign in that historical context, "to continue the long march of those who came before us." He has chosen to run for president "at this moment in history" because the American people are enacting an unfinished story, moving toward "a better future."

Up to this point, Obama has invoked a grand historical sweep. Now he personalizes this theme by invoking "my own American story." The dynamic here is bought home and brought to life. We see that the great historical struggles are reflected in the immediacy of our own lives, and as a people we are invited to engage that struggle. Obama sets out to show us this through his own history. As he does so, he mixes personal and historical: the grandfather who worked in World War II, a wife who shares directly the inheritance of slavery.

Obama turns now to the immediate issue before him: the controversy surrounding his former pastor. He denounces the worst of the pastor's remarks, and then turns again to history, quoting from one of his own best-selling memoirs his reaction to hearing Pastor Wright for the first time. The passage he quotes evokes history on an even grander scale than before: "I imagined the stories of ordinary black people merging with the stories of David and Goliath, Moses and Pharoah, the Christians in the lion's den . Those stories … became our story, my story; … until this black church, on this bright day, seemed once more a vessel carrying the story of a people into future generations and into a large world."

Turning to the bitter feelings that have been stirred up, Obama counsels his audience that we cannot turn away from issues of race, because that would mean turning from the country's past. And here he very directly invokes the sense of past as present, of time as unitary, choosing to do so by quoting a white southerner, William Faulkner, "The past isn't dead and buried; in fact, it isn't even past." Returning to the wrongs done the black people in generations past, he makes a link between those past wrongs and present racial tensions, describing "a legacy of defeat [that] was passed on to future generations—those young men and increasingly young women who we

see standing on street corners or languishing in our prisons, without hope or prospects for the future."

As the speech continues, Obama returns again and again to the way that past shapes present toward a future that can be only be transformed through connecting to a time greater than past or present or future, that links and transcends them all. He speaks of the experience of whites in America, children of immigrants who today are anxious for their future. In a few broad brush strokes, he paints in several decades of politics as a response to these concerns and seeks to recharacterize the political questions of the moment in terms consistent with the sweeping temporal dynamic he has presented. He asks his listeners to "embrac[e] the burdens of our past without becoming victims of our past," ready to "write their own destiny," ready to change. And it is here that the link to a temporal dynamic is truly made. For it is not enough to sketch out a sweeping history and use it to explain what is going in now. What matters is to engage the dynamic of that history. Obama embraces history in order to transform it, "not just with words, but with deeds." That is where the transforming power of leadership most truly emerges.

It may help to make this point if we compare briefly a still more momentous historical moment that we have also all lived through: the horrific attacks of September 11, 2001 and their aftermath. This time it was George W. Bush leading his nation at a moment of transformation. The attacks on the World Trade Center in 2001 were so shocking, on such a scale, that they changed the course of history and the very fabric of time. Time in the aftermath of 9/11 was not the same as time in the days before it. In such moments (others from American history would include December 7, 1941 and November 22, 1963), time itself changes in a unitary way. Transformative leadership at such times means something different: it is the leader along with his people who is transformed, and his transformation confirms the transformation of the larger group.

Yet some leaders rise to such occasions more successfully than others. One reason for the difference, the one that I am exploring here, is the ability or lack

of ability to embrace in a sustained way the temporal dynamic as a whole. That is one way of looking at what happened with President Bush, who ended his term of office with some of the lowest approval ratings on record. Carried forward initially by the events of 9/11 into a new world with a new temporality, he proved unable to connect with that temporal dynamic. It is a different dynamic that emerges from his words and deeds.

We can see this in Bush' speech to the Joint Houses of Congress on September 21, 2001. The President acknowledges that the course of history has changed, and he says, tellingly, that "in our grief and anger we have found our mission and our moment." But his primary message to the American people is not an invitation to embrace this change and let it transform them. Instead, he asks them to remain as they are, strengthened in resolve and patience, but essentially the same:

> Americans are asking: What is expected of us? I ask you to live your lives, and hug your children. I know many citizens have fears tonight, and I ask you to be calm and resolute . . . I ask your continued participation and confidence in the American economy….It is my hope that in the months and years ahead, life will return almost to normal. We'll go back to our lives and routines, and that is good. (http://archives.cnn.com/2001/US/09/20/gen.bush.transcript.)[1]

Now, it would be a mistake to make too much of this example. The situations faced by President Bush and candidate Obama were entirely different, and in the charged atmosphere that prevailed after the World Trade Center bombings there were certainly good reasons to encourage stability. In fact, one could argue that under such circumstances a return to stability was in fact a transformation, and that President Bush, in leading the American people away from their fears and concerns was playing the role of the transformative leader to perfection. It is what happened afterwards that seems more telling. Having restored the listing ship of state to an even keel, Bush seemed unable to embrace the new temporal dynamic that had emerged out of 9/11—a new past, present, and future emerging as an integrated whole. Had he done so, he might have been able to become an instrument of transformation in an entirely different. But that did not happen. A "return to normality" too quickly became "business as usual," differing chiefly in a heightened sense of danger. The Bush presidency and the American people alike eventually came to suffer the consequences.

Time Beyond Words

Evoking the dynamic of time in a way that allows other to engage it may be at the heart of leadership, but— as Obama's critics often argue— speech is often a medium inadequate to work this alchemy. As Macbeth put, "Words to the heat of deeds too cold breath gives." Leadership requires action, and though words are a form of action, they will often not be enough.

Here again the present political circumstances are instructive. As I write, candidate Obama, having become President Obama, is called on to lead the nation and the world toward recovery from a global economic crisis. The nation waits, its patience perhaps wearing thin, for plans that can guide the economy and the structures of government through the slough of financial despond. The more Obama's administration seems to evidence uncertainty about what action to take, the less helpful words become.

Yet the opposite of fine speeches here is not new plans to rescue the economy. Such plans are of course vital as means to accomplish ends, and the wrong kind of planning could sink the economy and vastly damage the nation. Yet in terms of the temporal dynamic, planning cannot be enough. For plans have as their goal to turn to the future into an accomplished past: to impose a previously worked-out structure on an unknown future and thereby tame it. In the words of Alfred Schutz (1972), they treat the future as 'future perfect' in the strict grammatical sense: as 'that which will have happened.' What is needed is a different way of being open to the future, a course of action attuned to time that can leave the future open and make of that openness the heart of transformation.

A valuable concept to describe the readiness of the leader to embark on such a course of action is that of "preadaptation," introduced in this context by

the well-known systems theorist Stuart Kauffman. Certain features of an organism, writes Kaufmann (2006), have the capacity to become useful in completely novel ways when environmental circumstances change: they are "preadapted" to such changed circumstances His example is swim bladders, organs that fill with air and that were used by certain ancient species of fish for maintaining

The ability to hold past, present, and future together as a unity is one aspect of a transformative relationship to time.

an equilibrium of buoyancy. When those fish found themselves spending time at or near the shore, their swim bladders proved unexpectedly useful as oxygen reservoirs. They were pre-adapted to become lungs.

Preadaptation in the biological sense is a blind (though not perhaps unknowing) process, but it can still serve as a metaphor for a leader's ability to act into time in a way that engages the whole of time. The leader makes use of the way things are, without being bound by how they have been. She is ready to turn the past toward the future, or to feed the future into the past, in a way that transforms the present. The preadaptive leader does not limit her situation in advance; does not take a position or accept an identity, for doing so only closes down the knowing that time in its wholeness makes available. Whereas Kurt Lewin's influential model of organizational change (1947) starts with a movement to "unfreeze" the existing situation, a preadaptive leader regards no situation as frozen to begin with (cf. Bergson, 1911).

A preadaptive approach to time suggests that the knowledge that guides the transformative leader is not something we extract from time, as a doctor performing a caesarean section extracts a baby from the womb. Long before we seek to manipulate it or tease it into the open, knowing is available *within* the

wholeness of time. The transformative leader is open to that knowing by being available for time. In Weber's (1947) terms, the charismatic leader embraces and manifests the temporal dynamic, while the move toward routinization that inevitable follows seeks to technologize time, to tame its dynamic through the instrument of the plan.

An availability to time starts on the basis of presence, a kind of wholehearted engagement. Tarthang Tulku (1990, 484-85) illuminates this alternative when he writes that each moment presents a 'point of decision':

> The 'decision point' gathers together all that is known and all that presents itself in [each] 'moment' of time. ... As a gathering together of all that contributes to its making, each 'point of decision' is the whole. ... In the gathered wholeness of the 'point of decision', nothing is left out, and choice is freely available. ... Between the rhythm of time and the 'decision points' of knowledge, a sustaining balance holds.

The availability of the gathered-together wholeness of time bypasses one of the great concerns that managers and leaders often express about time: that time is always in short supply. To illustrate this, consider an all-too-typical story I heard recently from a business consultant working with a mid-level manager who was having trouble with an employee. Perhaps, the consultant suggested, it would be helpful to look at things from the employee's perspective, to get a sense of how the employee felt about the massive changes the company was trying to implement. The manager exploded with impatience: "I don't want to know how she feels! I don't have time to deal with her feelings."

This outburst reflects a characteristically limited view of time. The manager was right: she did not 'have' the time she needed. But this was not because of the pressures of her work. Rather, the manager had lost touch with the temporal dynamic, lost sight of the knowing available within the wholeness of time. Suppose that in her interactions with her subordinate she had been more fully present to what was happening, present in a 'wholly engaged' way. Would a separate act of "dealing" with her employee's feelings have been necessary? Would dealing with those feelings have 'taken' time?

Cultivating Whole-Hearted Presence

A whole-hearted, 'timely' knowing emerges in the present, so the leader interested in transformation must above all be present (Senge, et. al., 2004). But do we even know how to be present in a timely way? Our usual approach is quite to the contrary, for it depends on taking a position in advance. First do the research, then act, first develop a plan of action and then follow the plan. Necessary as such procedures may be for a variety of practical reasons, they are neither whole-hearted, timely, or present to what is happening. The transformative leader cannot act in this way. Rather, she must work to free herself from all positions. For such a leader, every moment becomes what Tarthang Tulku (1990, 484) calls an "ongoing emergency," in the quite literal sense that the present always 'emerges' anew in each moment. This does not mean lurching from one crisis to another, though it may be in crisis situations that transformative leadership is most required. Rather, it means treating each situation, each day, each new encounter, as a new opportunity.

Let us consider what it means to be present by focusing on the element of intention. How can intention merge with presence in such a way that the leader is available to the whole of time? Here are three important elements: First, the leader must be clear on his or her own intentions: they must be and remain present. Second, those intentions must accord with the leader's own highest values. Third, the intention to act on those values must be inseparable from the action itself: the leader can neither forget nor waver.

The last of these three elements may seem self-evident, but in fact it is precisely here that leaders often falter. Like the rest of us, leaders are often distract-ed from their intentions; put differently, they are not present in a timely way to what they care about most. They fall back into business as usual, or else get caught up in the next immediate concern. The perfect contemporary symbol for this is the cell phone, whose presence in pocket or purse implies a commitment to interruptibility, and whose use gives rise to the recurring reality of divided attention.

The enemy of being present to each new circumstance in an intention-filled way is fear, for fear overrides care and commitment to one's own values. For a leader bound to the past or (which amounts to the same thing) to carrying out plans decided on advance, fear comes close to being the default state, for each emerging moment threatens departure from what has been pre-established. But presence is the antidote to fear, for engaging openly the temporal whole means accepting that you do not know what comes next. To choose decisive action and the ongoing emergency means being ready to start from this mystery. As Tarthang Tulku (1994b, 199) writes:

The enemy of being present to each new circumstance in an intention-filled way is fear, for fear overrides care and commitment to one's own values.

Touched by awareness, time expands ... Simultaneously creating and focusing on what we experience, we can relax into each event ... The more awareness opens, the more time opens, revealing new dimensions of awareness.

In this innovative way of being, there is no rushing past what is so, no trading the present for an image of the future or a reaction to the past. You act in the timeliness of what presents itself, act when the moment for action arrives.

Touching Time

The ability to hold past, present, and future together as a unity is one aspect of a transformative relationship to time. But there is another aspect, equally important: the ability to touch the dynamic of time. We have all known people, natural leaders, who seem larger than life, more closely attuned to the dynamic of being alive. And we have all known occasions when we are so much in tune with what is happening that we act swiftly, decisively, and accurately. The transformative leader can touch time in that way; what is more, she can make that experience available to others.

To know whether you are touching time, you can ask some simple questions. When moments of decision come up, can you see the past and future that emerge within or as part of the decisive moment? Can you experience directly and openly the 'arising from' and 'going to' of this 'now'? To look in this way is to invite the dynamic of time. From there, the path toward transformation unfolds by itself.

The Organization in Time

Because they depend on presence and intention, timely action and timely knowing are intensely personal: they involve the leader's own way of being. Yet the leader's role is trans-personal: it involves the organization. What is the link between these two ways of being? Can the leader help structure the organization so that it too can anticipate, adapt to, and bring about change? How can the organization engage the whole of time? That is where the leader can be most effective: in creating opportunities for transformation for others. This does not mean simply sharing and communicating the temporal fullness of the vision that shapes the organization's mission, though that is part of it. It also means sharing and communicating a vision of what constitutes timely action and timely knowledge, of transforming the organization so that ongoing transformation becomes the matrix of its being. Here are a few preliminary thoughts, rooted in what has gone before, on how this could be done.

First, the leader must communicate the clear intention that the organization cannot hold on to a fixed identity. Transformation happens in every moment, and, at least potentially, transformation is total. Of course, this does not mean turning away from what is so, from what has led up to his moment. But it does mean accepting the truth of change, which is also the dynamic of time. It means operating from the future rather than the past. This is a radical shift. It means more than being ready to give up what is no longer working. It means having nothing—nothing at all—to lose.

Second, the leader must encourage others to challenge identity at the personal level as well, and must create structures for decision-making and planning within the organization that make this possible. People are ordinarily afraid of change. But if they have no positions to hold on to, then this fear loosens, for without positions and conditions, change is the 'stuff' of being. At another level, people fear that change is not possible. But again, timely action, grounded in timely knowledge, demonstrates that there is *only* change.

Third, the leader needs to create an organizational culture that rewards a full embrace of time. The more stakeholders welcome transformation and the less people are rewarded for holding on tightly to what is so, the more innovative and creative the organization can be. With the right kind of intention, organizational structures can be established that foster such an approach and help to give it birth.

Organizations are not machines; they are not even organisms. Created by human beings, organizations participate in the human capacity for freedom from positions, for transformation as the boundless truth of what is so. In each moment, a different intention can reign, a new world can take form. At one level, the change that results from this shift will be subtle, almost impossible to notice. At a deeper level, however, the organization guided toward transformation will experience the fullness of freedom (and freedom of fullness) that make the most profound forms of accomplishment possible.

A World Ripe for Change

In a world streaking with ever accelerating momentum into the unknown—the world we occupy now—this open, timely way of engaging what is so, of acting on what the situation requires, seems to be precisely what is called for. In such a world, leadership that can transform the organization toward a new and more timely knowledge, new and more timely ways of acting, becomes a life and death matter.

If we transform the organization toward the fullness of time, we transform the possibilities for those who inhabit the organization. We give them the possibility to go beyond their own limitations. And this too seems deeply important, for we live in a time where, despite surface appearances, the choices for all of us are growing steadily more confined.

The true transformative leader may be the one who can combine these two perspectives. Whatever the conventional metrics for measuring organizational success, the test of successful transformation is whether both knowledge and freedom grow—for the organization and for its stakeholders alike. If they do, accomplishment will follow.

References

Arendt, H. (1957). *The human condition.* New York: Anchor Books.

Arendt, H. (1963). *Between past and future: Six exercises in political thought.* Cleveland: World Publishing.

Bergson, H. (1911). *Creative evolution.* New York: Henry Holt.

Fields, R., with Taylor, P., Weler, R., & Ingrasci, R. (1994). To work is to pray. In C. Whitmyer, *Mindfulness and meaningful work: Explorations in right livelihood* (pp. 83-89). Berkeley: Parallax Press.

Gronn, P. (1995). Greatness revisited: The current obsession with transformational leadership. *Leading and Managing 1*(1), 14-27.

Kauffman, S. (2006, November). The evolution of future wealth. *Scientific American, 295* (5), 44.

Kotter, J. (1990). What do leaders really do? *Harvard Business Review 68*, 103-111.

Lewin, K. (1947). Frontiers in group dynamics. *Human Relations 1*(1), 5-41.

Schutz, A. (1972). *The phenomenology of the social world.* Evanston, IL: Northwestern University Press.

Senge, P., Scharmer, C. O., Jaworski, J. ,& Flowers, B. S. (2004). *Presence: Human purpose and the field of the future.* Cambridge, MA: Society for Organizational Learning.

Tulku, T. (1987). *Love of knowledge.* Berkeley, Dharma Publishing.

Tulku, T. (1990). *Knowledge of time and space.* Berkeley: Dharma Publishing.

Tulku, T. (1994). *Mastering successful work: Skillful means wake up.* Berkeley: Dharma Publishing.

Weber, M. (1947). *The theory of social and economic organizations.* New York: The Free Press.

Footnotes

(1) Compare also Arendt, 1963, 169: "[T]he faculty of freedom, the sheer capacity to begin, . . . animates and inspires all human activities and is the hidden source of production of all great and beautiful things" (1963, 169).

(2) It is natural to think here of Bush's famous injunction to the American people to respond to the attacks by "going shopping." However, Bush never actually made such a statement (though Tony Blair in the UK did). The closest he came was a statement in a speech at O'Hare airport in November, 2001: (http://www.whitehouse.gov/news/releases/2001/09/20010927-1.html) "Do your business around the country. Fly and enjoy America's great destination spots. Get down to Disney World in Florida. Take your families and enjoy life, the way we want it to be enjoyed."

The Heart of Hearing

A Story of Transformative Leadership and Sustainable Development

Shoshana Simons

The world is emerging from eight long years of the Bush Administration. On Tuesday, January 20th, the day after the Martin Luther King Jr. holiday, Barack Obama was sworn in as the first African-American President of the USA. Elected at a time of global economic meltdown, US troops still at war in Iraq and Afghanistan, unprecedented human-made, potentially cataclysmic ecological changes and the unintended social and political consequences of these and other forces, Obama's election brought to fruition the hopes of the millions of us, hungry for change, who've participated in multiple ways over these last years in creating the conditions for the mass grassroots movement that evolved in support of his candidacy.

However, Obama isn't distinctive simply because he is Black. He is also the son of a poor white Midwesterner-

Shoshana Simons is the Chair of Expressive Arts Therapy at CIIS and core faculty in the Transformative Inquiry Dept. Her background in work with communities and organizations began in London in the late 1970's when she worked for several years with women surviving domestic violence, homeless families and disenfranchised youth. Since coming to the USA in 1990, she has applied her education and skills in counseling psychology, social and emotional learning, drama therapy, and human & organizational systems to her work as a trainer, organizational consultant and educator. She has a particular interest in arts-based research and the power of the arts in fostering social change.

turned global citizen; a single mother, Peace Corps volunteer & social justice activist who eventually gained a PhD in anthropology. She married and then divorced a Kenyan student, remarrying an Indonesian man with whom Barack Obama and his half sister, Maya, lived for several years. He grew up in the rich soil of an atypical multicultural family, its roots and branches stretching from the Midwestern USA to Kenya, Hawaii and Indonesia. Obama is, in essence, a "third culture kid", someone who spent a significant amount of time in childhood in one or more cultures. The research on "third culture kids", suggests that rather than identifying with any one nation, they tend to be adaptable, flexible, finding a sense of belonging everywhere and nowhere. (Hill Useem in Eakin 1998).

As such, it seems like Obama's background positions him outside the confines of multiple conventional discourse communities, particularly as they relate to race, class, ethnicity, religion and nationality. Perhaps this factors into his ability to reach seamlessly beyond the either/or dichotomies of party affiliations, racial identities and the tendency to side on social issues. Instead, he invites us to come together in the service of identifying our common goals and aspirations in the interest of establishing and sustaining our collective future on this planet.

Furthermore, unlike prior Presidents,

Obama's roots are in community organizing, founded on the kinds of skills that make successful community development possible. These include the skills of openness to listening to multiple perspectives, emotional intelligence, facilitation skills, advocacy, mediation and the rhetorical skills necessary to mobilize people into action.

Obama's presidency soars on a message of hope in the face of the extreme problems facing our country and planet. He is perhaps the most high profile example we currently have of the emergence of what we trust will prove to be the right leader in the right place at the right time.

This article, however, is not about Barack Obama, though it draws inspiration from his example. Instead it is the story of a lesser-known transformative leader called Yiota Ahladas who has played a key role in creating a vibrant culture of participation and partnership in the small city of Burlington, VT. Ahladas shares with Obama multiple outsider statuses, which, like he, are intrinsic aspects of her leadership style that she draws upon as sources of strength as will be described later in this article.

This article is also rooted in my own personal relationship with the city of Burlington, where I lived from 1992-1998, and with Yiota, who is also a friend. She and I shared the generational influence of the second-wave of feminism, the essence of which is captured by the phrase "the personal is political". In so saying, this article tacks between social and geographic contexts and the personal context of Yiota's life, elevating and exposing the relationship between a given leader's personal experiences, beliefs and values and how these might manifest in actual practices of leadership. Furthermore, a fundamental premise of this article is that there is a mutually reciprocal relationship between a given community, the kind of leadership to which it gives rise and the effects of that leadership back on the community – a social ecology of leadership, so to speak.

I spent three days with Yiota in the spring of 2007 on a "retreat" of our own creation in Sedona, AZ, inviting her into a conversation about the relationship between her background, beliefs, values and her approach to leadership.

A journal article is a particular form of story telling, one that traditionally has not done justice to the actual territory of lived experience. Poetry and other forms of creative writing have the capacity to weave together social facts, interpretations and the more nuanced texture of life-as-lived. I therefore integrate some poems written by both Yiota and myself, in response to some of the most striking of the conversations that we shared.

The Landscape of My Interest

The impetus for writing this article began almost two years ago when I had no conscious awareness of the possibility of electing a visionary African-American president, not to mention an electoral campaign rooted in a searing vision of hope and community-building across difference. At the time I was interested in the fact that, despite the prevailing ultra-right wing political climate of the USA under George W. Bush, many communities across the country were nonetheless deeply engaged in practicing what Frances Moore Lappe

(2007) calls "living democracy", rooted in the principles of sustainable social, economic and environmental development, equity & social justice.

I've been keenly interested in participatory forms of community development and governance since my beginnings as a community worker with homeless

A fundamental premise of this article is that there is a mutually reciprocal relationship between a given community, the kind of leadership to which it gives rise and the effects of that leadership back on the community – a social ecology of leadership, so to speak.

families in inner city London in the early 1980's. Influenced by the conscientization theories and practices of Paulo Freire (1970), the ideals of a partnership society (Eisler, 1987) and the vision of a sustainable planet (Goerner, 2008; Moore Lappe, 2007), I wanted to take a more intimate look at a community that was making real strides towards creating partnerships between government and community in the service of sustainable social development. In particular, I was interested in exploring the relationship between the social ecological landscape of a given community, the type of leadership that might flourish against that landscape, and the reciprocal relationship between that formal leadership and the community that it serves. In so saying, I was interested in exploring the possibility of a social ecology of leadership. As Clandinnin and Connelly (2000) express it, stories need to be understood against the background of already existing "storied landscapes" without which they are not fully intelligible.

I also wanted to share a hopeful and successful story of sustainable development and sustainable leadership practices from within the US context at an historical moment when hope seemed thin on the ground. It's therefore with some irony that this article pushes up from its roots to break through at this particular juncture.

On Landscapes and Stories: Burlington, Vermont

Burlington, a city of 40,000 residents, is the largest city in the small state of Vermont. It is situated in the Champlain Valley on the shores of the magnificent Lake Champlain, framed on its far side by the towering Adirondack Mountains of New York state. Lake Champlain winds it way some 110 miles up into Canada where it meets the St. Lawrence River. The city has a long and impressive history of progressive leadership, beginning with the election in 1981 of socialist mayor Bernie Sanders (now Vermont's Representative in the US Congress), extending for a further fifteen years under Mayor Peter Clavelle. Vermont, the "whitest state in the Union" after Maine and the last state to actually join the original thirteen states of the union, was the first state to outlaw slavery in 1777. Vermonters played a key role in the Underground Railroad, providing refuge to slaves fleeing the South as they made their way to freedom over the Canadian border. However, this is not to romanticize either the state or the city of Burlington. Slavery persisted informally well into the 1800's and racism is still alive and well in the city.

Despite its small scale, contemporary Burlington shares similar problems to those in larger cities especially related to poverty, unemployment, environmental degradation, public transportation, affordable housing, domestic violence, mental health problems & drug and alcohol abuse. In recent years, the racial and ethnic mix of the city has begun to shift dramatically, largely as a result of the Vermont Refugee Resettlement Project. Approximately 52 different European,

African and Asian languages are now spoken in the Burlington school system. The public sector is under great pressure to develop culturally appropriate services in response to the overwhelming challenges confronting these communities and dominant populations have a steep learning curve in terms of developing cultural awareness.

However, Burlington has a strong commitment to equity, participatory governance and community partnerships and the small scale of the city is well suited to such initiatives. A core principle underlying this commitment is the inclusion of the voices of populations, traditionally excluded from having a say in government.

The city is recognized both nationally and internationally for its model of sustainable community development, deeply rooted in a partnership model. A highly participatory Legacy Project was initiated in 1999. This project has involved thousands of residents across ages and backgrounds in creating a common vision for the future of Burlington. This ongoing project informs the city's vision of sustainable development, grounded in four foundational areas: environmental protection, social equity, education & economic development.

Collaborative, Community Partnerships

The year was 1981. Rooted in a deep understanding of the politics of social class, the then mayor, Bernie Sanders (2), launched Burlington's ambitious agenda for social justice and equity. This initiative was supported by a diverse coalition of city stakeholders including low-income residents, local police officers as well as academics from the University of Vermont (UVM). The Progressive Party emerged as the vehicle for advancing what was now a widely supported social change agenda. The Progressive party has more or less dominated Burlington's political scene ever since, offering Burlington a rare opportunity within the USA to pursue the goals of social justice and equity over the long term.

In 1989 Sanders founded the Community and Economic Development Office (CEDO) in order to implement the Mayor's sustainability and social equity agenda. CEDO has been the "power behind the throne" so to speak in operationalizing the Progessive's agenda.

Transformative Leadership for a Transformative Organization

The Center for Community and Neighborhoods (C-CAN) is one of CEDO's three primary divisions. C-CAN is the vibrant arm of the city's government offering multiple programs that promote civic engagement in the community. These include a community justice center that implements a restorative justice approach; a neighborhood center; conflict resolution projects; study circles focusing on racism; clean up and service days; offender and re-entry programs; reugee assistance programs; Neighborhood Planning Assemblies; a first-response team of volunteers that takes action to clean up after acts of vandalism and much more.

C-CAN is deeply rooted in a partnership approach to addressing the community's needs, working with social groups whose lives are often overlooked including families living in poverty, recently resettled immigrants, and people of color in general. It is an integral part of city government and offers a unique spectrum of initiatives that inspire and support community participation, citizen action and responsible municipal government.

Yiota Ahladas is the Co-Founder and Director of C-CAN. She brings a sense of passionate commitment and possibility to her work.

According to Ahladas

People make happen what they help to create. So we invite people into conversation about the possibility of the future. It's the responsibility of government to ask the right questions because the quality of what you create is going to reflect the quality of the questions you've been asking. (Ahladas, 2006)

Ahladas plays an instrumental role in the ongoing processes of transformation that Burlington is so deeply engaged in. C-CAN recruits 40 Americorps VISTA volunteers a year. VISTA volunteers are not traditionally recruited by city governments to work in local neighborhoods. However, Ahladas played a central role in envisioning the building of an army of VISTA volunteers who could jump-start the engine for revitalizing the com-

munity which, at the time of C-CAN's inception had a poverty rate of 39%. The use of VISTA volunteers is seen as a key element of a conscious capacity building strategy. It develops leadership potential within the volunteers, with many of them subsequently taking on important offices in both the non-profit and local government sectors in Burlington. Ahladas sees VISTA workers as crucial to the Burlington Neighborhood Project that actively seeks to involve local residents in shaping their communities.

In 2006 Ahladas won a prestigious Eisenhower Fellowship that took her to South Africa and New Zealand to exchange ideas with local community leaders concerned with sustainable community development.

An announcement in the Burlington Free Press of Ahladas's fellowship described her as having "inspired her city government colleagues and hundreds of AmeriCorps VISTA workers who have reached a little higher because of her spirit and infectious can-do attitude. A friend of hers says that it's the "Zorba" in her that makes her wholeheartedly embrace whatever life brings her way." (Reid, 2005).

Leading from the Outside-In and the Inside-Out

Yiota Ahladas was born in 1960 in Utica, NY. She spent most of her childhood in Springfield, MA, a solidly working class city to the west of Boston. She is a first generation North American, born to Greek immigrants.

My grand mother's grandmother was a village healer/midwife and the Greek tradition says that in every other generation, the healing legacy gets passed along. My grandmother used to pick the plants and do healing. My mother grew up in the shadow of this very tiny but very powerful woman who had dreams and actualized her dreams. She was very smart and a fierce feminist. She was the first girl in the village to go to school – girls in the village don't go after the 3rd grade – and my grand mother said why not? I'm going to go to school! And she went to school and she became the town clerk.

Yiota inherited her grandmother's fiery spirit. She played a key activist role in city government, initiating the movement to draft Domestic Partnership policy in 1993 when Burlington became the first city in the country to pass a retain a policy to provide equal benefits to domestic partners regardless of sexual orientation. Her central role in this initiative led to her being targeted in a reaction to the policy within the city's administration, which at the time was under the leadership of a one-term Republican mayor, Peter Brownell elected as a result of a citywide backlash against the domestic partnership legislation. She told me that when she organized around the issue she

> really felt the extent to which I was an outsider. Before that I wasn't as aware of it because I was in such a progressive bubble. But that's when the true colors came out – in millions of ways – in hate-filled phone calls and even one death threat– but ultimately it manifested in the municipality when the Republican mayor, Peter Brownell, got elected.

Her key role in formulating this landmark legislation left her in a vulnerable position. She found herself being publicly attacked by Brownell who wanted her dismissed from her job. This strategy backfired as the community powerfully rallied around Ahladas. Not only was her position saved, she was eventually promoted. However, rather than taking an oppositional stance to Brownell in the face of this hostility, Ahladas built a personal connection with him, striving toward building a relationship based in mutual respect. Brownell, who went on to take a seat in the Vermont State Senate, eventually ended up voting for passage of the Civil Union legislation in the State of Vermont in 2000, affording same-sex couples the same rights, privileges, obligations and responsibilities as Vermont gives to heterosexual married couples.

In hearing this story, I am struck by Yiota's ability to stay in relationship with folks through the most difficult times and in the most difficult places. She says that

> as soon as you know anybody and begin to share your life a little bit – become human beings instead of labels, you know – for whatever reason we started to relate around our commonalities rather than our differences.

For many leaders, this statement can sound clichéd. However, for Yiota, relationship building across differences is

the stuff of her everyday existence, not only in relation to her ethnicity and sexual orientation but also because she is "late deafened" third generation deaf.

Counterpoint

In my head buzzes the sound of
                                    disease
A tiny hiss, a rubble, a roar that
                                    haunts me.
A part of me leaves me
I notice it more each day.

I am left alone
With only the noises in my head
Perhaps it's time
For me to be alone.

I put my ear to your lips
The whispers on the pillow
Safe in your arms I cry
Because the man in the store repeats
                                    himself
Three times before I hear him.
I cry because I cannot hear
The bass tones of the Bach Cantata
Or the howling wind outside our
                                    bedroom.
I cry for when
I will not hear
Whispers on the pillow.

You say it's okay, I love you
Think of all the other ways we are.
But will you still love me
When all words are beyond my
                                    reach?

At the theater you sit close
And the words of the stage come to
                                    me.
What if I did not have you
To speak the world into my ear?

With the sounds that fade away
I am fading too.
Perhaps I shall disappear into a shell
                                    from the sea
A nautilus spiraling inward
To a quiet center point.
                            - Yiota Ahladas

Yiota shares:

My father's father was deaf, my father's aunts and uncles were deaf, and my father refuses to admit to my deafness. My father, a deaf man, lives alone in a silent house, lives alone in a silent world. A life, like his, I will not live.

I wondered to myself about the cost to Yiota not only of living a life in a silent world, like her father, but the alternative she has chosen of being in a high profile professional position that places such a huge demand on her to acculturate to the hearing world. I asked her about her outsider status, particularly as it related to deafness and the pressure to assimilate, recognizing the fear of my own potential for deafness, lurking behind my question. She states

> Outsider and insiderness only work if you recognize them. Part of the gift of having been deaf and of growing up with a deaf father...I think there's a way that I miss a lot of the ways the inside world responds to my outsiderness – and I don't care! (we both laugh) it's sort of like everyone else's problem.

As we talk about her deafness over time, a more complicated picture emerges. In a recent e-mail to me Yiota writes

> I've had a challenging week on the hearing front w/ accommodations not being met even when I've asked for them and the technology is there etc..., being excluded not because I can't belong but because the dominant paradigm can't step out of itself...times like these...you don't just lose your hearing you lose your own voice.., you begin to take responsibility not only for your own need but for the discomfort of the persons around you.., It's easy to develop a "culture/habit of not understanding". You have been punished for not understanding, so you stop trying. If you keep trying and keep not understanding, you keep being exhausted and stressed.., you simply stop trying and enter the culture of make believe.., the frustrating side of hearing loss.., some many gifts too I know..,

To be in relationship with Yiota is an exercise in connection; we need to be mindful of extraneous noise in the environment, to where we position our faces in relation to each other. She lip-reads and often has to turn down her hearing aids. Yiota said

> You don't hear with your ears at this stage... you hear with your brain and your eyes (lip reading) my left ear has next to no hearing left... my right ear has something with the hearing aid but is considered profound loss...my speech discrimination and ability to function on the crumbs of hearing I have in my right ear are beyond what is usual with this degree of loss.

One night I dreamed that Yiota's hearing got dramatically worse. I had to sit right up in her face so that she could "hear" me. She had to touch my lips to know what I was saying.

Through the dream I realized that to maintain a relationship with Yiota, both of us had to make a leap that necessitated greater intimacy. No real connection could be sustained without our direct, close eye- to-eye contact.

Yiota speaks of disclosing to members of her work community that she cannot hear in large groups. The circle of the group therefore has to move in close in order to be able to hear. I note that in this, her deafness is the gift that she gives to the whole community, but one which takes a huge personal toll.

Managing by Walking Around

She says that she likes to walk about
city hall

Stopping to chat
So joyous in her curiosity
Where are you from?
Who are your people?
How did you get here?
How can I help?

After hours
The janitor stoops
bucket and mop in hand
transformed and transported
he, an intrepid traveler who trekked
over
dangerous mountain paths
crossing enemy lands
The only shelter the canopy
of Tibetan Buddhism

OM GATE GATE PARAGATE
PARASAMGATE BODHI SVAHA

A picture of the Dalai Lama folded
into his papers
His mother cannot speak English
and is deaf
He needs to help her through the
thickets and tangles
that line the steep passes
of US immigration bureaucracy
mama cannot hear nor speak on the
telephone/deaf

She says:
I hear your mother
for I too am deaf

She writes a magic letter
Called Grant Proposal
The fairies deliver with a hearing aid
-Shoshana Simons

Yiota considers spending time just hanging out with folks, getting to know their experiences and concerns, to be the most important part of her role. She demonstrates a seemingly insatiable, genuine curiosity about people – particularly folks who are generally overlooked. She shared the example of a conversation

Yiota Ahladas's story illustrates the inextricable relationship between the personal landscape of a given leader's history and experience and that of the community that she serves.

she had when she stopped to chat with a janitor, after hours, at City Hall. He described to her the long and treacherous journey he undertook that brought him from Tibet to Burlington, VT. In the course of this informal conversation, she learned that this man's mother, visiting from Tibet, was deaf.

I arranged to get her hearing aids – money, testing etc. – no way to get hearing aids in Tibet. Before she arrived to visit him in the US, this man hadn't seen or talked to his Mom in 15 years - since he was 15 and had to flee in the night. After she returned to Tibet from the US he was able to talk to her by phone...when she was in the US and got the aids she grabbed my hands in a tearful/prayful clasp saying the light had been turned on in her life again and she would live a new life, not only be able to talk to her son but also her grandchildren. Tattered shreds of the Dalai Lama's robe were pinned to her robes...quite a sight.

Cultural Fusion: Creating New Traditions

You come into a room in City Hall
which would usually be
stuffy public hearings and stuffed suits
and there's 400 people there
Children are painting
People eating food together
it's Black and it's Yellow and it's
White
and it's people with disabilities and

it's elderly and it's kids
- Yiota Ahladas

Yiota states that one of the most important of C-CAN's initiatives is the creation of new traditions that celebrate, hold and recognize the space of communities that are emerging as multiple ethnic, religious cultures and histories become newly intertwined in this small city.

Because we're a mixture of so many cultures and histories and a lot of our own indigenous traditions are getting diluted and lost and convoluted – communities need to develop their own traditions – it's one of the pieces of my work I love and one of the things that started organically and small but has grown into this huge annual event of about 300-400 people into Neighborhood Night of Successes. We just put out the word everywhere – little corner stores – who's doing really cool stuff right next door to you that should be recognized – and it's like everyone from kids in the street to folks who've created welcoming committees for their new neighbors to a refugee who's really taken on a role to serve as interpreter for her people. We've put together a group of neighbors who receive nominations and we have this award ceremony at City Hall. It included a play that one of the citizens wrote about being a victim of a crime and how in creating a system of restorative justice we can transform and heal the community. We give out a growing number of awards every year. We create this huge slide show with images of the people and their quotes – creating an iconography of the community's experience.

The creation an iconography of the community's experience through images serves to make real, affirm and concretize the emergence of the growth of a new collective sense of community even as multiple ethnic and language communities live side-by-side, growing a positive sense of community proactively.

On Sustainability

Yiota hosts many visitors from other cities who come to Burlington in order to gain a blueprint for how to develop a sustainable community. For Yiota, the first step is to help visitors give up their search for a blueprint so that they can develop a more holistic and context-based approach, rooted in the social ecological landscape of their own communities.

> Where sustainability really counts is in culture, is in people. That's where it really counts. Where the police chiefs and the state's attorney and the activists and the priest and the refugees all sit in the room and talk about racial profiling. That's a huge transformation and evolution of consciousness for the culture to be able to do that. And that's what allows things to happen. It's like - you can't plan it. You have to organically create the environment that allows it to emerge. That's what makes it sustainable…you need to have an unshakeable faith in the people you're working with…it's a combination of the vision, the bigger political commitment - all of those things but there's a bigger possibility that emerges through being a learning community. Learning your way into the future, discovering your way into the future – not trying to just plan.

Learning into the Future

46 years old
approaching menopause
she is entering into a time of not
                                    knowing
losing the anchors in her body
that keep her in tune with
rhythms
cycles
moon
stars
tides
days
months
years
to lead now
is to surrender to not knowing
getting lost in the darkness
In the silence.
It is scary to breathe in here.
Is the world in menopause?
Ice melts out of season
hot oceans swollen like breasts
break onto the shores
flooding our homes
long sporadic menstrual periods that
                              will not subside.

What crone wisdom will invite
world leaders
To plunge into the dark
empty womb of not knowing
encounter the grief at the prospect of
                                    infertility
before the possible shedding of the
                                    last egg?
                        - Shoshana Simons

I ask Yiota about where she sees her leadership going over the coming years. She talks about noticing patterns of cycles that seem to last about five years. However, the next step seemed to be about getting lost and feeling comfortable with that. She related this to menopause

> because the whole orientation of your body has been toward giving birth and your body's suddenly saying "you can't do this anymore" – you're entering a different era and in a way your whole orientation has been about the future, even if you haven't had children. You hit this point when it isn't about that anymore in your body – but I think it's a spiritual journey, too, where you get more comfortable with being lost – not that you're ever comfortable with it but you've got to be in the unknown.

We wonder together as to how this poignant statement seems to relate so closely to the challenge of leading in these times, more generally. Theories abound in leadership and management texts about sustainable development, but when all is said and done, we are off the map. We don't know where we're headed.

Yiota Ahladas's story illustrates the inextricable relationship between the personal landscape of a given leader's history and experience and that of the community that she serves. She holds out the possibility of being comfortable with uncertainty whilst leading with a sense of hope, faith and trust in the power of inclusive, participatory governance.

Yiota's leadership on the local level models what President Obama is now modeling on the national and international level. Both leaders appear to have cultivated the humility to be able to tolerate the collective anxiety associated with not-knowing, are able to co-exist with uncertainty, to move out from there to connect with others in ever-widening circles and webs of inclusion as part of the complex process involved in taking right action.

References

Reid, S. (2005, November 15). Burlington Free Press.

Clandinnin, D. J., & Connelly, F. M. (2000). *Narrative inquiry: Experience and story in qualitative research.* San Francisco: Wiley.

Eakin, K. B. (1998) According to my passport, I am coming home. Retrieved February 1, 2009 from http://www.state.gov/documents/organization/2065.pdf

Eisler R. (1988) *The chalice and the blade.* New York:Harper One.

Freire (1970) *Pedagogy of the oppressed.* New York: Continuum.

Goerner, D. R., & Lagerroos, D. (2008). *The new science of sustainability: Building a foundation for great change.* Chapel Hill, NC: Triangle Center for Complex Systems.

Moore, L. (2007). *Getting a grip: Clarity, creativity, and courage in a world gone mad.* Cambridge, MA : Small Planet Media.

Footnotes

(1) For more information, see www.cedo.ci.burlington.vt.us/legacy/index.html

(2) Americorps VISTA is the national service program established in 1965 as Volunteers in Service to American in order to fight poverty. For more information see www.americorps.org/about/programs/vista.asp

Teaching Innovation and Entrepreneurship

The Singapore Experiment

Charles Hampden-Turner

In 2002 the Economic Development Board of Singapore sponsored a series of 4 month experimental programmes in "technopreneurship". The word is a hybrid of entrepreneurship and the kind of high tech development which Singapore has been promoting for decades. The EDB is one of the most creative departments of government in the world. It wanted to discover whether entrepreneurship could be deliberately taught in its universities to its own citizens and whether such programs would lead to new start-ups. The answer was "yes we can!" to echo Barak Obama. This chapter tells the story of the last six years of this programme which we also carefully evaluated. Our methods of capturing this innovation are also potentially important.

The Nanyang Technopreneurship Cen-

Charles Hampden-Turner was an associate of the Judge Business School, Cambridge University for 17 years and is currently a Visiting Professor to Nanyang Technopreneurship Centre at Nanyang Technological University in Singapore and an associate of the Insitute for Manufacturing at Cambridge. He has just published *Teaching Innovation and Entrepreneurship* with Cambridge University Press in August. He is completing an 80 minute documentary entitled "Innovation and the Fate of Nations" which he narrates. Its premiere is in June in Singapore. In 2003 he was Hutchinson Visiting Scholar to China and toured eleven universities there. Riding the Waves of Culture with his business partner Fons Trompenaars has passed 250,000 copies in English alone and has been translated into 19 languages. He co-founded Trompenaars-Hampden-Turner in Amsterdam in 1986.

tre was purpose-built as an interdisciplinary programme, apart from other graduate schools at Nanyang Technological University in Singapore. The course was designed and run by Professor Tan Teng-Kee, a Singaporean-American alumni of NTU, an ex-entrepreneur and corporate executive who obtained his PhD from Cambridge University in 2002, under the supervision of Charles Hampden-Turner. The design of TIP (Technopreneurship and Innovation Program) was crucially influenced by his thesis and by the ideas set out in this book. Dilemmas methodology is at the heart of this initiative. Recently a second programme in Mandarin for students from the People's Republic of China has been started. This remains to be properly evaluated although early indications are very positive.

The programme was not confined to the classroom. Innovation cannot be enclosed in a specific place. Rather "Prof. Tan" as he is called, designed an "innovative ecosystem", stretching from Singapore to China to the USA. The idea was to confront students with an environment, which had highly contrasting stimuli, great *hopes* great *disappointments*, great *riches* great *poverty*, a *past* heritage that had been invaluable and *future* prospects that must be brighter still, as the torch was passed from the entrepreneur founders of Nanyang to the

second generation and the third. (Words italicised indicate strong contrasts).

"You will go from zero to millions and back to zero" Prof. Tan tells his students. Why back to zero? Because they will all end up dead and can take nothing out of this world. Everything they *get* they must *give* and the only legacy they can leave behind is the bestowal of the wealth they have created to enrich the lives of others.

An eco-system is characterised by a great *variety* within a single *unity*, like the coral reef that plays host to a thousand species of tropical sea creatures. The program begins with three days in an Outward Bound exercise wherein *individuals* are taught to bond in *teams* as they discover *opportunities* in *crises*. It is also intended to join *minds* with *bodies* and *challenges* with *responses* to these.

The next stop is the Chinese Heritage Centre at the heart of campus, a museum of the struggle of early Chinese immigrants. Nanyang is an authentically Chinese university built not simply by wealthy entrepreneurs but by the pennies of rickshaw drivers who wanted their children to have a better chance than they. The key to *change* is *continuity* stresses Prof. Tan. You can only transform yourself if you know where you came from and where you want to go, a "red line" joins your *heritage* to your *legacy*.

Throughout the entire 16 weeks the teams of students engage in a *simulation* of *reality* and *play* at the *serious* task of running their own businesses. The exercise speeds up the process of *trial* and *error,* with *strategies* created and *results* fed back to improve those strategies, in a process of *error* and *correction.*

Students are also put "on stage" there to *imagine* and *dream* a scenario they want to *come true* and to *realize*. Theatre is a mark of higher civilization which allows us to imagine shocking *failures* so that we can avert these to *succeed.* To imagine disaster is to suffer only vicariously while experiencing life vividly, dramatically and memorably. Students exposed to twenty common reasons of business failure, experienced while rehearsing can avoid such mistakes in their futures.

Students of Chinese ethnicity are raised to be *modest* and *shy*. There is no problem in having such feelings within you, but those seeking to be entrepreneurs must be at least outwardly *bold* and *confident,* even while questioning themselves. After all if they need others to believe in them, they must believe in themselves.

Another strong contrast within the classroom is between being a *competitive arena* in which participants vie to think up better ideas and having a *family atmosphere* in which all have close memberships. "What are we?" cries Prof. Tan rhetorically. "A family!" respond the class. One result of everyone being so *different* in their aspirations is that they are the *same* in their need for attention, warmth and support. They need to be *supported* as persons, yet *critiqued* as innovators and trust that this feedback is authentically intended to help them succeed.

What this programme does is to transcend a zero-sum game in which good grades are inherently scarce and others' brilliance spells your own eclipse. Because success is multidimensional and every success is unique, students are no longer win plaudits at each others expense. There are still failures, a great many, but these are steps in the process

of improvement. Better by far to be told that your product is not good enough by a member of your "family" than by a distant angry customer demanding a refund.

Not only is Nanyang Technopreneurship Centre full of new products, trophies and pictures of successful product launches but visitors come there most days. These are entrepreneurs willing to share their secrets, venture capitalists willing to explain their judgements, government representatives with details of incentive programs and soft loans to the enterprising, "Angel" investors looking less for personal gain than a noble cause, experts on the acquisition of small companies by larger ones (a common strategy for start-ups is to get acquired and begin again).

There are visitors from other universities, loan officers specialising in smaller businesses, corporations seeking to renew themselves and hosts of the curious. Students come to realise this is *their* programme, a new venture in itself and one for which they share responsibility with their mentors. They interview the next intake, choose the speakers they want to hear from and help improve the programme design for next year.

But if the world comes to NTC, NTC also goes out to meet the world. The entire class travels to Shanghai, to the eco-suburb nearby, to incubators near Fudan and other universities there and around Beijing. It travels to Seattle on America's West Coast to visit Google, Starbucks and others. Students discover and champion inventions created by the Bioengineering School at the University of Washington, where the *disciplines* biology, medicine and engineering meet *cross* each other. Students write up business plans for the *commercialisation* of these *inventions* and pitch them before real venture capitalists, who are not simply *sharing their knowledge* with students but also *practicing* their profession. Some inventions were funded.

The tour moves on to the Bay Area

around San Francisco, down the peninsula to Silicon Valley and to Stanford University's innovation courses, while visiting IDEO, the world's best known consultancy on innovation started by Tom Kelley. The $2 billion Kauffman Foundation, America's fourth largest foundation, which commits all its funds to innovation is also part of this extended Learning Journey. Carl Schramm CEO of Kaufmann has designated this programme the best in the world outside the USA and among the best even there.

This extensive tour contrasts *developed* with *developing* economies, those calling themselves *capitalist* with those proud of *socialism*, relative *affluence* with relative *poverty*, innovation driven by *self-fulfilment* with innovation driven by *necessity*, a system of *laissez-faire* with a system of *government oversight*, a culture of *individualism* and a culture of *communitarianism*. The contrasts could hardly be stronger.

After their return home the students are exposed to the contrast between supply innovation and demand innovation. Supply is something novel and valuable to customers, typically a technological development, but demand innovation is more subtle and well suited to tough times. You search out the "pain-points" in the customer's system and try to relieve these. A hospital's surgery unit that used instruments was forever running back to the sterilizer when one instrument was dropped or mishandled. The company supplied twenty foot rolls of sterilized towelling with the instruments inserted in pockets in the order in which they were used by that particular surgeon. The hospital's problems were solved.

Developing a Methodology

Given our belief that innovation consists of being presented with highly contrasting values at powerful levels of intensity and learning to reconcile these, how could the success or otherwise of the program be measured? We took a single dilemma transforming ideals into realities and created a questionnaire around this theme.

Despite the risk of doing so we decid-

Innovation cannot be enclosed in a specific place.

ed to contrast the pedagogy of the TIP program with the 3 year bachelor degree program the same students had received earlier. This was risky because students are typically nostalgic about their undergraduate days and grateful for the degrees conferred upon them, which is the gateway to a career. In contrast, the TIP diploma had scant recognition. Any university fundraiser will tell you that alumni funds are more forthcoming for undergraduate than for graduate studies. Comparing TIP to the university at large and with courses and head teachers the students had selected for themselves was going to be tough. Below are the kinds of instruction we gave to our respondents.

Question X

Please indicate your judgement of the values attained by NTU (U) and NTC (N) as measured against the following statements.

a) My education has been realistic. It readies me for the world as it is, not necessarily as it might be. It is practical and effective.

Not at all (value 1) to Very much so (value 10)

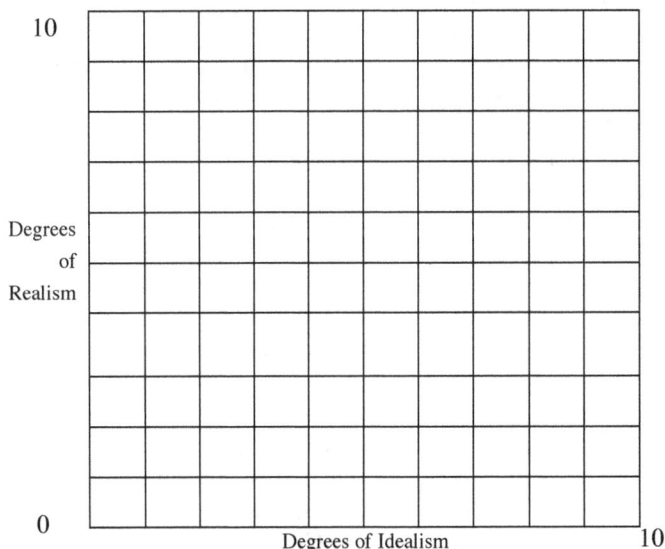

Degrees
of
Realism

Degrees of Idealism

b) My education has been idealistic. It shows me how realities can be changed, so as to create new values. It is inspirational.

Not true at all (value 1) to Very much so (value 10)

Suppose for the sake of argument that you have judged NTU (U) to be slightly more realistic than NTC (N), so you give

NTU a score of 6 and NTC a score of 5. Suppose that you have judged NTC (N) to be slightly more idealistic than NTU (U), so you give (N) a score of 6 and (U) a score of 5. Please place "N" and "U" on the scales above. With these scores in mind please consider transferring them to the Grid below. This gives you an opportunity to record whether "realism" and "idealism" have been integrated or whether these have been polarised. For example a score of 8/1, 2/9 or 5/5 would indicate polarisation while 9/9 or thereabouts would indicate integrity. Were you to copy your scores of 5 and 6 straight on to the Grid they would appear as below.

As you move your cursor across the grids various pop ups appear as balloons. These are there to prompt your choices, so that at top left we have non-idealistic realism and at bottom right we have idealistic unreality. Do NOT worry if you change your mind. After all we have changed the question. We will count your scores on the grids only. Please make sure there is only ONE (U) score and one (N) score for each grid. Please place your score inside a square. We now proceed with the questionnaire.

We posed ten sets of dilemmas, but there is space here to report only five. This is not a serious omission because the answers to all ten different questions were remarkably similar. What seems to matter are not the particular values referred to in the questionnaire but whether the respondent experiences the pedagogy received as polarising or integrating. There is persisting pattern crossing *all* dilemmas posed. As we shall see NTU's undergraduate pedagogy was largely polarising in its effect on respondents, while TIP's graduate course was largely integrating in its effect. The differences were very large indeed and highly consistent across all questions. Two very

different styles of education are being assessed here. The first is quite sterile. The second is highly innovative. No less an authority than the new President of the United States is an advocate of this integrative view. The five pairs of values are summarised below.

The Results

We now turn to the evaluation of TIP as compared to NTU undergraduate courses. We found 153 qualified respondents. Many others had attended other universities. These were omitted. Many qualified respondents were out of the country and preoccupied with business. We received 68 usable replies. All questions were on the theme of Realism vs. Idealism. We regarded the first as a traditional value, which NTU was pledged to uphold. We regarded the second "progressive" value as one essential to innovation and acclaimed by TIP and many creativity experts.

We first used the Likert Scales to measure from 1-10 how *intellectual* the pedagogy was in the mastery and organization of key ideas. We next used the same scale to measure how *experiential* the pedagogy was, in working with feelings and emotions. Respondents were then presented with the grid below and asked to locate themselves upon it.

We were looking for those who could experience emotionally what they were thinking about at the top-right of the Grid. We were also looking for those who failed in this attempt, at top-left and bottom-right or compromised in the middle. To this end pop-up balloons prompted their choices and nudged them to consider whether these values had been integrated. The results are below.

Dilemma 1

Intellectuality vs. Experience

The responses are set out below and we see that "Prof. Tan" and his TIP education has not only exceeded other university courses, but has done so by landslide proportions. This is not on one axis only, as we might have supposed, but on BOTH. If you use your intellect to be innovative you not only have your heart in your mouth, you strive to be more rigorously intelligent still, since your whole future now depends upon it. Although vivid emotional experiences can detract

Grid 1   Intellect vs. Experience

The atmosphere is remote, abstract and "ivory tower". Feelings play no part.

Because we are experiencing what we think about our ideas come alive

10

NTU: 11
16.18%
TIP: 0
0%

NTU: 3
4.41%
TIP: 30
44.12%

How intellectual is your education?

NTU   TIP

NTU: 0
0%
TIP: 3
4.41%

0

How experiential is your education?

10

The culture is "feel good", "touchy-feely". Not exactly rigorous!

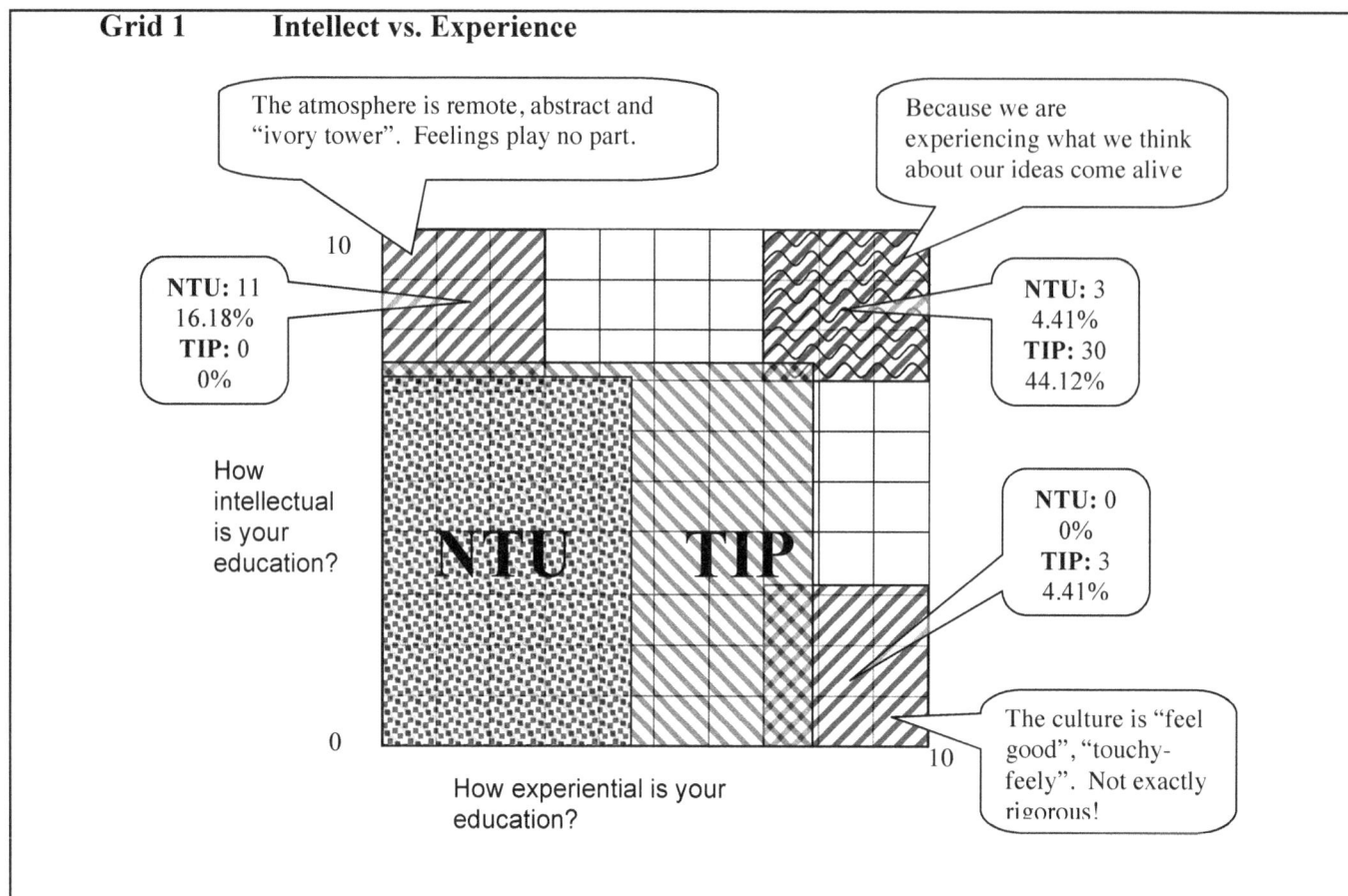

from intellectual rigour and although intellectual activity at universities often occurs in a moratorium from stressful experiences, intellect and experience can develop together. This is strongly suggested by TIP's scores recorded below.

The different locations on grids 1-5 need to be explained. There are two "pathology zones", the nine squares at top left and the nine at bottom right. There is one Reconciliation Zone, the wavy pattern across the nine squares at top right. The average scores for the NTU pedagogy are clearly marked as are average scores for the TIP pedagogy taught at NTC. In virtually all cases the number of squares occupied by TIP is substantially larger than those occupied by NTU. We see that the intellectual attainment in the "Technoprenuership" course was judged to have exceeded the NTU average. The TIP course scored 7.20 out of 10, compared to the university average of 7.06. Yet as expected, TIP won hands down upon the intensity of emotional experience, scoring 7.97 to the university's 4.78. The simplest comparison is to count the number of squares covered in the Grid above by NTU and by TIP. When we do this NTU covers 33.26 squares and TIP 57.38, the latter is 74.2% higher ($R2 = 34.23\%$, $P<0.01$).

We laid two deliberate traps for TIP and the University respectively. These are represented by the "pathology zones" top left and bottom right. We prompted respondents to say that the TIP program was "feel good" and "touchy feely", see bottom right of the diagram above. We wanted to smoke out any anti-intellectualism. But only 4.41% agreed with this verdict. We also prompted respondents to say that NTU courses were "Abstract, ivory tower and remote." Fully 16.18% agreed that this was so.(see Appendix II). It is important to stress that NTU as a university DOES succeed on its own terms. 42.65% of its students rated their education as 8, 9, or 10 on intellectuality, see Appendix III. What it does not do so well is to bring intellectual order to its own personal experiences. Only 4.41% of respondents succeeded in scoring their undergraduate learning in the Reconciliation Zone, see wavy square at top right, while 44.12% of TIP graduates reached this zone, their "ideas coming alive". Hence on Question 1, TIP's capacity to combine intellectuality with emotion the programme scores ten times higher.

Dilemma 2

Learning by absorbing top-down information
vs.
Learning by thinking and acting for yourself

Our second dilemma, one that affects all pedagogy, is to consider how learning is communicated. Is it transmitted top-down by educators "filling up" students with information and knowledge? This was the view of John Locke that educators "wrote" upon the *tabula rasa* of the mind. Or are there innate structures of the mind (Platonic forms) that educators elicit so that in a sense we already know? Clearly both visions have some validity. Those who wish to think and act for themselves need information *with* which to think and they might be wise to listen first, or they may jump to a wrong conclusion. Those who only absorb conventional wisdoms filtering down upon them may take on the characteristics of a sponge. Since this accusation had been made against traditional Chinese education, we wished to see if it had lingered.

Grid 2. Absorbing information vs. Thinking and doing.

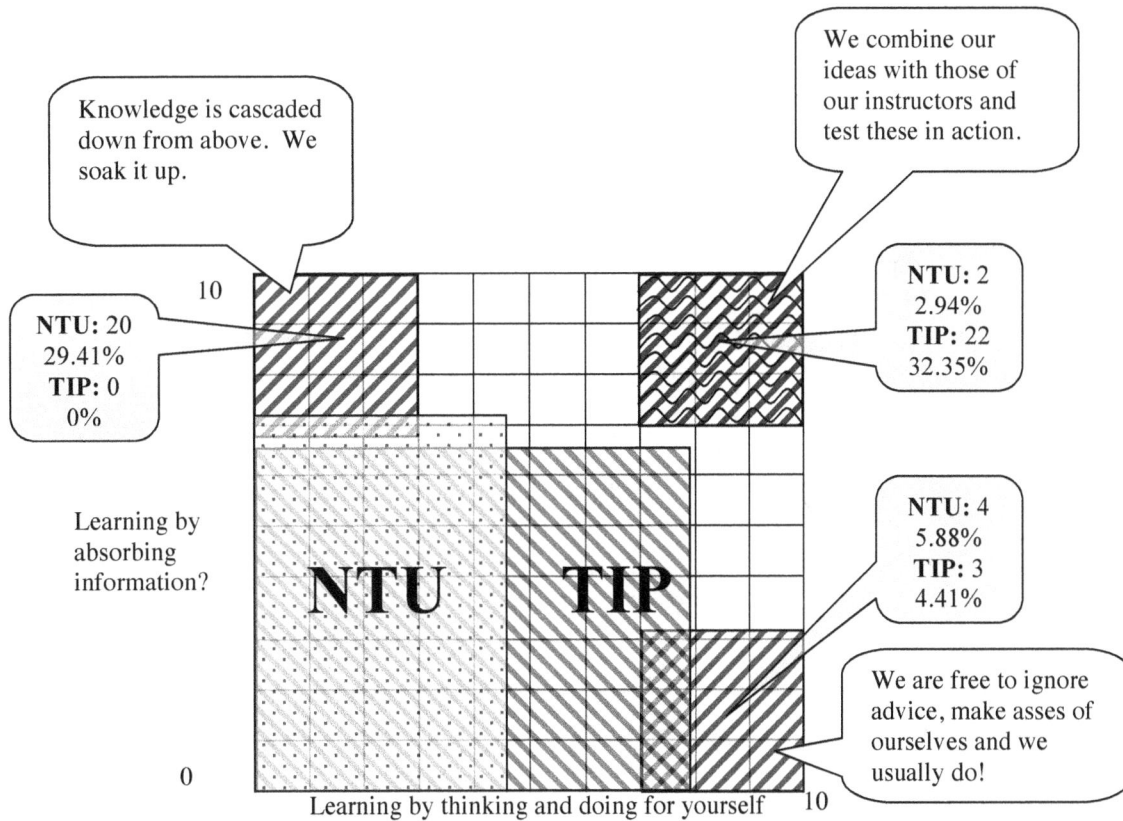

Genuine innovation requires us not just to listen and absorb, but to select, convince ourselves and act. We obtained the following results.

Once again the pathologies are cross-hatched at bottom-left and top-right , while the wave-forms characteristic of the Reconciliation Zone are top right. Comparing the number of squares covered gives NTU a score of 33.66 and TIP a score of 53.52 squares covered. This is a 60% advantage ($R2 = 25.36\%$, $P<0.01$). As we had anticipated NTU scored higher on the top down transmission of knowledge, but the difference was surprisingly small, considering how much less time TIP spends lecturing, compared to the university at large. NTU scored 7.24 and TIP 6.74. Anyone wishing to think and act using information would need first to absorb the information. It seems TIP students did this. When it came to "thinking and acting for oneself ", the University scored only

4.66 and was swamped by TIP scoring 7.94, almost three squares higher. Again we tested the authenticity of "thinking and acting" for oneself. Was it just pretending? We prompted the answer above "We are free to ignore advice, make asses of ourselves and we usually do!" Yet only 5.88% taxed TIP with this fault. We prompted respondents to complain of NTU "Knowledge is cascaded down from above we soak it up". 29.41% believed this to be the case so the concerns about passive memorisation are upheld.

Yet the university succeeds in its aims with 58.82% testifying that information from above is absorbed in the degrees of 8, 9 and 10 (Appendix III), yet only 2.94% felt that they could use that information to think for themselves! In contrast 32.35% of TIP scored in the Reconciliation Zone by absorbing information *and* using it to think.

Dilemma 3

**Level playing field for competitive for competitive efforts
Are we good enough?**
vs.
Extended family of brothers and sisters who root for you

Whether business enterprise is "basically" competitive or cooperative is one of the oldest arguments. But no one witnessing the rise of Asian countries with Confucian family-based ethics can doubt that familial relationships play an important part. The case is even stronger for creativity and innovation. Great writers, artists, scientists for the most part, knew and respected each other and were members of a salon or group.

Creative eras tend to come in bursts of one or two generations. There occurs an inter-stimulation of like minds, a mixing of intimate strangers. There are signs of this today in such places as Amsterdam, Seattle, the Bay Area, Helsinki, Dublin, Taipei and Shanghai.

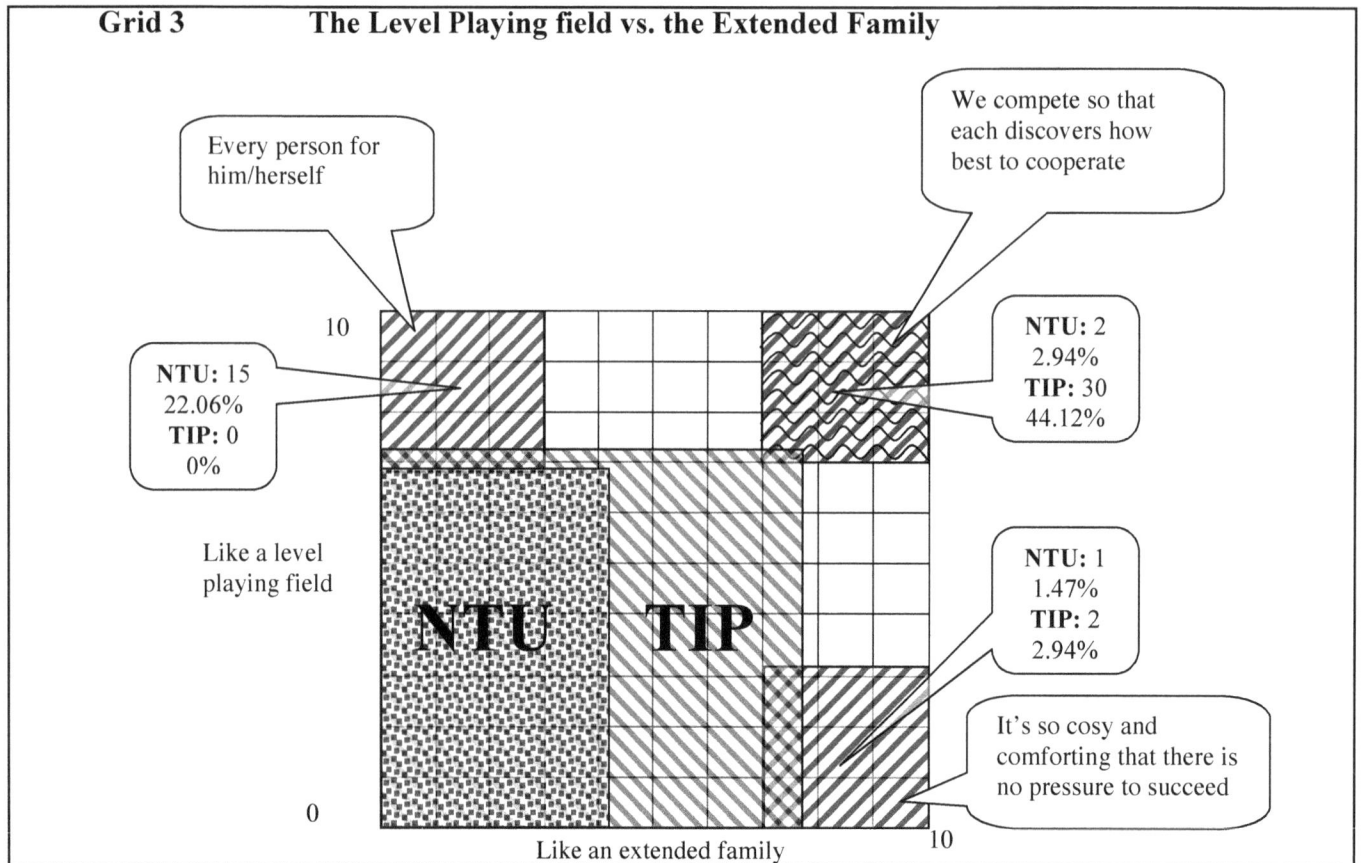

Every person for him/herself

We compete so that each discovers how best to cooperate

10

NTU: 15
22.06%
TIP: 0
0%

NTU: 2
2.94%
TIP: 30
44.12%

Like a level playing field

NTU   **TIP**

NTU: 1
1.47%
TIP: 2
2.94%

It's so cosy and comforting that there is no pressure to succeed

0

Like an extended family   10

Singapore follows the American "level playing field" axiom, so faithfully that it may be a purer meritocracy than its mentor. Yet innovation is crucially different because what constitutes "merit" has not been defined before hand. You need an extended family of colleagues to champion and to give significance to what you are trying to do, which authorities may not recognize. It may be recalled that we wanted to test the proposition that where those in the class wanted something *different* from each other, that head-on rivalry would be less and most would wish each other well. We believed a "family" of innovators might well rejoice at each others fortune. Players needed coaches. Might programme members willingly coach each other, mixing cold criticism of the work with warm support for the person?

It was, at any rate, our hypothesis that TIP might be more competitive *and* more cooperative and familial than NTU. We believed this to be true of creative communities historically, a crucial blend of personal striving with interpersonal supportiveness, a co-mingling of contrasting minds..

NTU covered in all 26.80 squares. TIP covered 56.37, or 103% higher (R2

=36.23%, P<0.01). TIP's average score on Competitiveness was 7.19, compared to 6.85 for NTU, so that NTC was even more competitive than the mean for the university-at large, but on the classroom environment resembling an extended family, the University scored but 4.22 compared with TIP's 7.84, a huge margin of 3.62. Once again the University "succeeds" in being competitive, 42.65% score the environment 8, 9 or 10 as a "level playing field" for competition, yet 44.12 % of TIP report "co-opetition", with competition and cooperation in a family-style culture reconciled at top-right. Once again we probed for dysfunctional extremes of too much familial atmosphere and too much "cut-throat" competition. (see crosshatched squares) We tempted respondents to admit that the family atmosphere at TIP was "cosy, comforting and free of pressure" but only 2.94% agreed. We tempted respondents to say that NTU's competitiveness placed "Every person for him/herself" and 22.06% agreed - a rather worrying proportion. NTU appears to have imported a large dollop of Western-style alienation into its pedagogy. Undergraduates feel apart,

absorbing information with their emotions not engaged.

Dilemma 4

Serious hard work
vs.
Playful enjoyment

Those who want to succeed in the world of free enterprise and opportunities-for-all had best take such challenges seriously. Few will make it without determination and perseverance. Hard work is the inescapable recipe. Yet countless studies of innovative persons note their playfulness. They have created something that gives them untold pleasure and they want to share it. They find joy in their work and are guided by secret delights. Moreover, much use is made of simulations, skits, role plays, prototypes and models, because these can fail inexpensively. Innovators practice with "toys" as the actual product takes shape.

Michael Schrage has suggested that innovation consists of Serious Play, i.e. a playful process leading to a serious outcome, light hearted experimentation in search of a crucial solution. We hypothesised that the University would tend towards Seriousness, even to the

Grid 4   Seriousness vs. Playfulness

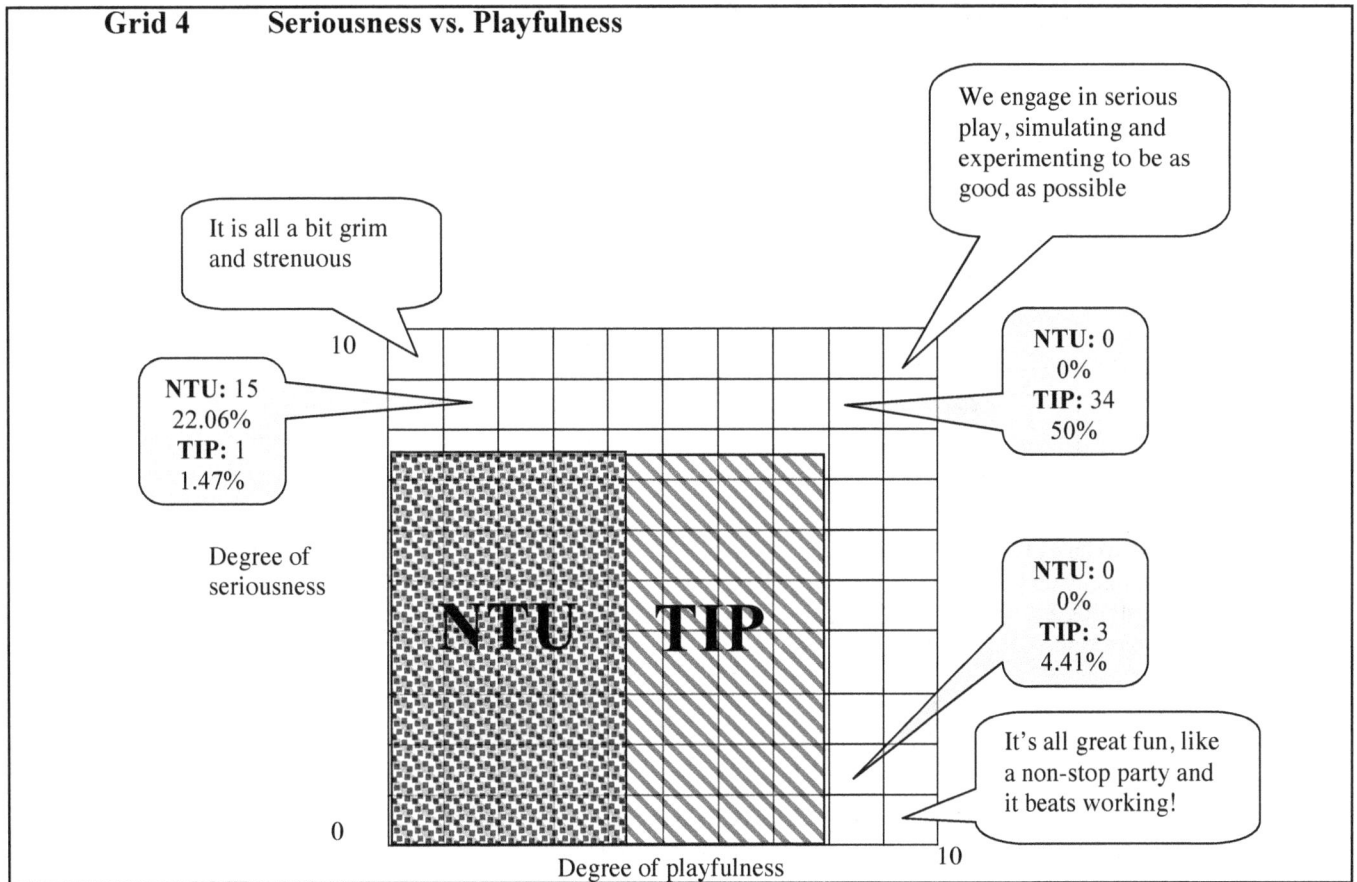

We engage in serious play, simulating and experimenting to be as good as possible

It is all a bit grim and strenuous

10

NTU: 0
0%
TIP: 34
50%

NTU: 15
22.06%
TIP: 1
1.47%

Degree of seriousness

NTU: 0
0%
TIP: 3
4.41%

NTU   TIP

It's all great fun, like a non-stop party and it beats working!

0

Degree of playfulness   10

---

point of strenuousness. We knew TIP was much more playful but were its participants aware of the serious purpose? The course has a business simulation running its full length. It has practice presentations to Venture Capitalists and many skits and plays, but were these games more than fun? Could seriousness and playfulness combine in a joyful rendezvous with reality? Could playful prototypes culminate in serious products and services? Could we take the problems seriously but not ourselves? Play inevitably involves error, but because models, simulations and prototypes are cheap, such errors are not "serious" as much as instructive. Piet Hein calls it *The Road to Wisdom*.

The road to wisdom – well it's plain
And simple to express
Err and err and err again
But less and less and less…(Quoted by Schrage, 2000)

What we are talking about is the "error correcting system".

The University scored 7.54 on Seriousness, but interestingly TIP is extremely close behind with 7.50, a non-

significant margin. TIP is quite as serious as NTU. But when it comes to Playfulness the difference is dramatic. The University scored 4.24 on Playfulness and TIP scored 7.97, over three squares above. NTU covered 31.54 squares and TIP 59.78, or 91% higher ($R2 = 34.53\%$, $P<0.01$).

We tested to see whether TIP's playfulness was "like a non-stop party", a trap it is easy to fall into, but only 4.41% agreed. We asked if the experience of university courses was not "a bit grim and strenuous" and 22.06% agreed. Once again TIP has demonstrated that playful processes can prepare for serious purposes as the hours slip by because you are enjoying yourself. 50.00% of respondents said that TIP reconciled work and play, but none (0%) claimed that the University managed this.

But note that once again the university succeeds on its own terms. 52.94% of its students score the teaching environment 8, 9, or 10 in Seriousness, even if fun is scarce. However this is lower than TIP's score on Playfulness.

Dilemma 5

Career continuity and mastering chosen paths
vs.
Transformation of yourself and reinvention

Universities still prepare people for careers, although how long certain careers can now last grows ever more problematical. Whole technologies may come to the end of their useful lives. Never-the-less continuity remains crucial, as does choosing your career path. Even innovations tend to advance certain disciplines and callings, with one innovation forming "the platform" on which the next is based and so on. The core competence of a company makes no sense without thematic continuities. The greater the whirlwind the more you must rely on sense of direction so as to ride upon it.

Increasingly those who learn will ride a new technology for perhaps five-to-ten years and then transform and re-invent themselves jumping from one form of competence to a contiguous one in variations on underlying themes. The TIP

Grid 5   Career Continuity vs. Periodic Transformation

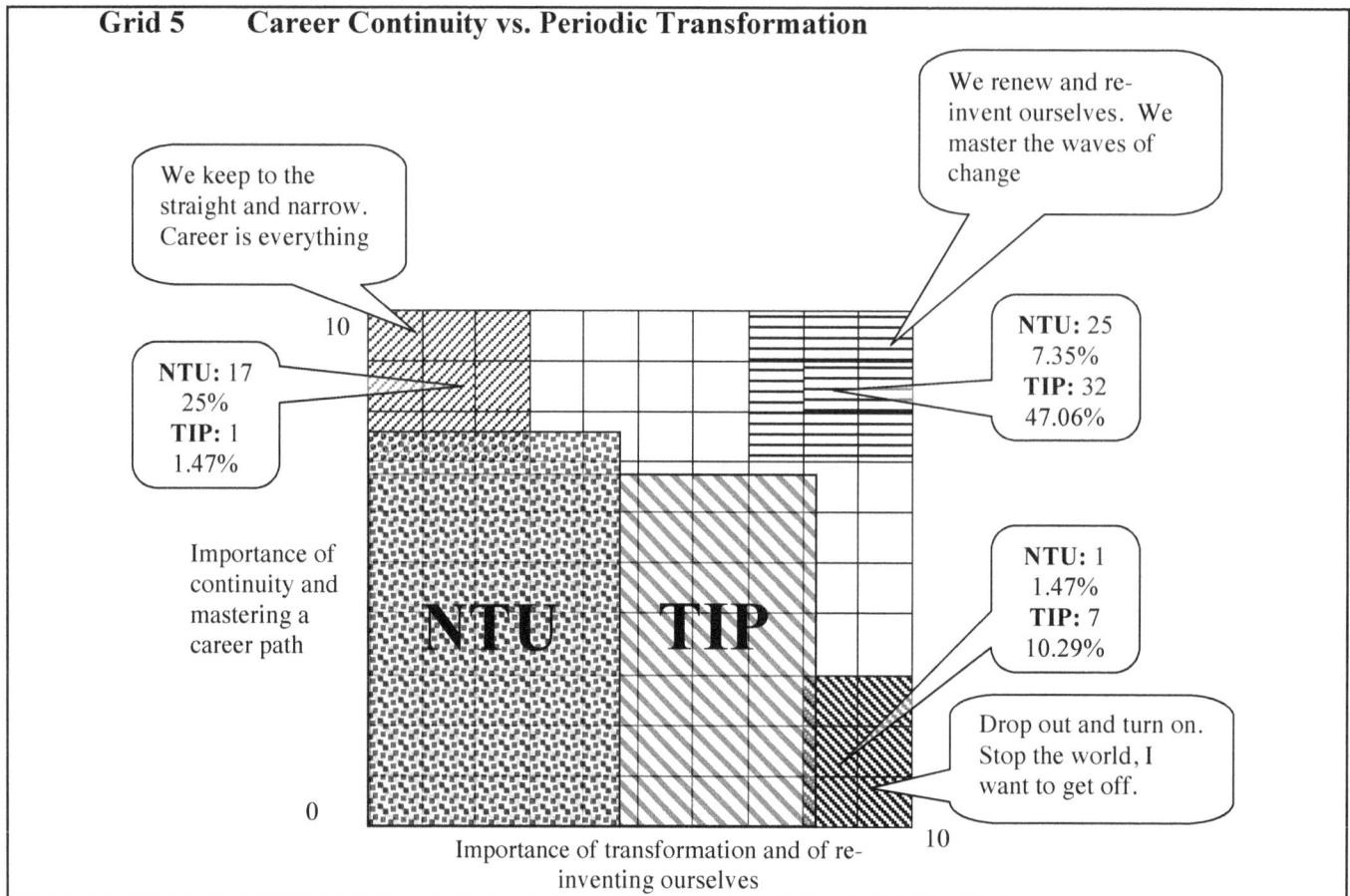

We keep to the straight and narrow. Career is everything

We renew and re-invent ourselves. We master the waves of change

NTU: 17
25%
TIP: 1
1.47%

NTU: 25
7.35%
TIP: 32
47.06%

10

Importance of continuity and mastering a career path

NTU   **TIP**

NTU: 1
1.47%
TIP: 7
10.29%

Drop out and turn on. Stop the world, I want to get off.

0

Importance of transformation and of re-inventing ourselves

10

course was designed to help students transform themselves, hopefully without losing an underlying sense of continuity. Is it possible to combine the two, changing radically while still retaining a stable identity? We believe it is. Transformation that sacrifices continuity takes you back to square one. In any true development there must be a path, however winding, that brings you to your destination.

We set out to discover how NTU and TIP balanced career continuity with self-transformation of the kind that outstanding entrepreneurs and innovators achieve. We expected NTU to stress continuity and TIP to stress transformation, but we hoped to discover whether TIP retained at least some sense of continuity, without which a sense of growth and the development of core capabilities over time may be lost. Knowledge is to an important extent cumulative. One verified proposition links to another. We generalise as far as we can and then examine the exceptions. Disrupt continuity and you break up knowledge into incoherent fragments. TIP must serve continuity AND transformation.

What "technopreneurship" means is that you simultaneously follow relevant

technologies in their most advanced states, yet take a stand between these, entre-preneur "to stand between". As we shall see, TIP succeeded in this. You take the most advanced work from at least two disciplines and create a novel synthesis between these. Here are their scores.

NTU covered 34.80 squares. TIP covered 49.45 or 67% higher (R2 =24.77%, P<0.01). NTU outscores TIP on career continuity by 7.76 to 6.81 or 0.95. Note how small this difference is and how emphatic is the TIP course on maintaining a sense of continuity. Since innovations often combine two disciplines, the entrepreneur needs to be aware of career trajectories that are converging or running parallel in a way that makes connections possible. The combination of two lines is often transformative, while still retaining the initial continuities.

When we asked how transformative NTU's courses were, the university scored 4.69 but TIP scores 8.35, nearly four squares better. 47.06% of respondents reported that TIP combined Continuity with Transformation the Reconciliation Zone, but only 7.35% made that claim for NTU. We checked that TIP was

not cheating in selling Transformation as "dropping out and turning on Hippie fashion" yet 10.29% agreed and there may be a little danger here. We asked whether students 'kept to the straight and narrow" at NTU and 25% agreed, see Appendix II. Yet this "straightness" meant that 63.24% of our respondents rated the university at 8, 9 and 10.

Final Proof of Success

We have looked at the scores for the five questions and found that TIP scores considerably better on all lateral dimensions, while not being below NTU on the traditional, vertical dimensions by any significant margin, so that TIP may be said to uphold the university standards. However, the most remarkable finding is that nearly 42% of all TIP students scored in the Reconciliation Zone, eight times more than achieved in undergraduate classes at NTU. This unique capacity to integrate contrasting educational processes would seem to be its greatest virtue.   Yet there remains one nagging question. The purpose of this programme was NOT primarily to be well assessed by those who participated in it, encouraging although this is.

The programme is not an end in itself but a means to making its members more innovative and entrepreneurial. Is there any evidence that they became so? There is.

By January 2008 out of 154 students 46 had started business ventures, employing about 75 of their numbers. This had happened despite the fact that:

a) Many had not joined the programme to become entrepreneurs.

b) Twenty or more had gone on to get their MSc degree of which this programme was a module.

c) Most are in debt when they graduate.

d) The course advises them to get experience in their selected area of innovation before launching their own ventures.

e) They have an average of only 2-3 years to launch such a venture..

We contend that 46 surviving start-ups is a very remarkable result. If only 10% of these eventually prosper they will have repaid the cost of the course several times over.

Can we Model the Innovative Process?

By what process do TIP students and innovators in general reach the Reconciliation Zone at top right of our Grids? In order to understand this we need a three-dimensional model, with the third dimension representing time. One way dilemmas are resolved is by emphasising first one dimension then another in sequence, and by achieving the second dimension *through* the first.

For example, when innovating we first feel excited, doubtful and emotional until such a time as we can intellectually order these fresh insights, see Dilemma 1(a). This results in an anti-clockwise helix. On the other hand most students must first absorb top-down information and only when they have enough of these resources can they think and act for themselves, see Dilemma 2(a). This results in a clockwise helix.

It is at least probable that students feel initially that they are competing with all other members, but as the extended family develops around them and team skills develop they start cooperating, see

Dilemma 3(a). This results in a clockwise helix. There is little doubt however that playfulness, experimentation and simulation precedes the serious business of creating finished quality and risking everything in the market, see Dilemma 4(a). In this event, the helix is anticlockwise once more. Finally, the mastery of your chosen discipline and career path precedes the intersecting and crosscutting with other disciplines to make new connections, see Dilemma 5(a). In this event the helix is clockwise. Note that we have retained our grid pattern

on the face of each cube and that helices flirt with pathology by skirting these zones. There is no innovation without danger. It is easy to go too far in either direction as our results show.

Is this nothing but the "Hawthorne Effect"?

Before concluding, let us address a likely critique of this article. "Here we have", critics will say, "nothing more than the Hawthorne Effect." This occurs when respondents grow to like their teacher and "give him what he wants", perhaps because his own enthusiasm is infectious and because they feel they owe him in return for a fun time, or both. What these critics fail to realise is the "Hawthorne Effect" is a *vital part of life itself.* We create nothing without hope and yearning, nothing without passion and optimism. So *what* if the prophecy is self-fulfilling? You believe in yourself, in part because your teacher does and that belief is vindicated. That is what being innovative is all about and if it breaks taboos on clinical detachment then the fault is with those taboos.

But in any event this was not research that measured a heady optimism at the end of the program. Students had, on average, been out in the cold, hard world of business reality for two and a half years when this research was conducted. It is more than likely that they had tried

and failed at least once since graduating. What is more likely than they would blame this program for any disappointment? That they do not seem to have done so in any numbers testifies to the lasting legacy of this educational experience.

Are we to have a science of only dead things that cannot respond to the investigator? *You discover innovation by engendering it.* There is no other way. Remain cold and unmoved and the world around you mimics your own demeanour. We hope to have demonstrated that innovation can be elicited, that it builds on what the university already teaches, while qualifying and augmenting this, that innovation requires dilemma-resolving, lateral type thinking. The capacity to create wealth resembles the ancient Alchemists' dream of creating gold from base metals. The world's current predicament is pretty "base" as we fight the credit crunch and the death of the Anglo-Saxon economic model.

An answer to world crises?

It is clear that innovation CAN be taught, that this builds upon the university's traditional mission to society by placing this in an innovative context. This is very exciting for students, transformative in its impact upon them, as witnessed by many moving accounts. It is hard to think of a more vital topic in world affairs than generating a capability to innovate spontaneously. This capacity can reconcile and generate abundance out of scarce resources, create satisfactions out of wants, agreements out of discord and realities out of ideals and imaginings.

The very process is joyful and playful, while the consequences are valuable and serious. It is hard to see how societies dedicated to innovation would have the time or the inclination to kill, how a mind that could be generative and thus get its "highs" could ever want to be befuddled with abusive substances. Teach our children and young people to be innovative and scarcities are transcended, ideas are joined and so are the people who believe in these. Innova-

> # Genuine innovation requires us not just to listen and absorb, but to select, convince ourselves and act.

tion needs not just diversities of ideas but diversities of people supplying those ideas. From their inclusion comes not only wealth but our best hope of tolerance and global dialogue. A world where imagination fathers new forms can solve its own problems.

Those who "give" each other knowledge still retain it within themselves. Romeo's words to Juliet become more nearly true, "The more I give you the more I have." There is a secret world of abundance within us that is widely shareable by those willing to gain-share and fate-share. To create makes of our lives a lasting legacy. The obscenely large salaries of bankers who proved to be incompetent can become things of the past. People who innovate do not need to be bribed to do so by extrinsic rewards. It is simply a better way to live.

To have shareholders' money to play with is a privilege.

References

Hampden-Turner, C. M. (2009). *Teaching innovation and entrepreneurship*. Cambridge: Cambridge University Press.
Schrage, M. (2000). *Serious play*. Boston: Harvard Business School Publishing.
Trompenaars, F., & Hampden-Turner, C. M. (2009). *Innovating in a global crisis*. Oxford: Infinite Ideas Press.

shadowtouch

featherglide chills
        the nape of my neck
    with a *shadowtouch* of wild

he is one of mine
    brags the wind

I fall into a fit of full hearted laughter
 as the swift soaring hawk outstrips all vision

    some *things* must be felt
    before they can be heard or seen
    and even then
    and even then
  reason refuses to believe
in anything not bracketed
        between its iron clamps
so no wonder *wonder* crumbles into doubt
        and yet
        and yet

        deepdown
an appetite awakes
        that seeks no proofs
    but blindly hungers
        for *another taste*
        another touch

                John Thompson

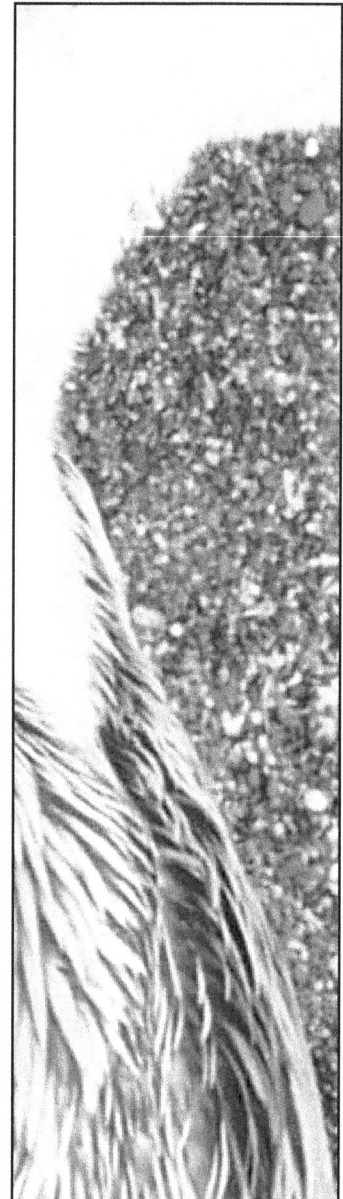

Leadership and Lace

Rita Durant

The following essay employs a roundabout weaving of themes, including leadership, feminism, discourse, and stories, in order to create a pattern of open spaces. I lace my observations of being a female scholar with verbal attacks on the system that prefers closed and linear logic, in large part in order to add zest to my story and observations. At heart, I hope to intertwine opposite edges of logic/emotions, male/female, theory/practice, truth/fiction, abstractions/bodies, and so forth. I gratefully acknowledge Marja Flory's (2008) courageous dissertation as a quilting, inspired by Ann Rippin's (2007) willingness to open herself to learning from threads.

Lengthy Introduction

I am female. I am thinking about my conundrum about writing a transformational leadership piece. I still imagine a man when I hear or use the term. That is something I'd like to transform. This masculine imagery is not accidental. As a child in the 1950s, I spent a great deal of my waking hours at St.

Rita Anne Genevieve O'Laughlin Durant learned from her parents to love books, children, lakes, and ideas. Through studies and teaching in Language and Management, and by practicing speaking safely in her group, she is learning to give voice to her points of view. She acknowledges the gifts of music, and dance thereto, in her life.

Peter's, school and church. My teachers were women, nuns and lay in alternating years, starting with Miss H. in Kindergarten, who labored to make and keep us holy to do the will of God, "the Big Guy upstairs." Our lessons included explanations of how Eve caused Original Sin, how women need to cover their vanity (hair) in church, how our failure to obey spoken and unspoken rules could land us in purgatory or hell, and how silence was the key to being good. My fifth grade teacher, therefore a nun, was pretty cool about drawing diagrams of sentences on the board and having us fill in the Subject, Verb, Direct Object, Adverbs, and Prepositional Phrases. Since I wasn't learning to talk at school, it was nice to at least see our language illustrated. At home, I was also pretty quiet, too. I loved to read and so I used that interest to keep from bothering my parents, who were busy raising us five kids and supporting my dad's career as a lawyer.

When I was in graduate school, I was taught scientific thinking with illustrated models that represented social systems. These epistemic models identified constituent parts, explained the behavior of the parts through cause and effect relationships, and thus identified the predictable ways that outcomes could be determined (Ackoff, 1974). Representations of the models tended to include arrows, which meant that change of the "depen-

dent" variable occurred through the force and power of the "independent" variable. Therefore, under these scientific assumptions, leadership was the disembodied (abstracted) identification of embodied (originally in a Great Man) presence of forces for change. Its prime exemplar was God (Ackoff, 1994, p. 5).

In the relationships-as-cause-and-effect-force models, definitions of leadership situated the leader as the independent force that causes changes in others: "to influence and inspire others to act beyond what their jobs or roles require" (Rhode, 2003, 159-160). Leaders are those who have power to cause others to do what they wouldn't ordinarily do (Dahl, 1957). This power could come in a variety of forms, including Expert, Coercive, Reward, Legitimate (bureaucratic), and Referent (French & Raven, 1959). I have appropriated the last of these to refer to interactive relationships, but mostly books refer to referent power as akin to charisma, getting someone to do something they wouldn't ordinarily do because you have charisma or other likeable traits.

Our job as academics, I was instructed, was to conduct scientific investigations in order to test others' theories and identify any problematic "gaps" in the cause and effect reasoning. "But," I protested, "I have theories, too." "Everyone has theories." "Why do we need to learn and test others' theories?' (I came to wonder about the phallologocentric imagery of the problem with "gaps" and their need to be filled. And arrows of course. But that was later. Back to class:) "Good point," the professor replied, and didn't answer the question.

In that class, our reading about Greenberg's (1990) finding that employees stole less from the plant whose leaders "adequately explained" why the company had to impose a temporary pay cut for all personnel gave me pause. The leader in the lower-theft plant had spent an hour listening and responding to employee concerns. The leader listening seemed to me to be important, but it wasn't mentioned. So I wrote my paper for that class on the cognitive, emotional, and symbolic meaning of leader listening. Later, when I mentioned to a visiting Economics professor what I was interested in, especially since the guy was an expert in Ethics, he told me to leave the topic alone. No one was writing about leader listening, he informed me, so I better get on board with making a real contribution to the literature. Ouch!

In an effort to counter-balance the linear and quantitative models in the business school, I enrolled in a series of Qualitative Research classes that introduced me to postmodern and post-structuralist concepts. At the same time I was in a fabulous leadership seminar led by my dissertation advisor. This was the same professor who was enthusiastic when, my first day in the first class I took in graduate school, I moved the tables and chairs to the side of the edges of the seminar room, wore all black, and sat on the grey carpet in order to illustrate the generative effects of paradigm selections. (Afterward one of my classmates came up to me and warned me I shouldn't do such outlandish things in graduate school.)

For my final paper in that leadership class, I wanted to write further about leader listening, but the Introduction to it grew to more than 20 pages as I compared the history of leadership research to the structure of the English language

sentence, which I knew inside and out from my fifth grade nun. Entitled *Leadership on the frontier: A new grammar of meaning*, it seemed to write itself it introduced the leader as the Subject of the sentence in research on the Traits/ of a Great Man (Stogdill, 1974; Yukl, 1998). The search for traits is an exam-

---

Lace, Definitions

An openwork fabric, patterned with open holes in the work, made by machine or by hand. The holes can be formed via removal of threads or cloth from a previously woven fabric, but more often open spaces are created as part of the lace fabric. (Wikipedia)

A string or cord serving to draw together opposite edges (OED)

A slender open-work fabric of linen, cotton, silk, woolen, or metal threads, usually ornamented with inwrought or applied patterns. (OED)

To intertwine, to place together as if interwoven (OED)

To put a 'lace' of spirits (or sugar) into (a beverage); to mingle or 'dash' (with spirits). (OED)

To add savor, zest, or spice to (Websters)

To compress or confine the waist (as with a corset) (Websters)

To admit of lacing or tying (Websters)

To make a physical or verbal attack --- usu. used with into (Websters)

---

ple of what Ackoff (1974) referred to as reductionism, the search for constituent parts.

After looking for Great Man traits, they looked for their behaviors [aka verbs] (Bowers and Seashore, 1966; Schriesheim, & Stogdill, 1975). Zaleznik (1970) noted that "leadership inevitably requires using power to influence the thoughts and actions of other people" (p. 126). Other leader behaviors included defining the problem; facilitating information exchange, evaluation, or analysis; controlling execution of plans;

initiating and directing behavior; developing plans for goal attainment or positive group atmosphere; enhancing task motivation, etc. (Lord, 1977). Similarly, Fayol's classical management functions list verbs: planing, organizing, commanding, coordinating, and controlling (Carroll & Gillin, 1987).

Just as Sister Mary H. would have predicted in her sentence diagram, after the verb comes the followers [direct object]. Tannenbaum and Schmidt (1958), Evans (1970), and Hersey and Blanchard (1977) looked at how the followers affect leadership. Similarly, contingency theories, such as those of Fiedler, rounded out the leadership sentence with prepositional phrases: Fiedler's contingency "theory was the first to specify how situational variables interact with leader personality and behavior" (House & Aditya, 1997, p. 421). So, decades of research on how the arrows could predictably cause intended change, with the followers as the mediating variable and contingencies moderating, merely replicated an English-language sentence.

My advisor, when he was in graduate school, had noticed that in Fiedler's theory, the quality of the relationship between leaders and members always trumped the other situational variables (Graen and Cashman, 1975). So I ended my class project whose introduction, now at 24 pages, was deemed to be the entire paper for the class. My closing argument was that we recognize that attempts at structuralism, standing outside of what we are looking at, leads nowhere. Instead, I proposed that we look at how language can be used to support respectful and supportive relationships.

With my look at listening and relationship quality, I might have avoided the trap of marching along the lines of grammatical constraints, but I still found myself dominated by gender expectations of my language culture. Maybe it was because I was designated "other" to the logocentric expectations of the "masculinist concern with personal power and the ability to control others and self" (Collinson & Hearn, 2003, p. 77).

I never played sports as a child. At that time "endurance, strength, and a competitive spirit were the proper qualities of manliness" (Goffman, 1977, p. 322).

"Since men in organizations take their behavior and perspectives to represent the human, organizational structures and processes [such as leadership] are theorized as gender-neutral" (Acker, 2003, p. 50). Power is conceived as "power over," and it may be the unarticulated assumptions of the "proper" superiority of men to woman that provides "a primary way of signifying relationships of power" (Scott, 1986, p. 51). Leaders compete, for leadership and with leadership: Who is on the leader board? Who leads the league in scoring? Who is the cost leader? Power, and therefore leadership, usually gets defined as the ability to make others do something they wouldn't ordinarily do. Is rape, therefore, power, and its perpetrators leaders?

In academics, demands in publication to include numerous citations of seminal (yes, the etymology is that it comes from the same source as semen) works means that I cannot say just anything. Instead, according to Foucault (1981), I need to follow expectations to make my work recognizable and standardized so that academic publishing institutions can successfully use their peremptoriness and decisiveness to hold back the sea of in-tranquility, so that all around me—no, all around us—can be like a calm, deep transparence infinitely open, where others will fit in with expectations and from which truths would emerge one by one. By including numerous citations, identifying a problem or gap in the theory, quantifying my results, and recommending action, I submit to a collective, masculine order of laws, in which everything is at least potentially under control, particularly if the discourse itself presumes to be able to identify patterns that lead to predictability, if it takes single individuals and closed anomic systems as the key variables, and if it presumes that power is the power to change other closed anomic systems.

I may not be cut out to write about leadership. I don't have any experience in the military or sports or corporations, places where we learn about strategy, campaigns, teamwork, and measurement of value. I do not easily fit the profile of "hegemonic masculinity, typified by the image of the strong, technically competent, authoritative leader who is sexually competent and attractive, has a family, and has his [sic] emotions under control" (Acker, 2003, p. 57), although I am "white, middle-class or upper middle-class" (Ely, 2003, p. 156), but only in some parts an "unblushing male in America: a young, married, white, urban, northern heterosexual, Protestant, father, of college education, fully employed, of good complexion, weight, and height, and a recent record in sports. Any male

> **Power, and therefore leadership, usually gets defined as the ability to make others do something they wouldn't ordinarily do.**

who fails to qualify in any one of these ways is likely to view himself—during moments at least—as unworthy, incomplete, and inferior" (Goffman, 1963, p. 128). And I am not personally convinced that it is either possible or important to predict the future, to force my views on others, or to isolate individuals from the whole.

The typical discourse of leadership and academia is designed to reinforce and reinscribe masculinist archetypes, as represented by the symbol for the planet Mars: a circle attached to an arrow. In such a conception, singularity is essential, deliberate transformation is valued, moving forward into the future is the key activity, and being able to influence others is a sign of power. The feminine archetype represented by the planet Venus is similarly represented with a circle, with the difference that the arrow is now a cross. In such a perspective, the values of reflection, praxis, embodiment, presence, and duality take precedence. The key to humanity, in our own emergence from the union of masculine and feminine, is likely to involve ways to balance these archetypes that give rise to our circumstances. At the present time, identification with, and preference for, the singular has yielded a two-column configuration of items that carry positive and negative signs respectively Masculine values of "mono" (singular) as in monotheism and monologue, assign the "other" the role of negative, wrong, substandard, even evil. The feminine is part of, some even say defines, this alterity. Hopfl (2000) adds to the typical two-column depictions of men/women, light/dark, day/night, culture/nature, reason/emotion, rich/poor, and true/false, to include scholarly conventions that privilege quantification over qualification, general truths over specific instances, answers over questions, completeness over gaps, the objective over subjective, and transforming over being transformed. In a world of such dichotomies, abstract language is greatly privileged over embodied experiences, and language that causes action is the best of all. Such language is commonly defined as rhetoric.

In traditional rhetoric that the purpose of talk is influence—to change another's view into one's own. "Embedded in efforts to change others is a desire for control and domination" (Foss & Griffin, 1995, p. 3). In the traditional rhetoric model, success is measured by the extent to which the audience changes "in the direction requested by the rhetor, who then has gained some measure of power and control over the audience" (Foss & Griffin, 1995, p. 6). Foss and Griffin (1995) coined the phrase "invitational rhetoric" to suggest an alternative view of rhetoric. Invitational rhetoric uses language to express a desire to understand the other, admits the inadequacy of language to express such an understanding, and indicates a willingness to learn from the other in order to build a new relationship, new structures, and new metaphors. I use it here, invitational rhetoric is a discourse strategy of partiality, gaps, contradiction, ambiguity, and careful attention on the part of the interviewer to what the respondent has to say.

In invitational rhetoric, change emerges out of the communicative interaction of the participants. Stories are "not told as a means of supporting or achieving some other end but as an end in itself—simply offering the perspective the story represents" (Foss & Griffin, 1995, p. 7). Such stories "represent an initial, tentative commitment to a perspective that is subject to revision as a result of the interaction" (Foss & Griffin, p. 8).

The story-essay below is an experiment in using a different, alternative language to express my internalized views of transformational leadership. In it, I necessarily violate social and scholarly norms, norms that privilege a certain set of conventions that enframe, and therefore limit, possible ways to conceptualize leadership and transformation. Specifically, I focus on a specific point of view rather than a general outlook, on a child's perspective rather than on an adult's, looking and thinking backwards rather than forward, on circular and open-ended logic rather than tight linear argument, on a story rather than verifiable facts, on the feminine rather than masculine, and on poetic emotional prose rather than academic logical reasoning. Finally, I do not provide an ending that wraps up my point of view with recommendations for future research and implications or predictions for the future. Instead, I invite the reader to share her or his own stories.

With the following essay I hope to show you an insider's view of what it meant to be a young girl in the 1950s-1960s, when all my role models of power and leadership were men. I hope to provide a glimpse into the kind of poetic language and self-categorization that resulted in my case when as a female I was relegated automatically to the "second" column, the place of emotions and questions and relationships and being changed by circumstances.

Even though the story ends with my inclusion into a circle of friendship, and even though all of the women named as my 7 friends are now leaders in philanthropic and educational and spiritual and health care fields, the point is to help you accompany you along the journey of my wonderment rather than to nail down a specific definition of transformative leadership. As I write the essay, and as you read it I invite you to join me as I wonder how love transforms and/or steadies one and many.

Because leaving the story open at the end is important to me, I will go ahead and introduce a scholarly proposition relevant to my discussion of leadership above. In today's increasingly hybrid and open-system world, sharing the same meaning with even one other person, or with an entire community of speakers, is likely to result in a Tower of Babel. Let me refine the previous statement to note that using language to promote singularity and cognition in an attempt to limit meaning to common definitions will probably lead to confusion, even hostility, and failed projects. Instead, sharing meaning by using language to illustrate our individual circumstances provides important clues to one another about

the reasons for our choice of words, values, and viewpoints. Understanding where one another "comes from" will likely help us with the inevitable equifinality of language: the same words meaning different things and different words meaning the same thing. Stories have been the hallmark of a community membership. Therefore, telling and sharing one's stories builds communities, even amidst heteroglossia (multiple languages). Telling stories invites relationship, and the mutual influence welcomed by such an orientation toward reciprocity and respect. In a world where meaning is variable, the future is uncertain, and control is experienced as an aggressive act, leadership itself is ripe for transformation. With my little story below, I offer my perspective that we are able to influence others to the extent that we are willing to be influenced. The solid ground on which to organize cooperative and functional organizations is provided primarily by relationships, reverence, compassion, acceptance, understanding, mutuality, humility, humor, and holistic inclusion.

The following story, therefore, gives voice to a child trying to make sense of the phrase transformational leadership.

Body

Could I write a transformational leadership piece about the 7 girls? I think I'll go with my own experience of my own leadership. About the Transformative power of love. The capital letter T in Transformative generates itself! Very weird!! I may speak in an ancient language, from waaay back in 1962 or 1965 or 1966 or sooner or later, when I was little and a little older and up to 19.

So, what's up with the word leadership? It sounds like lead, like lead in a pencil which is really graphite, but which if it were really lead and you

Photo: Jürgen Werner Kremer

really did chew on it you would end up dead like babies who get retarded from eating the paint chips in their tenement or antique homes. It sounds like a ship, like the 3 ships that Christopher Columbus sailed to our new world to kill our Indians, who didn't even know they were Indians instead who thought they were just regular people.

I am sorry, but even though I am a critical scholar I am still very, very hard to change my mind. My mind is lead, you might say. Or is lead a little bit soft. I think gold is softer. I think it may have been lead that the alchemists that Jung talked about were trying to turn to gold. I don't remember much chemistry. So that is an empirical question that I could probably research by looking up "lead" in Google. Anyway, let's consider it harder than gold and certainly heavy and certainly certainly much uglier than gold. So leadership is heavy and unattractive, insofar as it is lead on a ship.

And it is definitely done by men. That is what I was trying to get to earlier. By Jesus who was a fisher of men and lead is often used as a sinker for fishing to get those of us to are bottom feeders because we like the coolness and the way the green plants ripple in the dappled light. I am not talking sunken treasure dead man's cove deep here. I am talking Lake of the Ozarks deep where Dad wore his cotton fishing hat with a narrow brim that wouldn't protect a fly from the sun and certainly not this wanna-be-Pinoccio but who never allowed himself to lie or cut up so I guess he thought his nose was short or maybe flat so who got to wear inadequate hats. And his scaly arms with that cute red hair among the freckles reaching around the outboard motor boat to help put the shimmering wriggly minnows where we could reach them. That deep. That's where the lead goes, down to the "put hands in water" mixture of coolness and warmth along the hillsides that got drowned so we could have the lake of the Ozarks and someone could have electricity. But the lake is 90 miles long and windey and it is easy not to be fooled and think this is anything but a clogged river.

Dad, and Jesus, and my two brothers, they are leaders. And I guess John F.

Kennedy, though he got shot. Kennedy Kennedy he's our man; Nixon in the garbage can. We are Catholic and so we are for Kennedy. And he won! And his pretty wife is part French, or at least her name and face seem so, Jacqueline, and my mother's people are French: Francour, or is it Francouer, which anyway means true heart. Women are not leaders. Leaders are pointy and they stick out and they go where no man has gone before. Women center. We go inward, to the kitchen to feed babies and make food and dry dishes and laugh.

So when Dad asked me whether I would consider going to the K-12 all-girls Loretto, I declined, rather politely I thought. Because, even though the nuns were so old, for the most part, at St. Peter's, that we needed an extra teacher for music and an extra one for recess and the younger nun who was even the

In a world where meaning is variable, the future is uncertain, and control is experienced as an aggressive act, leadership itself is ripe for transformation.

principal for New Math, this was 1964-1965, anyway we did have boys. And Loretto didn't have boys. And I liked boys. For the most part. I kind of hated Tim W. because he sat at the near wall to the door to the classroom, the wall that our progress chart was placed, and he was just mischievous enough to glint at me when his construction paper star seemed to mysteriously be a couple of squares ahead of where it had been and we hadn't been asked to move them as a reward for doing good on our papers, such as spelling or sentence diagramming. Dang, that nun could sure diagram a sentence. I loved her for that. Linking up the prepositional phrases, having them slide down from the parts of the

sentence that supported them. And having the separate parts of the sentence with their own little cubby: Subjects in the subject place, verbs in the verb place, and direct objects pulling up the rear. So cool!

And speaking of boys, I had liked Mike T. a lot the year before. Naturally, we were never allowed to talk to each other. None of us were, I mean. Not in class, ever, and not during lunch because imagine how noisy it might get. Though I think they started to let us talk in the lunchroom but I found I didn't have any idea what to say after so many years of being quiet all the time. I remember one day they had told us there would be a contest on writing a song. And I wanted to and wanted to and so I spent all lunch tying to think up a song. And now I am married to a composer. And I have three sons. I have always liked boys. But at the time I am remembering I am still liking boys and remembering how Mike T. would quietly lean over his desk and tap a linoleum tile on the floor and then tap the one next to it and we would quietly marvel at the different sounds the two tiles made. I think he liked me. Though we were not allowed to talk, to anyone and especially not to boys. They got to be altar boys and we might contaminate them. Or we might kiss or hold hands or have sex walking to school. That would be bad.

So I didn't go to Loretto that year. Or in 6th, when Tim and I got to be friends because we both liked crusty Miss W. who lived in a duplex with a turret and a Scottish terrier with a bow around his neck. I think Miss W. liked Tim better, and I was a little jealous, but he was handsome and smart and he was a boy. I liked boys enough to stay at a not so good school in comparison to a good school, so I understood nearly completely.

But by 7th when I was scheduled to not be in classes with boys anymore—at that age they couldn't trust us together even in the classroom not talking—and I was scheduled to have the oldest and meanest teacher nun there, I let myself get shipped off to Loretto. I took the bus at 6:50 in the morning and rode around further north in Kansas City where we got the singing girls and others and then back to pick up others and then out the 10 miles to Loretto's new building. I remember Sister Mary V., "call me Sister Vicky," who was young and nice and quite a change in pace for a nun and who showed my mom and me around the school. They didn't have the carpeting in yet in the building, which gave me terrible bronchitis the next year but I had other problems that year anyway but at the time I thought it was interesting how Loretto was up on a big hill. And there was a cemetery from the Santa Fe Trail just over the hill with old graveyards including of babies.

Maybe the first day I was there I was interested and pleased to have Black girls there, too. And I sat next to a very very nice girl who I liked right away. I didn't talk much to my parents, but I did tell my mom about this nice girl. Turn out she was Beth Z., who my mom knew was going to be there because my mom and her dad had dated, as had my dad and her mom. My mom had decided not to tell me to look for Beth, because she didn't want to prejudice me against her. Beth lived in Kansas and had a lot of brothers and sisters and a ranch style house. Beth and I would pretend we were gazelles and run long legged leaping into the air and laughing. Beth was friends with Susie K. from Cure of Ars, but I didn't see her as much as I saw Beth. And I liked Mary N., who had two very handsome brothers, and who being an N last name got sat next to me, an O, since the classes were pretty small. I think Mary might have been from Cure of Ars, too.

What is leadership when there aren't any boys? It is playful, for one. I tried out for Cheerleader, even though I could never do even a cartwheel and even though Darcy could do like a triple aerial somersault. I got it, and we would cheer our 7th grade volleyball team. And we picked class colors, and we chose bright neon pink and orange, this was 1967-

1968 mind you, and we laughed and laughed.

When one of our seniors got chosen to be the homecoming queen for Rockhurst, the Jesuit all-boys school a few miles away, we were very proud. She was our queen!

The next year was hard. I'm not real clear on what exactly happened, but the best I can figure Beth and Susie K. and Mary N. just stopped talking to me. That's it. For two months. They would

Photo: Jürgen Werner Kremer

turn and walk away when I came up.

Fortunately, I had made friends with Diane G. from Spanish class. Diane was a private person whose sister was real wild and whose brother had some disability so who had a perspective on life. Diane was kind to me and we would be the kind of smart loners and social losers who end up being the heroes or at least the interesting characters in the teen movies of today, like Mean Girls. I'm not saying that Beth and Susie K. and Mary N. were mean. Like they didn't go out of their way to spite me or anything. They just refused to talk to me.

In the meantime, the bus ride was tiring but had some interesting mornings, like the day that someone brought doughnuts to share or the morning they threw water balloons and even hit a guy in a buckskin suede jacket, a guy one of them knew. They said that the water would damage the jacket. And we would sing when Kathy pulled out her guitar. Kathy was the lead singer in a

rock group that sang Jefferson Airplane songs.

And Barbara I think it might have been, but I am fuzzy on names and she was mostly in the other class though she might have been from Cure of Ars, too, anyway, Barbara's brother got killed in Vietnam. And our Religion teacher nun who had a wide smile and sometimes mean eyes got arrested for pouring blood on some files in Washington, D.C. And she brought her war protester friend who burned his draft card in one of our seminars and wore a black arm band. I was surprised that he would light a fire in our school and surprised that the sprinkler system didn't come on. I hear later that he had a supply of draft cards that he burned for effect, but I don't know what to believe. I do know that Dad got real mad and other parents too and they almost pulled me out of Loretto but they didn't because it was a good education and sometime that year Susie K. and Mary N. and Beth started talking to me again. They said they were mad because they thought I thought they were stupid because I had pointed and said, "There's the convent door" when it was perfectly obvious to them and why would I think I had to tell them. I didn't quite know how to explain that I didn't exactly know how to talk or what to say. I just said what was on my mind, and I had been thinking about how those were the convent doors and I voiced my thoughts. I think now it was from all those years of not talking. Like in church you never talked even when the priest, who I guess you could say was a leader though he certainly had his people over him, like the Monsignor and the Bishop and maybe an Archbishop and certainly the cardinals and definitely the Pope, who was always already over everybody because he had authority in a direct line from St. Peter, which was the name of our Church and School, the first Pope because Jesus appointed him. So even when the priest asked a question we weren't supposed to answer, even if we had an idea and just wanted to raise our hand and try out our thought. And not at home, because there were so many kids and Mom was busy with them and Dad had work to do, talking into his Dictaphone and not to kids, except once he taught us how to borrow and carry with math and he would read stories and poems from the book, A Father Reads to His Children. I really liked a couple of the stories, A Highwayman Comes Riding Riding Riding, and she shoots herself in the breast to warn the man she loves. And another story was like from the Middle East about some character named Abou Ben Adhem, but when I tried to share the story with my class once during show and tell everyone laughed at me because it sounded like I was saying, "A Boob." Like I said, I didn't know how to talk or what to say.

In fifth grade, I guess I regress now, I used to draw little houses, little five sided shapes, around the holes at the edge of my notebook paper.

In eighth grade I went a few weeks with Tim W. to an inner city Head Start program. I was proud that he asked me. And I was real humbled by his dad's willingness to drive us down to 12th and Vine so much. No really, I know it is the name of some jazz song but it was also the approximate location of the Head Start School. I think my mom and dad drove us sometimes, too. I wasn't always real sure my mom was entirely safe there, dropping us off and then driving by herself in the car. Although being Saturday mornings that we did it I can imagine another kid or two in the car. She sure did drive us around a lot. We all had swimming lessons since a little more than when we could walk. The boys had little league. Boys play sports and girls cheerlead them, or eat 19-cent hamburgers with tiny chopped onions on them behind the bleachers in the dirt and wait for the many baseball games to end. I am

so proud of Title 9 I could just pop. Of course, it was after my time but it is cool.

Tim was a leader, too. He played the organ in church and so would lead us in song, sort of. Later he was a jazz pianist and singer in a club very near 12th and Vine, where we went to Head Start. I guess that was to begin to train children from the inner city to be leaders. Maybe there is something to the trait theories of leadership. I mean, there were two kids there who needed a tutor

Photo: Jürgen Werner Kremer

or a Big or whatever we were. One was thin and dark skinned and looked bright. The other was sort of pudgy and had relatively lighter skin and didn't look as smart. Tim naturally made a bee-line for the smart kid and they would read books together and discuss them, while I would try to keep my Little from just running out the door.

At the end of 8th grade Beth called me and told me she had decided to go to public school in Shawnee Mission, Kansas, for high school. Kansas had good schools, but Missouri did not. Being from Kansas City people always ask me, Kansas City Kansas or Kansas City Missouri? They think they sound smart but they certainly don't. There is only barely a Kansas City Kansas. I think there may be a warehouse there and train tracks and probably a river. And liquor stores. But Kansas City is Kansas City Missouri. Good old KCMO. It had the sense to sprawl out and gobble up all the towns to the south, like Westport and Waldo.

And so it had a bad school system. If you are from Kansas you have a suburban town name that sounds like you are from an Indian Reservation but really you are from a pretty wealthy place with good schools and nice parks and lots of swimming pools. Places like Prairie Village and Overland Park and Shawnee Mission, and now even Lenexa but that was a separate town when I was a kid.

That's what I find kind of weird about Transformative Leadership, the title of this paper though it is really an introduction to a dream of writing with and about us 7 girls. Transformative leadership is usually about men trying to make others change in ways they think are good for them. That seems to think that it is hard for things to change. That things tend to stay the same unless acted upon, like some physics equation we had with Sister M. my senior year at Loretto. But they don't, stay the same I mean. No matter how much you try. Best friends move to different schools. I cried; my heart was broken. It took a lot of courage for me to walk back in that school my Freshman year. Or 9th grade, the year after 8th grade, the year that Beth was gone. Maybe that is being a leader. I had been sad the three months she didn't talk to me, but I still could see her. Now she was gone. And there were new girls, lots of them. Girls whose nuns maybe weren't as bad in 7th and 8th, or who got to still sit next to boys in those dangerous years. The nun at Cure of Ars was worse, I heard she pulled at boys ears until they bled. But of course, those Cure of Ars kids were already there. Beth was one. Now she was leaving now that she had a chance to go to a good school and even have it be for free.

Once the new girls arrived, we old girls seemed to know one another better than we did before. Mary and Susan were good friends. I think maybe I felt shy about being their friend when they already had each other. I admired them both. I felt shy and almost inadequate when I got invited to Susan's house, especially because she had silkscreen on her pool table and she was an artist and beautiful and smart and had a friend in Mary. I couldn't ever live up to Mary, who could talk easily. One of my problems you may remember was my difficulty talking.

So here I am coming to 9th grade and I am scared. I don't have Beth. New girls to the school include Kathy D., who was my favorite friend in some baby grade, like Kindergarten or first, though her brother did chase us around the yard with a rake held high. And she had albums of musicals that I wanted to hear, like Gigi. And her big brother got killed one day in the parking lot at church which was also our St. Peter's school playground because he got hit by a car and couldn't stop bleeding. I think he was in 6th and my mom said "poor mother who lost her baby" and I asked her because I didn't understand, about how he could be a baby when he was so old, me being the oldest of five and so being as big as we got in my family and being certainly no older than 2nd grade because I don't think I was real good friends with Kathy D. anymore because even though we looked almost the same she ended up popular and I did not... Anyway, I asked mom how could he be a baby when he was in 6th and she said that he was a mother's child so would be her baby, even as big as 6th.

So, here comes Kathy D. to my school, and a couple of other St. Peter's girls: Claudia K. and a different Claudia K. and Loretta O. They knew I couldn't talk and wasn't popular. But I was here first at Loretto so I had to have some credit for that. So I didn't talk to them much but I tried not to feel too bad about myself around them.

Why did Patty F. talk to me? She was beautiful and very popular with boys. And Susie B. did, too. I couldn't believe it. And Sheila C., too, who had the most blue eyes and the cutest freckles on the planet. Boys loved those girls. And they

talked to me like I was a normal human being, who could talk. I tried to talk to them, too. Our moms did some driving. We were from all over town, Kansas City Missouri and Prairie Village and Overland Park and Fairway, or was it Roeland Park? When did we know we were seven? Maybe someone knows. Patty was kind enough to walk to my house and we would walk to the Landing Shopping Center together. We could be found in pairs, sort of, certainly by location. Patty and me lived in Kansas City, Missouri. Susie B. and Sheila lived next door to each other in Overland Park off of Nall, and Susie K. lived that way and

Photo: Jürgen Werner Kremer

further. So she was with them geographically. Susan and Mary lived near each other, and further than Susie and Susie and Sheila, so Patty and I were kind of with them, too.

We are still friends more than 30 years later, across different states—even countries at times—and different politics and religions and values. World events don't mean the same things to us, but we know we mean the world to each other. And that gives me strength and joy and courage to allow my life to be meaningful in other ways. And to share myself with others.

Will you please tell me a story?

I have spent 9 years as a scholar trying to understand organizational leadership. My dissertation was about the power of meaningful relationships to co-create the kinds of social systems that nourish and support us. They key to such leadership is listening to stories.

The 7 girls listened to me when no one had before. I got transformed, and I continue to be transformed, in our love. Marja Flory's (2008) dissertation was about quilts, about piecing together our various remnants or re-cycling cuttings from the fabric of our lives. She was empowered to write about quilts by Ann Rippin (2007), who wrote about alternative post-masculinist, post-heroic ways to consider emergent processes in an otherwise "leaderless" quilting circle. And so now I have offered some observations on leadership and lace.

Why have I bothered to include a narrative from my "inner child" in a scholarly discourse on leadership? One reason is that I like to look at and for the origins, assumptions, and frameworks around concepts. I am suspect of "taken for granted" concepts that "go without saying." I believe that any concept gets its meaning in the interplay of context and convention. And the context of leadership studies, in fact of scholarship in general, has the potential for a gender bias, given the predominance of studies by and for and about men in the 20th Century. I have sought to deconstruct some common themes of the intermix of leadership, power, and rhetoric, particularly what it means to me as one who is still a little girl inside. Therefore, it was a synchronicity last night when I read the following in a workbook about the inner child: "The wolf also shall dwell with the lamb, and the leopard shall lie down with the kid; and the calf and the young lion and the fatted calf together; and a little child shall lead them" (Isaiah 11:6, American King James version, http://bible.cc/isaiah/11-6.htm).

To me, this quote refers to holism, to a union of opposites, that can be accomplished if I honor my inner child and her sense of newness, spontaneity, acceptance, wonder, joy, discovery, and movement. In my reading of traditional leadership, power, and rhetoric, such childlike capacities are often demeaned in the pursuit of competition, predictability, and control. In my upbringing as female, I would perceive myself as the lamb, the kid, the fatted calf—the one in a "power down" position according to institutional and cultural expectations of the co-alignment of traditional male values and my "Other-ness" to them. The game was fixed, in my mind. So, to me, the invitation of the biblical quote is to find the courage to meet and interact with the wolf, leopard, and young lion. In fact, under the guidance of my inner child, I might find a source of strength and comfort in finding a place in my heart for my own inner wolf, leopard, and young lion.

In traditional rhetoric, the end of the essay is where I turn aside from my own musings and get to the point of telling what I think you should do based on my observations. Similarly, as I watch cable sports (mostly men's teams) shows, a lot of time is spent by the male commentators discussing the likelihood of future events, as well as providing advice to the coaches, viewers, teams, etc. My inner child wonders if that isn't more of the same desire for prediction and control by and for masculine archetypes. And so I try to coax her that she holds the key to leading me to a better understanding of how to reconcile the predator and the prey. "You are a leader," I coax her. "You are very good with words. As a poet, you can find opposite meanings in the same term, so surely you can find a way to make these terms your own." I suggest that she think about feeling safe, about being okay with being who she is, and about her special talents in seeing holism, even (or maybe especially) in situations that seem to be imbalanced. "What does leadership mean to you," I ask her, "if it is done by a child and helps people and animals put aside fears and hungers in order to enjoy one another's warmth?"

She replies, Well it comes from the inside responding to cues from the outside, and to seeing the outside change as our insides do. It starts in bodies, in finding my breath and my spine and my heart, and in the spirited life of leaning back into the constant source of leadership from each of our individual and collective higher Selves. It comes from being happy to be human, to be a girl, or a boy. It is about asking a question, and knowing that the answer comes in a

time of waiting for it, of planning for it, of celebrating it. Leadership and lace are about patience, about a willingness to double back to pick up neglected threads of conversations or relationships. Leadership and lace are about being open—open-minded, open-hearted, open to suggestions, open to change. Leadership and lace comes from loving so much that it adorns windows of my heart, and lights up my soul, and provides a safe place for others to do the same. From there, in friendship and trust we experience an abundance of feelings and light that transform a barren wasteland into oases of greenery and safety and nourishment and quenching and beauty that relaxes desire into joy. We have enough. We don't have to be afraid of being eaten. Our transformation is transpersonal. We take turns being many ways, lion and calf, active and restful, winner and loser, certain and dazzled. Can you come out and play? Will you please tell me a story?

References

Acker, J. (2003). Hierarchies, jobs, bodies: A theory of gendered organizations. In R. J. Ely, E. G. Foldy, M. A. Scully, & The Center for Gender in Organizations Simmons School of Management (Eds.), *Reader in gender, work, and organization* (pp. 49-61). Malden, MA: Blackwell Publishing.

Ackoff, R. L. (1974, *December*). The systems revolution. *Long Range Planning, VOLUME?*, 2-20.

Ackoff, R. L. (1994). From mechanistic to social systemic thinking. *Systems Thinking in Action Conference, 11/93*, transcript: V5N1.cover. transcr, 1-22.

Bowers, D. G., & Seashore, S. E. (1966). Predicting organizational effectiveness with a four-factor theory of leadership. *Administrative Science Quarterly 11*(2), 238-263.

Carroll, S. J., & Gillen, D. J. (1987). Are the classical management functions useful in describing managerial work? *Academy of Management Review 12*(1), 38-51.

Collinson, D. L., & Hearn, J. (2003) Breaking the silence: On men, masculinities, and managements. In R. J. Ely, E. G. Foldy, M. A. Scully, and The Center for Gender in Organizations Simmons School of Management (Eds.), *Reader in gender, work, and organization* (pp. 75-86). Malden, MA: Blackwell Publishing.

Dahl, R. A. (1957). The concept of power. *Behavioral Science 2*, 201-215.

Ely, R. J. (2003). Leadership: Overview. In R. J. Ely, E. G. Foldly, M. A. Scully, & The Center for Gender in Organizations Simmons School of Management (Eds.), *Reader in gender, work, and organization* (pp. 153-158). Malden, MA: Blackwell Publishing.

Evans, M. G. (1970). The effects of supervisory behavior on the path-goal relationship. *Organizational Behavior and Human Performance 5*, 277-298.

Flory, M. (2008). *The never-ending story: Narrating the paradox of self-management in organizations*. Rotterdam: Erasmus University

Foucault, M. (1981). The order of discourse. In R. Young, *Untying the test: A post-structuralist reader* (pp. 48-78). Boston, MA: Routledge & Kegan Paul. (Lecture given in 1970)

Foss, S. K., & Griffin, C. L. (1995). Beyond persuasion: A proposal for an invitational rhetoric. *Communication Monographs, 62* (2-18).

French, J., & Raven, B. H. (1959). The bases of social power. In D. Cartwright, *Studies of social power* (pp. 150-167). Ann Arbor, MI, Institute for Social Research.

Goffman, E. (1963). *Stigma: Notes on the management of spoiled identity*. Englewood Cliffs, NJ: Prentice Hall.

Goffman, E. (1977). The arrangement between the sexes. *Theory and Society, 4*, 301-331.

Graen, G. B., & Cashman, J. F. (1975). A role-making model of leadership. In J.G. Hunt & L.L.Larson (Eds.), *Formal organizations: A developmental approach* (pp. 143--165). Kent, OH: Kent State University Press.

Greenberg, J. (1990). Employee theft as a reaction to underpayment inequity: The hidden cost of pay cuts. *Journal of Applied Psychology, 75*(5): 561-568.

Hersey, P., & Blanchard, K. H. (1977). *The management of organizational behavior*. Upper Saddle River, NJ: Prentice Hall.

Hopfl, H (2000). On Being Moved. *Studies in Cultures, Organizations, and Societies 6* 15-34.

House, R. J., & Aditya, R. N. (1997). The Social Scientific Study of Leadership: Quo Vadis? *Journal of Management 23*(3).

Kimmel, M. (2004). Masculinities. In Michael Kimmel and Amy Aronson (Eds.) *Men and masculinities: A social, cultural, and historical encyclopedia*. Santa Barbara, CA: ABC-Clio Press, 503-507.

Kristeva, J. (1983). Stabat mater, In T. Moi (Ed.) (1986). *The Kristeva reader*, Oxford: Blackwell translated by L. Roudiez, 160-186.

Lord, R. G. (1977). Functional leadership behavior: Measurement and relation to social power and leadership perceptions." *Administrative Science Quarterly 22*: 114-133.

Oxford English Dictionary (OED). *OED Online*. Oxford: Oxford University Press. Accessed August 2009.

Rhode, D. (2003). The difference "difference" makes. In R. J. Ely, E. G. Foldy, and M. A. Scully, and The Center for Gender in Organizations Simmons School of Management (Eds.), *Reader in gender, work, and organization*, Blackwell Publishing, Malden, MA: 159-180.

Rippin, A. (2007). Stitching up the leader. *Journal of Organizational Change Management 20*(2), 209-226.

Schriesheim, C. A., & Stogdill, R. M. (1975). Differences in factor structure across three versions of the Ohio State Leadership Scales. *Personnel Psychology 28*: 189-206.

Scott, J. W. (1986). Gender: A useful category of historical analysis. *American History Review 91*, 1053-1075.

Stogdill, R. M. (1974). *Handbook of leadership: A survey of theory and research*. New York, Free Press.

Tannenbaum, R., & Schmidt, W. H. (1958). How to choose a leadership pattern. *Harvard Business Review 36*(March-April), 95-101.

Webster's Third New International Dictionary, Unabridged. (1993) Springfield, MA: Merriam-Webster, Incorporated. Published under license from Merriam-Webster, Incorporated.

Yukl, G. (1998). *Leadership in organizations*. Upper Saddle River, NJ: Prentice Hall.

Zaleznik, A. (1970). Power and politics in organizational life. *Harvard Business Review, 55*(5). 67-78.

One Day

Everyday the sun rises
And every evening it sets again
A small girl tumbles on the ice and cries
Her mother offers comfort
In the square a disabled veteran begs for money
He is left with an empty hat
The narcissus grow so tall they bend
Touching the Chinese plate
In India 2,000 people are massacred
Over a voting issue
Sweet Honey in the Rock sings of civil rights and love
The crowed goes wild
After 44 years, 4 months a 29 days
I rest and enjoy a cup of tea

Michael Sheffield

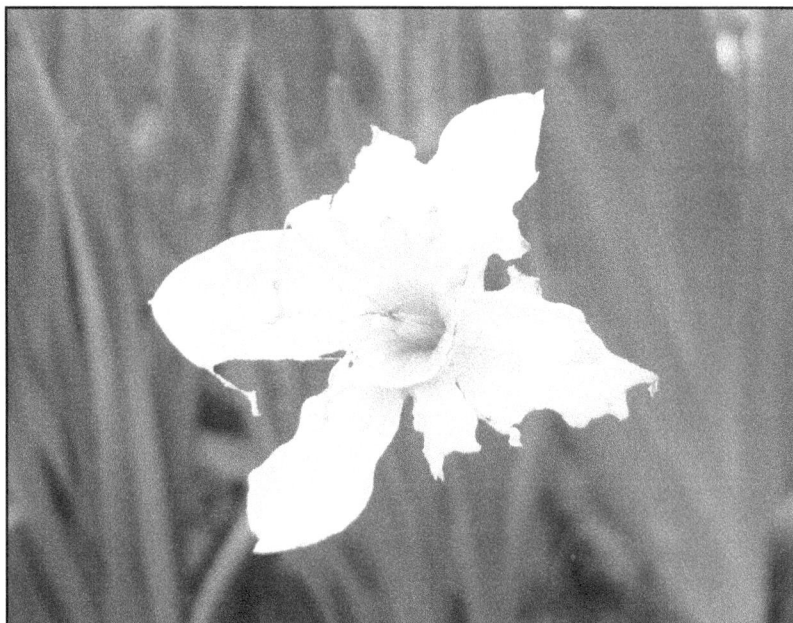

Photo: Jürgen Werner Kremer

Embedded Spirituality as a Leadership Foundation for Sustainable Innovative Learning

David A. Cowan

T he turbulence of a diverse global economy increasingly reveals new fault lines in organizational, community, and societal foundations that increasingly and unexpectedly shift (e.g., Davis & Botkin, 1994). Seemingly small events in one part of the world flow more readily in myriad directions - some intended and others not - and reverberate back in altered forms. The speed of information moving around the globe seemingly increases the rate, scope, depth, and uncertainty of such complex interconnections. Consequently, organizations guided by ideas that are even somewhat isolated or slow to adjust are becoming notably less able to participate constructively in today's world. Part of the challenge of thriving, or just surviving, in the 21st century involves creating, employing, and updating mental models (e.g., Wind & Crook, 2005) that are in sync with shifting tides, not just to realize decent profits, but also to instill common good and enhance quality of life (e.g., Davis & McIntosh, 2005; Sternberg, 2003).

David Cowan is a Professor in the Management Department at Miami University and has research interests in strategic sense-making, higher-order consciousness, and nontraditional inquiry. He is currently serving a sixth term on the editorial review board of The Academy of Management Journal, and teaches leadership, cross-cultural management, and organizational change.

With premonitions decades ago of rising turbulence (e.g., Toffler, 1970), scholars began forecasting significant change on all fronts, including technological, social, economic, political, and environmental. Accordingly, a project commissioned by the Club of Rome emerged in the 1970s to gather data from communi-   ties around

Embedded spirituality evokes anticipatory & participatory ways of knowing leadership, doing leadership, and ultimately being a leader.

the globe   (Botkin, Elmandjra, and Malitza, 1979) in search of core competencies that might enable humanity to sustain over the long run in reasonably good ways. Conclusions drawn from these data led its designers to propose that self-centered, re-active

ways of learning, which still predominate many organizations and societies, would need to be replaced with innovative learning, defined as an integral mix of anticipation and participation (cf. Sternberg, 1996). Whereas "anticipation is a mental activity [that] encourages solidarity in time ... participation is a social [activity that] creates solidarity in space." "Anticipation is the capacity to face new, possibly unprecedented, situations ... to deal with the future ... to account for unintended side effects ... creating new alternatives where none existed before." Alternatively, participation involves "the individual's aspiration to be a partner in decision-making ... people's claim to influence both local and global decisions that shape their environment and lives ... [and] people's aspirations for equality as well as their refusal to accept marginal positions or subordinated status" (Botkin, et al., 1979: 25 and 29).

Botkin et al.'s (1979) argument compels realization that ways of learning that sufficed in previous eras, such as industrial and informational, are increasingly inadequate as the world becomes dynamic and interdependent. Strategic advantages of the 20th Century, largely focused on outworking or out-thinking others, are falling prey in the 21st Century to advantages focused on out-learning others. Against this backdrop, my contribution is to identify tendencies that may help leaders become agents of innovative learning. I begin with a premise that initial conditions needed to create this kind of agency differ from those that led to traditional forms of leadership. For example, a strategy of outworking others led leaders toward authoritarianism and control, and a strategy of outthinking others prompted the pursuit of omniscience. Meanwhile, a strategy of out-learning others cannot emerge from either of these paths. Instead, the requisite path involves specifying conditions that genuinely sustain participation and anticipation. I propose that this foundation exists in well-grounded spirituality, i.e., spirituality rooted in real-world appreciation of all life. More specifically, I propose that an embedded spirituality - similar to Capra's heightened aliveness (2002) - evokes anticipatory and participatory ways of knowing leadership, doing leadership, and ultimately being a leader (Leader-to-Leader Institute, 2004).

In the following section, I begin in the domain of indigenous philosophy, which is arguably one of the most valid sources of insight for understanding embedded spirituality because it experiences Spirit as present on earth in each and every entity and relationship. Native Americans, as well as other indigenous communities such as African, Maori, and Celtic, live in close relationship to Earth, which is significantly different from most Western Europeans. Indigenous peoples tend to employ not only different metaphysics, but also different epistemologies and ethics, as I explain in the next section by highlighting defining characteristics of each. In doing so, I am not suggesting that indigenous ways are superior or inferior to Western European ways, but only that they provide a helpful foundation for innovative learning (cf. Maybury-Lewis, 1992). I use the concept of embeddedness to mean co-existing with nature, not necessarily living in the wild (cf. Whiteman & Cooper, 2000). Ultimately, embeddedness is more of a continuum than a duality. I also frame embedded spirituality as an emergent consciousness (e.g., Feuerstein, 1997; Wilber, 1995). In

subsequent sections, I translate salient dimensions of embedded spirituality into leadership tendencies that naturally promote participation and anticipation, thus helping to sustain innovative learning. To structure this process, I include a long-standing triadic framework with roots to Aristotle (1963) - truth/science, beauty/arts, and goodness/morality - that manifests in ways that are deeply meaningful to leadership. A prime example is the being-knowing-doing framework (Leader to Leader Institute, 2004).

All corn photos in this article: Jürgen Werner Kremer

Embedded Spirituality

The only real hope of people today is probably a renewal of our certainty that we are rooted in the Earth and, at the same time, the cosmos. This awareness endows us with the capacity for self-transcendence. ... Transcendence as a hand reached out to those close to us, to foreigners, to the human community, to all living creatures, to nature, to the universe; transcendence as a deeply and joyously experienced need to be in harmony even with what we ourselves are not, what we do not understand, what seems distant from us in time and space, but with which we are mysteriously linked, because, together with us, all this constitutes a single world. Transcendence as the only real alternative to extinction. (Vaclav Havel, 1994, p. F4)

Unique insight for enriching our understanding of constructive leadership

derives from close attention to native leaders (e.g., Neihardt, 1991), native storytellers (e.g., Underwood, 2002), native philosophers (e.g., Pennick, 1997), and native scholars (e.g., Cajete, 1994), who live and learn in close, interdependent relationships with nature. For this reason, I highlight practical values for today's leaders to possess "spiritual embeddedness," but not necessarily "ecological embeddedness," which is closely related. Whereas ecological embeddedness is the "degree to which a manager is rooted in the land - that is, the extent to which the manager is on the land and learns from the land in an experiential way" (Whiteman & Cooper, 2000: 1267), embedded spirituality is a way of life that is rich in appreciation for the aliveness, sacredness, and interconnectedness of all life, not just human. Embedded spirituality can co-exist with Western European, not just indigenous, modes of living as long as threads of connection to vital roots are not severed. The possibility of mending severed threads is a valid question that lies outside the scope of this paper (cf. Hurst, 1991).

Embedded spirituality is basically a progression toward real-world realizations of Spirit (with a capital S; see Wilber, 2003, for further explanation) flowing through all life, not separate from the tangible world. With significant progression, boundaries among spiritual, physical, emotional, and mental realms of consciousness tend to blur if not also diminish. A revealing description of such consciousness comes from a master tracker, Tom Brown, Jr., who was raised in part by an Apache elder known as Stalking Wolf, whom Brown, Jr. affectionately refers to as Grandfather. As a tracker, Brown Jr. excels at discerning subtle patterns of connection, which others often miss, that enable him to follow paths where evidence seems lacking. Through many books that he has written about such processes, as well as classes he has designed and teaches about presence and mindfulness in the real world, he educates on strategies and tactics for reading signals along our life journeys. At the same time, he educates with pragmatic philosophy - a way of being in the world - that increases mastery (cf. Lehrer, 2006; Kuhn, 2001). Integral to his teaching, Brown Jr. describes living in a way that does not isolate, marginalize, or discard spirituality. According to Brown Jr.'s mentor, Stalking Wolf, tracking occurs in concert with natural laws and rhythms so that as awareness of the physical world deepens, so does one's spirituality, and vice versa - a true indicator of embeddedness. As Brown, Jr. explains:

> Grandfather often stated that awareness is the doorway to the spirit. ... So integral to the spiritual domain was this intense level of physical awareness that Grandfather told us that the best way to identify a spiritual fraud was to determine how aware he or she was on a physical level. Lack of awareness on a physical level was tantamount to no spiritual ability (1999: 13).

In this metaphysic and epistemology, embedded spirituality depends on perceptions but includes deeper awareness of connections that comprise the web or totality of life (Capra, 1996). Explaining more about this developmental journey, Brown, Jr. adds unifying insight:

> [T]he more that we know about a particular species of animal, the better we will see it physically and spiritually. Tracking [brings] us face-to-face with the spirit-that-moves-through-all-things and the dimensions beyond. To be aware is to understand

the interwoven fabric of life. It is then the track that expands the awareness, but so too the awareness that expands the track, where all becomes one…[T]o understand the oneness, the fabric of life, through tracking is to comprehend more than each individual strand…The track is a universe in itself, reaching beyond its own parameters to encompass the grander universe of all things…When we track, we pick up a string. At the far end of the string a being is moving, existing, still connected to the track that we gaze upon…As we follow these tracks, we begin to become the very animal we track…Soon our spirit mingles with that of the animal and we lose our isolated human identity. We become the animal, and a deep spiritual bonding and communication begins…Our awareness expands from the animal we have become to the landscape it reacted to and is played by…A relationship to the grand fabric of consciousness we call the spirit-that-moves through-all-things" (1999, pp. 8-11).

Although I argue that embedded spirituality does not necessarily require living or working directly in nature, it obviously does require close contact with nature. This means living eye-to-eye and heart-to-heart with nature in ways that engage, respect, and comprehend the

earth as alive. Increasingly, such integral awareness is becoming appreciated and promoted by scientists, such as Fritjof Capra, who claims, "Spiritual experience is an experience of aliveness of mind and body as unity. Moreover, this experience of unity transcends not only the separation of mind and body, but also the separation of self and world. The central awareness in these spiritual moments is a profound sense of oneness with all, a sense of belonging to the universe as a whole" (2002: 68).

Cornerstones of Embedded Spirituality

In this section I identify cornerstones of embedded spirituality that derive from indigenous philosophies. Although I draw insight primarily from Native-American philosophy - because I live in the U.S. and have worked more extensively with Native Americans than with any other relatively indigenous groups - I also employ African and Celtic philosophies to some degree. Cornerstones that anchor such philosophies act like strange attractors (e.g., Wheatley, 1992)

Table 1
Cornerstones of Embedded Spirituality, Each with Representative Descriptive Quotes (1)
I. Metaphysical (Way of Being): Holistic, Living Systems:
Life is whole, understanding always partial. ... All things contain energy and therefore are alive. There is no inanimate world. Life . . livingness . . is happening everywhere . . all the time. Everything is alive ... connected. ... related. (Underwood, 2000, pp. xiv-xv)
The Circle is completion ... wholeness. The Circle – the Medicine Wheel – was seen as a complete entity ... reveal[ing] the relationship and integration of all things created. (Storm, 1994, pp. 191-192)
II. Epistemological (Way of Knowing): Interdependent, Dynamic Understanding:
Anthropologists have shown that management practices of indigenous peoples rely on a personal and cultural storehouse of traditional ecological knowledge, which is gained through firsthand interaction with the surrounding ecosystems. (Whiteman & Cooper, 2000, p. 1267)
Traditional American Indian education occurred in holistic social contexts that developed the importance of each individual as a contributing member ... in reciprocal relationships between social groups and the natural world ... [engaging] all dimensions of being to provide human development and skills through participation in community. (Cajete, 1994, p. 26)
III. Ethical (Way of Doing): Principled, Pro-active Behavior:
To Lakota, virtues such as respect, sacrifice, and honesty carry different weight and substance than in western culture. For us these qualities are not elusive goals [but] essential parts of daily life. ... we survived by living by virtues we learned. (Marshall, III, 2001, p. xiii)
In our way of life, our government, every decision we make, we always keep in mind the Seventh Generation to come. It's our job to see that the people coming ahead, the generation unborn, have a world no worse than ours – hopefully better. When we walk on Mother Earth we plant our feet carefully because we know the faces of future generations are looking up at us. We never forget them." (Oren Lyons, in Wall & Arden, 1990, p. 68)

to shape the character and integrity of life that results from embedded spirituality. In this manner, they are comparable to unique ingredients that distinguish a salad as Greek or a dessert as Brazilian. Particular cornerstones often lose their identities when combined to form such patterns, much the way cream cheese, eggs, and sugar seem to disappear when stirred and baked into a cheesecake. Nevertheless, it is helpful to distinguish key ingredients. Before describing the key ingredients or cornerstones of embedded spirituality, I must note that although each cultural group possesses unique defining characteristics, there also exists considerable within-group variation. Thus, there are significant differences not only among cultural groups, such as Native Americans and Western Europeans, but also among subgroups and between individuals within each subgroup. Thus, there are more than 150 Native American nations alone (Waldman, 1999) and each contains notable variation among its people. It is not my intent to outline all these patterns of uniformity and diversity, but rather only to illuminate cornerstones that generally comprise embedded spirituality. Such patterns are more similar among indigenous cultures than between indigenous and mainstream cultures, such as U.S. and European (Mander, 1991).

In Table I, I highlight three cornerstones of embedded spirituality. I select these three among other candidates (e.g., Suzuki & Knudtson, 1992; Wall, 1993) because they provide an internal consistency that helps to understand leadership catalysts for innovative learning. These three cornerstones are certainly not collectively exhaustive, but I believe they are meaningfully representative. One cornerstone is the metaphysical hub (cf. a way of being a leader in today's world), while the other two are derivatives, one epistemological (cf. a way of knowing about leadership), and one ethical (cf. a way of doing leadership).

As proposed previously, embedded spirituality resides on a developmental continuum suggesting that we can acquire more of it over time. Embedded spirituality also manifests in various combinations of metaphysics, epistemology, and ethics, creating many integral ways of living in harmony with

the world. As it becomes increasingly developed, it guides decisions and actions toward greater alignment with nature, and through more inclusive consideration of all relevant perspectives (e.g., Underwood, 1991). To the degree that embedded spirituality develops, it increasingly embraces the integrity of natural law (e.g., Lyons, 1991; Whiteman & Cooper, 2000) more than, or at least in addition to, socially-contrived law, as Cajete explains:

Indigenous people have preserved ways of ecologically based living that have

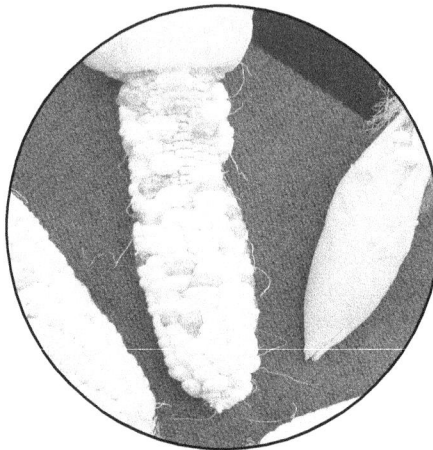

evolved over 40,000 years of continuous relationship with special environments. Their understanding and application of relating to their land represents models for the 'art of relationship' that must be re-taught through modern education. (1994, p. 78)

One of the challenges in understanding the impact of embedded spirituality on leadership involves translating its cornerstones into human and social processes such as awareness, perception, valuation, prioritization, and decision making. Although no one can completely understand the consciousness of another person or culture, respectful effort inevitably increases understanding (e.g., Hall, 1994). Thus, reading about native life, observing it in its own context, discussing apparent premises with native people, and engaging in native ritual and ceremony are helpful ways of clarifying and deepening understanding, stated in increasing order of engagement, each providing potentially deeper understanding.

Metaphysical: Holistic, Living Systems

I was standing on the highest mountain of them all, and round beneath me was the whole hoop of the world. And while I stood there I saw more than I can tell and understood more than I saw; for I was seeing in a sacred manner the shapes of all things in the spirit, and the shape of all the shapes as they must live together like one being. And I saw that the sacred hoop of my people was one of many hoops that made one circle, wide as daylight and as starlight. (Black Elk, in Neihardt, 1991)

When the "whole hoop of the world" is understood, not just conceptually but also physically, emotionally, and spiritually, the other cornerstones of embedded spirituality fall fairly readily into place. The hoop - or sacred circle as it is sometimes called - is a core metaphysical realization from which values and beliefs flow. Appreciation of holistic living systems involves understanding interconnectedness in life. This cornerstone is shared not only by Native Americans (e.g., Meadows, 1989), but also Native Celts (e.g., Cruden, 1998), Native Africans (e.g., Fu-Kiau, 1991), and other indigenous cultures (e.g., Suzuki & Knudtson, 1992). With this fundamental understanding in place, everything on earth is considered alive, with earth serving as the literal Mother or source of all. Everyone and everything is conceived as part of an intricately complex being continually flowing through cycles of birth and death (e.g., Crowley, 1998). Consistent with emerging scientific realizations, this sacred circle is a web of interrelationships (e.g., Capra, 1996), meaning not only that all parts are members of the same whole, but also that relationships are more essential or real than are the supposedly separate parts (e.g., Zohar, 1997). As Suzuki and Knudtson describe:

The Native Mind tends to view the universe as the dynamic interplay of elusive and ever-changing natural forces, not as a vast array of static physical objects. It tends to see the entire natural world as somehow alive and animated by a single, unifying life force, whatever its local Native name. It does not reduce the universe to progressively smaller conceptual bits and pieces. (1992, p. 17)

Relative to Western consciousness, native consciousness is more of a living, flowing stream of rhythms and energies than a warehouse of pieces and categories (e.g., Little Bear & Heavy Head, 2004). Such understanding necessitates awareness of connections, providing a meaningful foundation for grounding values and beliefs in real-world contexts. As an individual's development proceeds, there emerges increasing awareness of, appreciation for, and sense of presence within increasingly inclusive realms of reality (Deloria, 1973), for example, from local to global or from Lakota to Indian to all humans. With maturity, attention increasingly aligns with intention (e.g., Cowan, 2007) and responsibility for leading inclusively increases, as exemplified in Black Elk's comment above about the Sacred Hoop (Neihardt, 1991).

Responsibility begins to derive less from personal and local desires than from natural laws that guide the rhythms and flows of all life. Understanding becomes a more dynamic process of orchestrating individuals and communities amid natural laws, typically guided by the wisdom of elders who keep such understanding moving from one generation to the next (Cowan, 2008). Ultimately, words fit into sentences, which fit into paragraphs, which fit into stories, and so forth - the threads of reality synchronize to promote long-term survival in healthy ways, rather than to create misalignments and troubles as described in the beginning of my argument. Break a thread in the tapestry, and the fabric weakens and sometimes tears. As Seminole elder, Susie Billie, attests, "We were always taught to try to keep the heritage and traditions because that was the strength of the land or the earth" (Wall, 1993: 91). In Native life, the past connects integrally to the future and leaders serve as bridges for meaning to travel the path intact.

Living as if all of life is integrally connected instills a consciousness that embraces equality, inclusion, and community more than hierarchy, exclusion, and egocentrism. All parts of reality contain valid perspectives that only together comprise the whole. Thus, "the relationship between grandparents and grandchildren is one of the most critical elements of Indian culture" (Mander, 1991: 213). Similarly, every child is a child of a whole community in African Bantu culture (Fu-Kiau & Lukondo-Wamba, 1988). In the words of Hoh elder and grandmother, Leila Fisher, "all children are my children" (Wall & Arden, 1990:72) - an exemplary embodiment of consciousness grounded in a metaphysic of holistic living systems. Without the Sacred Circle as foundation, it is far easier to become self-serving, ethnocentric, human-centric, and so forth.

Epistemological: Interdependent, Dynamic Understanding

Mitakuye Oyasin, 'We Are All Related,' personifies the integrative expression of what Indian people perceive as Community. Understanding the inclusive nature

Embedded spirituality also manifests in various combinations of metaphysics, epistemology, and ethics, creating many integral ways of living in harmony with the world.

of this perception is key to the context in which traditional Indian education occurs. Context is essential in education and determines both the meaning and application of teaching and learning. (Cajete, 1994, p. 164)

Native people ideally live in a world bubbling with life and potential, communicating and interacting freely, engaging myriad adventures and insights along the way. Epistemological keys to access these benefits are found by paying close attention to both the micro and macro threads that connect what is seen and unseen. "There's only one price I ask you to pay - and, I'm sorry, but it's a very high price. I ask you to pay the price of attention," (Wall & Arden, 1990: 49). These words of Ojibway elder, Eddie Benton-Benai, illuminate substantive differences between an epistemology of interdependent, dynamic understanding and typical Western-world education of compartmentalization and specialization. As Gregory Cajete describes:

In Indigenous community everyone was a teacher, and everyone, at one time or another, was a learner. By watching, listening, experiencing, and participating everyone learned what it was to be one of the People, and how to survive in community with others. Learning how to care for one's self and others, learning relationships between people and other things, learning the customs, traditions, and values of a community: all of these understandings and more were the daily course of Indigenous education (1994:176).

By embodying this way of knowing, we are more likely to avoid pitfalls that derive from Western tendencies to talk more than listen and to restrict learning to formally designated people and times. By contrast, with an epistemology grounded in interdependence and dynamism, learning comes from all directions and times (cf. Dames, 1992; Meadows, 1990).

Following in the footsteps of the first cornerstone, the second emphasizes naturally unfolding processes of development. Unlike other species, humans must figure out for themselves what it means to be human. We have to discover and develop identities, purposes, talents, agendas, and so forth. When natural law is fundamental to life - to uphold rather than to circumvent or evade - human and societal development evoke a practical spirituality, where experiences and lessons gathered over time reveal a wholeness to life (e.g., Brown, Jr., 1999). Thus, learning continually dives below surface appearances to discern subtle but vital patterns (e.g., Glassman, 1998). Life becomes inherently empirical, not because books tell us so, but rather because we employ means of understanding that reveal the practical importance of natural law and the rich tapestry of living systems.

Because of its metaphysical grounding in holistic living systems, learning is more naturally dynamic than it would otherwise be, involving syntheses of multiple sources across multiple points in time (e.g., Wheatley, 2002). For a species whose defining characteristic is learning, there are few boundaries to understanding such as book covers and classroom walls. Furthermore, learning tends to avoid the otherwise common pretense of pretending to have all the answers (cf. Argyris, 1991; 2002). Instead, it retains the vibrancy of curiosity and the wisdom of patience to let patterns of meaning reveal themselves in their own due time (cf. Bassett, 2005). It makes little sense to hurry the process - the key is to remain aware and mindful at all times. Thus, competence is needed to attend vigilantly to what is unfolding in the present (Black Elk & Lyon, 1990) without becoming overly distracted by the past or future (Tolle, 1999). Socially, this means listening to each and every person - not just to supposed authority figures - to discern the value that each adds to the fabric of community (e.g., Zimmerman & Coyle, 1996).

Ethical: Principled, Pro-Active Behavior

Native wisdom tends to assign human beings enormous responsibility for sustaining harmonious relations within the whole natural world rather than granting them unbridled license to follow personal or economic whim. It regards the human obligation to maintain the balance and health of the natural world as a solemn spiritual duty that an individual must perform daily - not simply as admirable, abstract ethical imperatives that can be ignored as one chooses. (Suzuki & Knudtson, 1992)

Consciousness grounded in a metaphysics of holistic living systems and an epistemology of interdependent dynamic understanding tends toward action that is principled and pro-active. Separating natural reality from social reality becomes unwise. Conversely, treating all reality - people, animals, plants, minerals, oceans, forests, and so forth - responsibly becomes practical and vital instead of idealistic or tangential. Helping to create sustainable relationships among all forms of life becomes everyone's responsibility in the role of caretakers instead of controllers or consumers. For example, "To the Lakota, virtues such as humility, respect, sacrifice, and honesty carry a different weight and substance than they do in Western culture. For us these qualities are not so much elusive goals as they are essential parts of everyday life" (Marshall III, 2001: xiii). Levels of development are determined by how well we interact with the real world, not by how we re-act on paper-and-pencil tests or how elegantly we argue a favored view. "The most profound reason for existence of Life is that each person has opportunity to experience Life and to learn Self-Responsibility. ... When we teach the Self, we recognize the Spirit of Mother Life and learn to respect the Energies that birthed us all" (Storm, 1994: xiv).

In a community where all life is sacred, principled pro-active behavior does not therefore mean that we must agree with all others or support the decisions of others. To the contrary, it thrives on realizations that nature needs diversity; that natural forces rise and fall; and that particular beliefs and values support life better than others. Storms in life are inevitable but when they come, we learn to act responsibly rather than to retreat into self-serving behavior. Principled pro-active behavior requires understanding conditions that support community, not just locally and currently, but among all life (e.g., Underwood, 2000) including life to come (i.e., future generations). "In our way of life, in our government, with every decision we make, we always

Table 2
Leadership Tendencies that Promote Innovative Learning (2)
Metaphysical Foundation – Holistic Living Systems:
1. *Systemic Visions.*
Leadership that manifests from clear, uplifting visions of collective well-being.
Epistemology of Collective Participation – Interdependence and Dynamism:
2. *Zooming In & Out.*
Leadership that balances detail with pattern, accounting not only for majority perspectives but also for outliers.
3. *Knowledge Webs.*
Leadership that weaves together myriad interpretations from all relevant directions into meaningful, energizing storylines.
4. *Living Libraries.*
Leadership that architects real-time advantages by seeking and using state-of-the-moment knowledge.
Ethics of Strategic Anticipation – Principles and Proactivity:
5. *Source of Values.*
Leadership that takes responsibility and initiative for employing principles that bring to life systemically healthy values.
6. *Expanding Care.*
Leadership adept at bridging today's possibilities with tomorrow's realities in increasingly inclusive ways.
7. *Mindful Action.*
Leadership that transcends pitfalls and sustains innovation by orchestrating potentialities with improvisational spirit.

keep in mind the Seventh Generation to come" (Oren Lyons, Onondaga elder, in Wall & Arden, 1990: 68). Thinking and acting in ways that are likely to sustain a healthy world and to enable quality of life for future generations are essential.

Leaders as Emergent Agents of Sustainable Innovative Learning

A healthy human mind respects the gifts of life - all nature gives life. There is no word for "nature" in my language. Nature, in English, seems to refer to that which is separate from human beings. It is a distinction we don't recognize. ... I would urge the whole concept of nature be rethought. Nature, the land, must not mean money; it must designate life. Nature is the storehouse of potential life of future generations and is sacred. ... Western society needs to prioritize life-supporting systems and to question its commitment to materialism. Spirituality should be our foundation. (Audrey Shenandoah, Onondaga; in Wall & Arden, 1990: 24-27)

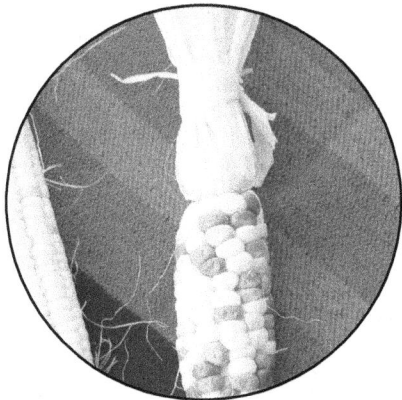

The central premise of my argument is that ample evidence supports the need for innovative learning on the part of today's leaders - if not all people - and that the philosophical cornerstones associated with an embedded spirituality provide a strong foundation for this to happen in a sustainable way. To complete the connections between embedded spirituality and sustainable innovative learning, however, we must understand how each cornerstone described above creates leadership tendencies to engage innovative learning. The degree to which leadership embodies an embedded spirituality, the more likely it is that participation and anticipation will emerge as natural leadership competencies to promote innovative learning. Although

certain outcomes in any leadership situation are unpredictable, certain tendencies - as depicted in Table 2 - are arguably more likely than others to arise from each cornerstones.

On a foundation of embedded spirituality, knowledge acquisition is a living process, consistently enacted in day-to-day community life (cf. Isaacs, 1993). It is not just church on Sunday or a new year's resolution in January that matters. To the contrary, the process tends toward a living library of knowledge that organizational members infuse with insights, interpretations, anticipations, in an ongoing, real-time manner (cf. Cowan & Adams, 2008). Each person is a vital contributor to, and steward of, the living library. In addition, customers, clients, investors, suppliers - all stakeholders - become valued sources of input. As a consequence, flows of knowledge become self-organizing and continually evolving, more like Facebook or Twitter than like a traditional, archived Dewey-decimal system (cf. Spender, 1996). Such knowledge-acquisition processes hold true potential for innovative learning and provide opportunities for wisdom rather than just knowledge (cf. Sternberg, 1998). The challenge of enriching leadership in such ways resides not only in reframing knowledge acquisition to be participatory, but also in providing technology to enable the focus to be anticipatory.

Assembling knowledge in a living library is one leg of a three-legged structure for innovative learning. If organizations cannot create effective ways to realize the potential of diversity, innovative learning will likely suffer. Assembling a living library, therefore, becomes a necessary but insufficient condition. The second leg involves ways of accessing the knowledge in real time, whenever and wherever needs arise. Cultures such as those mentioned earlier perhaps have an advantage in this regard over traditionally designed organizations because of their less mechanistic patterns of interaction among themselves as well as with their environments (e.g., Cowan, 1995). A helpful way to illuminate healthy access is to consider the difference between knowing what we know, which tends toward innovative learning, and knowing on a need-to-

know basis, which has long been the typical organizational approach.

A living library enables knowing what we know so that we can use what we know prior to threats, rather than only in reaction to them. With a living library, we increase anticipation within a system without having to justify particular reasons for knowing what we know. Thus, a process that might otherwise appear inefficient in the short-run, becomes an asset over time as people learn to participate and to anticipate. Somewhat like Special Operations forces, organizations can therefore become better prepared to handle threats and/or opportunities as they appear on the horizon, without knowing details in advance. Alternatively, in a "knowing-on-a-need-to-know" system, participants tend to wait until crises or opportunities arrive before they realize them and seek knowledge. For example, many people wait until their health is threatened before treating it responsibly. Differences such as these lie at the heart of what Botkin, Elmandjra, and Malitza (1979) claim mainstream organizations and societies need to address.

The third leg of this system for handling knowledge more collectively (cf. participation) and proactively (cf. anticipation) involves acting in ways that are consistent with a living library. This leg highlights the integrity and often courage needed to be consistent with what one stands for, rather than merely thinking and talking about doing so. Possessing a living library and using it in ways that enable innovative learning provide essential feedback to guide and sustain the system. Chiefs of native communities seem to recognize these connections more readily than others do

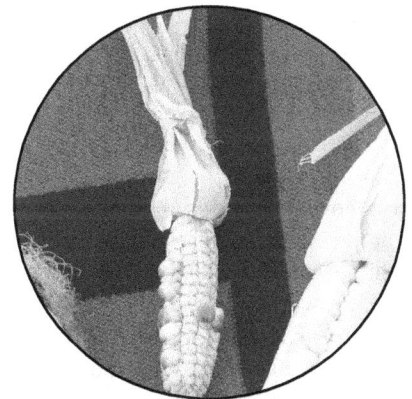

(Cowan, 2008), leading them to promote rituals and ceremonies as ways not only to practice such processes but also to increase the likelihood of remembering to act wisely when relevant needs and opportunities approach. The difference between knowing what to do and actually doing so remains a troublesome gap in Western education and society alike (Pfeffer & Sutton, 2000). Schools and organizations tend to emphasize knowing about, but frequently lose sight of the follow through needed to use one's knowing (cf. Lehrer, 2006). What leaders gain from an embedded spirituality is increased seamlessness between knowing the talk and walking the talk. Thus, native people tend to employ practical questions such as, "will this activity put food the table during the upcoming winter" (Little Coyote, 1994). In other words, they tend to avoid acquiring excess baggage that has no connection to sustainable life.

Acting on real-time knowledge in a living library presents a challenge for the design and operation of many organizations (cf. McGregor, 2005). Nevertheless, processes tending toward that direction are arising in exemplary companies such as Gore (Deutschman, 2004), IDEO (Nussbaum, 2004), and Montefiore Children's Hospital in New York (Labarre, 2002). In each of these three, knowledge is assembled, accessed, and employed in ways that are reasonably participatory and anticipatory. Movement in this direction requires appropriate leadership. It also requires creating uniquely supportive cultures (e.g., Brown & Isaacs, 2005; Wheatley, 2005) to share and support such values. To the degree that leaders possess an embedded spirituality, my argument suggests that the chances for such outcomes increase. Leaders who embrace the value of all life and build systems to give voice to all members arguably have the best chance of harnessing innovative learning in today's world, thus providing the greatest likelihood of a healthy world for coming generations. Adding embedded spirituality to conversations of leadership and leadership development can help to illuminate subtle but practical and important terrain for organizations and communities to evolve wisely in a turbulent world. Leaders who believe that sustainable innovative learning is important to such conversations are the stewards needed to help transform the world into a healthier and more supportive home for all life.

References

Adler, M. (1985). *Ten philosophical mistakes*. New York: Macmillan.

Argyris, C. (1991). Teaching smart people how to learn. *Harvard Business Review, 69*(3), 5-15.

Argyris, C. (2002). Double-loop learning, teaching and research. *The Academy of Management Learning and Education, 1*(2), 206-218.

Aristotle. (1963; original 322 B.C.). *Metaphysics* (Richard Hope, Trans.). Ann Arbor, Michigan: University of Michigan Press.

Bassett, C. (2005). Emergent wisdom: Living a life in widening circles. *Revision, 27*(4), 6-11.

Black Elk, W., & Lyon, W. S. (1990). *Black Elk: The sacred ways of a Lakota*. San Francisco: Harper.

Botkin, J. W., Elmandjra, M., & Malitza, M. (1979). *No limits to learning: Bridging the human gap*. New York: Pergamon.

Brown Jr., T. (1999). *The science and art of tracking: Nature's path to spiritual discovery*. New York: Berkley Books.

Brown, J., & Isaacs, D. (2005). *The World Cafe: Shaping our futures through conversations that matter*. San Francisco: Berrett-Koehler.

Cajete, G. C. (1994). *Look to the mountain: An ecology of indigenous education*. Durango, Colorado: Kivaki Press.

Capra, F. (1996). *The web of life: A new scientific understanding of living systems*. New York: Anchor Books.

Capra, F. (2002). *The hidden connections*. New York: Doubleday.

Cowan, D. (1995). Rhythms of learning: Patterns that bridge individuals and organizations. *Journal of Management Inquiry, 4*(3), 222-246.

Cowan, D. (2007). Don't move until you see it.: Searching for intellectual maturity. *Journal of Management Inquiry, 16*(2), 174-178.

Cowan, D. (2008). Profound simplicity of leadership wisdom: Exemplary insight from Miami Nation Chief Floyd Leonard. *International Journal of Leadership Studies, 4*(1), 51-81.

Cowan, D., & Adams, K. (2008). Talking circles, leadership competencies, and inclusive learning: Expanding the frame of business education. *Journal on Excellence in College Teaching, 19*(2&3), 135-165.

Crowley, V. (1998). *Celtic wisdom: Seasonal rituals and festivals*. London: Thorsons.

Cruden, L. (1998). *Walking the maze: The enduring presence of Celtic spirit*. Rochester, VT: Destiny.

Dames, M. (1992). *Mythic Ireland*. New York: Thames and Hudson.

Davis, S., & Botkin, J. (1994). *The monster under the bed*. New York: Touchstone.

Davis, S., & McIntosh, D. (2005). *The art of business*. San Francisco: Berrett-Koehler.

Deloria, V. (2003). *God is red*. Golden, CO: Fulcrum Publishing.

Deutschman, A. (2004). The fabric of creativity. *Fast Company*, December, 54-62.

Feuerstein, G. (1997). *Lucid waking*. Rochester, VT: Inner Traditions International.

Fu-Kiau, K. K. B. (1991). *Self-healing power and therapy: Old teachings from Africa*. New York: Vantage.

Fu-Kiau, K. K. B., & Lukondo-Wamba, A. M. (1988). *KINDEZI: The Kongo art of babysitting*. New York: Vantage.

Glassman, B. (1998). *Bearing witness*. New York: Bell Tower.

Hall, E. T. (1994). *West of the thirties: Discoveries among the Navajo and Hopi*. New York, Doubleday.

Havel, V. (1994). A troubled quest for meaning. *The Cincinnati Enquirer* (Forum section, Sunday July 10, pp. F1-F4).

Hurst, D. K. (1991). Cautionary tales from the Kalahari: how hunters become herders (and may have trouble changing back again). *Academy of Management Executive, 5*(3), 74-86.

Isaacs, W. N. (1993). Dialogue, collective thinking, and organizational learning. *Organizational Dynamics*, Fall, 24-39.

Kuhn, D. (2001). How do people know?. *Psychological Science, 12*(1), 1-8.

Labarre, P. 2002. Strategic Innovation: The Children's hospital at Montefiore. *Fast Company*. Accessed on March 5, 2009, at www.fastcompany.com/magazine/58/innovation.html.

Leader to Leader Institute. (2004). *Be-know-do: Leadership the Army way (adapted from the official Army leadership manual)*. San Francisco: Jossey-Bass.

Lehrer, J. (2006), How we know. *Seed*, September, 68-73.

Little Bear, L., & Heavy Head, R. (2004). A conceptual anatomy of the Blackfoot word. *Revision, 26*(3), 31- 38.

Little Coyote, S. (1994). Personal communication.

Lyons, O. (1991). *The faithkeeper Oren Lyons* (video). Cooper Station, NY: Mystic Fire Video. PRODUCER & DIRECTOR NEEDED INSTEAD OF LYONS

Mander, J. (1991). *In the absence of the sacred: The failure of technology and the survival of the Indian nations*. San Francisco: Sierra Club Books.

Marshall III, J. M. (2001). *The Lakota way: Stories and lessons for living*. New York: Viking Compass.

Maybury-Lewis, D. (1992). "Tribal wisdom: Is it too late for us to reclaim the benefits of tribal living?. *Utne Reader*, July-August, 95.

McGregor, J. (2005). The architect of a different kind of organization. *Fast Company*, June, 66-70.

Meadows, K. (1989). *Earth medicine*. Rockport, MA: Element.

Meadows, K. (1990). *The medicine way*. Rockport, MA: Element.

Neihardt, J. G. (1991). *Black Elk speaks: As told to John G. Neihardt* (audio, read by John Contreras). Berkeley, CA: Audio Literature.

Nussbaum, B. (2004). The Power of design. *Business Week*, May 17, accessed July 27, 2006, www.businessweek.com/print/magazine/content/04_20/b3883001_mz001.

Pennick, N. (1996). *Celtic sacred landscapes*. London: Thames and Hudson.

Pennick, N. (1997). *The sacred world of the Celts*. Rochester, VT: Inner Traditions International.

Pfeffer, J., & Sutton, R. I. (2000). *The knowing-doing gap: How smart companies turn knowledge into action*. Boston: Harvard Business School Press.

Rosch, E. (1978). Principles of categorization. In E. Rosch & B. Lloyd (Eds), *Cognition and categorization*, 27-47. Hillsdale, NJ: Lawrence Erlbaum.

Spender, J. C. (1996). Making knowledge the basis of a dynamic theory of the firm. Strategic *Management Journal, 17*, Winter (special issue), 45-62.

Sternberg, R. J. (1996). *Successful intelligence: How practical and creative intelligence determine success in life*. New York: Simon & Schuster.

Sternberg, R. J. (1998). A balance theory of wisdom. *Review of General Psychology, 2* (4), 347-365.

Sternberg, R. J. (2003). WICS: A model of leadership in organizations. *Academy of Management Learning and Education, 2*(4), 386-401.

Storm, H. (1994). *Lightningbolt*. New York: Ballantine Books.

Suzuki, D., & Knudtson, P. (1992). *Wisdom of the elders: Honoring sacred native visions of nature*. New York: Bantam Books.

Toffler, A. (1970). *Future shock*. New York: Random House.

Tolle, E. (1999). *The power of now*. Novato, CA: New World Library.

Underwood, P. (1991). *Who speaks for wolf: A Native American learning story*. Bayfield, CO: A Tribe of Two Press.

Underwood, P. (2000). *The great hoop of life, vol. 1: A traditional medicine wheel enabling learning and for gathering wisdom*. San Anselmo, CA: Tribe of Two Press.

Underwood, P. (2002). *Three Native American learning stories: With information about the nature of a learning story*. Bayfield, CO: A Tribe of Two Press.

Waldman, C. (1999). *Encyclopedia of Native American tribes* (rev. ed.). New York: Checkmark Books.

Wall, S. (1993). *Wisdom's daughters: Conversations with women elders of Native America*. New York: Harper Collins.

Wall, S., & Arden, H. (1990). *Wisdomkeepers: Meetings with Native American spiritual elders*. Hillsboro, OR: Beyond Words Publishing.

Wheatley, M. (1992). *Leadership and the new science*. San Francisco: Berrett Koehler.

Wheatley, M. (2002). *Turning to one another: Simple conversations to restore hope to the future*. San Francisco: Berrett-Koehler.

Wheatley, M. (2005). *Finding our way: Leadership for an uncertain time*. San Francisco: Berrett-Koehler.

Whiteman, G., & Cooper, W. H. (2000). "Ecological embeddedness." *The Academy of Management Journal, 43*, 1265-1282.

Wilber, K. (1995). *Sex, ecology, spirituality: The spirit of evolution*. Boston: Shambhala.

Wilber, K. (2003). *Kosmic consciousness: The Ken Wilber sessions* (compact disk set). Boulder, CO: Sounds True.

Wind, Y., & Crook, C. (2005). *The power of impossible thinking*. Upper Saddle River, NJ: Wharton School Publishing,.

Zimmerman, J., & Coyle, V. (1996). *The way of council*. Ojai, CA: Bramble Books.

Zohar, D. (1997). *Rewiring the corporate brain: Using the mew science to rethink how we structure and lead organizations*. San Francisco: Berrett-Koehler.

Footnotes

(1) See Leader to Leader Institute (2004) for a description and explanation of the "be, know, do" foundation of leadership development. The cornerstones employed here are similar to defining characteristics (Rosch, 1978), initial conditions (Adler, 1985), strange attractors (Wheatley, 1992), and hidden connections (Capra, 2002), each of which frames a system's identity. For detailed examples of Native identity, see chapter 12 in Mander (1991).

(2) The structure of these ideas derives not only from the cornerstones of embedded spirituality outlined in Table 1, but also from a blend of two other sources. One is Botkin, Elmandjra, and Malitza's (1979) framework of participation and anticipation as components of innovative learning. The other is the triadic leadership structure (e.g., Leader-to-leader Institute, 2004) of being (cf. metaphysics), knowing (cf. epistemology), and doing (cf. ethics).

Three Haiku

Michael Sheffield

the muffled strike
of a wood-splitters ax—
morning mist

around the tree roots
compost of a century
only inches deep

morning fog
above the hills
a promise of blue

Two of the haiku (on left) were previously published in *Geppo: Journal of the Yuki Teikei Haiku Society*. The haiku on the right was previously published in *Haiku Poets of Northern California Newsletter*. Photo: Jürgen Werner Kremer

Transformative Leadership

From Domination to Partnership

Riane Eisler and Susan Carter

During his campaign, and now as U.S. President, Barack Obama's rallying cry has been consistent: leadership for change. Certainly, in our rapidly changing world, a world of escalating environmental, economic, and social crises, leadership for change is urgently needed.

But the underlying question, particularly for those of us committed to transformative change, is: change from what to what? A related question is: what kind of leadership can bring about *real* change

Riane Eisler is president of the Center for Partnership Studies (http://www.partnershipway.org/) and is best known for her international bestseller *The Chalice and The Blade: Our History, Our Future* and other books on the partnership system identified by her research. Her most recent book is *The Real Wealth of Nations: Creating a Caring Economics*, hailed by Archbishop Desmond Tutu as "a template for the better world we have been so urgently seeking." Dr. Eisler is cofounder of the Spiritual Alliance to Stop Intimate Violence (http://www.saiv.net/), teaches at CIIS, and can be reached at center@partnershipway.org.

Susan Carter is an Associate Professor at the California Institute of Integral Studies, San Francisco, CA, where she teaches in the Transformative Leadership and Transformative Studies graduate programs, as well as the Philosophy and Religion/Women's Spirituality graduate programs. She has developed courses with action, experiential, and community engagement components, which are structured to expand the dynamic possibilities of academic studies and collaborative community activism/social change work. She may be contacted at scarter@ciis.edu.

– transformative rather than simply surface change?

These critical questions are central to a new focus on Partnership Studies we developed for the California Institute of Integral Studies' Transformative Leadership graduate degree program. Our aim has been to offer a new framework that not only addresses these questions but also empowers students to go deeper and further in the development of their individual potentials, particularly their capacities as "partnership leaders."

By partnership leaders, we mean two things. First, using leadership to inspire rather than control, to engage others and empower others. Second, using leadership to accelerate the shift from what one of us, Eisler, has identified as a domination system to a partnership system.

We have been teaching online courses in Partnership Studies since January 2008. The four courses that constitute the main Partnership Studies offerings place both leadership and transformation in a larger historical and social context.

The students who have taken these classes have engaged in deep dialogue as well as intense study on both a theoretical and practical level. Many have been deeply affected, both personally and in their career and leadership paths.

One PhD student reported that: "The

Partnership concentration is proving to be the most worthwhile and transformative educational opportunity I've encountered. It presents practical, accessible and holistic solutions to the most urgent challenges and myriad problems we face on a personal, interpersonal, national and global scale. I am excited to continue growing with this material and using it throughout my life - enabling me to be an even more effective leader and the best social change agent I can be."

Another wrote us that: "As an activist and community leader, I am thrilled to have the opportunity to study such powerful, transformational theories as addressed in this class. . . This class is a must for anyone with a penchant for leadership, politics, and change."

One of the great joys of our work has been coming into contact with women and men interested in probing issues not generally taken into account in conventional discussions of fundamental social change. They are eager to go deeper, to even venture into emotionally charged terrain that is rarely explored, such as the link between the private sphere of family and other intimate relations and the public sphere of politics and economics – and how these relate to urgent global problems such as violence and poverty. Above all, they are excited to apply the new system of social classifications that is the framework for these courses to better understand what kinds of cultures support, rather than impede, the realization of our great human capacities for caring, consciousness, and creativity: the partnership system or the domination system.

Holistic Social Categories

When most of us think of social systems, the categories that spring to mind are right or left, religious or secular, Eastern or Western, capitalist or communist, North or South, or industrial or pre- or post-industrial. The problem is that none of these categories describe whole social systems. None of them describes the totality of a society's family, educational, religious, political, and economic institutions and its guiding system of values. And it's only when we examine societies from a perspective that takes all this into account that we can see two underlying configurations that transcend all the old social categories.

One configuration is all too familiar. It's what research identifies as a domination system, a way or structuring relations – from intimate to international – as top-down rankings of control. The other is a configuration that can support a more equitable, peaceful, and sustainable way of life: a partnership system (Eisler, 1987, 1995, 2000, 2002, 2007).[1]

No society orients completely to either system. But the degree to which it does has profound effects on all relations – from intimate to international. And it profoundly affects how leadership is constructed and exercised.

If we look at Khomeini's Iran, Hitler's Germany, Stalin's U.S.S.R., the Samurai of pre-industrial Japan, and the Masai of nineteenth- and early- twentieth century Africa from this larger systemic perspective, we can see that while they are different in many respects, they all have striking commonalities. They are characterized by strong-man rule in both the family and the state or tribe, rigid

male dominance, and a high degree of institutionalized violence, from child and wife beating to chronic warfare. They are also societies where so-called masculine values, such as toughness, strength, conquest, and domination are given high social and economic priority, as in the emphasis on weapons and wars. So-called feminine values, such as caring, compassion, empathy, and nonviolence are, along with women, relegated to a secondary, subservient sphere cut off from the "real world." These four characteristics – strong-man rule, rigid male dominance, institutionalized violence, and the devaluation of women and the "feminine" (whether in women or men) – are the core configuration of the domination system.

In partnership-oriented societies, whether in the family, the workplace, or society at large, so-called feminine qualities and behaviors, whether they reside in women or men, are not only held in high esteem but also incorporated into the operational values system.

In the domination system, caring for those who are not members of one's in-group, as well as caring for our environment, are not priorities. On the contrary, the whole system is based on using the environment and people to benefit those on top. Relations conform to in-group versus out-group rankings in which difference – beginning with the most fundamental difference in our species between male and female – is equated with superiority or inferiority, being served or serving, dominating or being dominated.

By contrast, in the partnership system difference is valued, as in the ideal of the more pluralistic society now gaining cur-

rency. In partnership-oriented societies, whether in the family, the workplace, or society at large, so-called feminine qualities and behaviors, whether they reside in women or men, are not only held in high esteem but also incorporated into the operational values system. There is a more democratic and egalitarian social structure, equal partnership between women and men, and less built-in violence, as it is not needed to maintain rigid rankings of domination.

The partnership configuration also transcends differences of time, place, and level of technological development. It can be found in technologically undeveloped tribal societies, such as the Teduray of the Philippines studied by University of California anthropologist Stuart Schlegel (1998), agrarian societies such as the Minangkabau of Sumatra studied by University of Pennsylvania anthropologist Peggy Reeves Sanday (2002), and technologically advanced industrial societies such as the Nordic nations.

If we look at our past through the analytical lens of these two underlying possibilities for structuring beliefs, institutions, and relations, we see that the tension between the partnership and domination systems underlies all of cultural history. It has affected all aspects of our lives, including how power is defined and exercised.

Today, there are strong trends worldwide toward the partnership system. All the modern progressive movements have challenged domination backed by force and fear. This is the common thread in the eighteenth- and nineteenth-century "rights of man," anti-slavery, anti-monarchist, socialist, pacifist, and feminist movements. The twentieth-century anti-colonial, anti-war, civil rights, women's rights, and economic justice movements are also part of a this larger movement: the movement to create a world in which – be it in our global family of nations or in our individual families – principles of partnership rather than domination and submission are primary. Indeed, although we have not been taught modern history from this perspective (and should be), underneath its many complex currents and cross-currents lies a powerful movement towards the partnership system, countered by fierce resistance and periodic regressions (Eisler 2000, 2007).

A key aspect of the movement toward partnership is a redefinition of power and leadership. Much has been written about the "new leadership." But to clearly understand what it is and what the hidden obstacles to it are, we have to go deeper: to areas that are not generally discussed.

If we closely look at the literature on new leadership, again and again we see that a major element is the adoption of behaviors such as empathy, listening, caring, nurturing, and consulting that are stereotypically considered feminine. When we say stereotypically feminine (or masculine), we mean just that. We are not talking about anything inherent in women and men. Some men are very caring and empathic. And some women are not.

In fact, historically when women have made it to the top of domination hierarchies, they often have felt they must show every inch of the way they are not too "soft" or "feminine." What we are talking about is the equation in dominator systems of "real masculinity" with domination and violence, the view that caring, empathy, and other "soft" traits are appropriate only for women, and the belief that women and "effeminate" men cannot be good leaders.

We also want to emphasize that there are characteristics stereotypically considered masculine that are positive, and are important leadership qualities. Assertiveness, logical thinking, venturesomeness, and courage are stereotypically considered masculine – and they are admirable, whether found in women or men.

But women have as a group been socialized for traits and activities men also need to be socialized for in a complex world where leaders who inspire, nurture, and empower others are essential. This is why, as John Naisbitt and Patricia Aburdene (1985) put it in their book, *Reinventing the Corporation*, more corporations are today taking advantage of women's "softer" leadership qualities. It is also why enlightened male leaders are embracing this more inspiring and caring, rather than authoritarian and coercive, leadership style.

Center for Partnership Studies www.partnershipway.org

Partnership Trends in Leadership, Management, and Social Policy

There are obvious differences between women and men. But much that is considered masculine and feminine is our heritage from earlier times when women were strictly barred from leadership and power. Accordingly, anything considered feminine was basically held in contempt. Philosophers like Nietzsche took this view, and it was central to 20th century fascism – a major regression to proto-domination.

Another part of this dominator heritage was the belief that a fear-based, institutionally insensitive, and all too often abusive and dehumanizing leadership and management style is a requisite for social order and economic productivity. This view still persists in many cultures and subcultures worldwide, even though increasingly this leadership and management style is recognized as a barrier rather than spur to social order and economic productivity.

Today's management and organizational development literature proposes that, particularly in the postindustrial knowledge economy, a new leadership and management style based on respect, accountability, and empowerment is needed for economic productivity, indeed, economic survival. We are told that effective leaders and managers are not cops or controllers whose commands must be unquestioningly obeyed, but people who facilitate, inspire, and elicit from others their highest productivity and creativity.

This is a partnership management style that models caring rather than coercion. While some leaders – male and female – have always recognized its effectiveness, it is becoming more prevalent today because of the rising status of women, and thus of qualities and behaviors associated with femininity, such as nurturance and empathy.

Nordic nations such as Finland, Sweden, and Norway are particularly interesting in connection with what happens as women make strong gains. In a very short time during the 20th century these nations changed from poor, famine-ridden countries to prosperous, creative economies.[2] A major reason is that their policies give value and fiscal support to the stereotypically feminine work of caregiving. Measures such as universal healthcare, childcare allowances, elder care, and paid parental leave, as well as major investment in education from early childhood on, helped produce the higher quality human capital that transformed them into prosperous nations.

It is sometimes said that the Nordic success is due to their homogeneity and relatively small size. But many homogeneous, smaller, and even wealthier, nations do not have these policies.

The Nordic nations always rank on the top of the U.N. Human Development Reports as well as the World Economic Forum's (WEF) Global Competitiveness ratings (WEF, 2009). These nations also pioneered the first peace studies courses. They pioneered laws against physical punishment of children in families. They pioneered a strong men's movement to disentangle male identity from violence. They also pioneered what we today call industrial democracy: team work in factories rather than turning human beings into mere cogs in the industrial machine. Environment initiatives, such as the Natural Step, came out of these nations. And of course women in the Nordic nations occupy a far higher percentage of political leadership positions than anywhere else in the world: between 40 and 50 percent.

None of this is random or coincidental. It is part of the cultural configuration characteristic of the partnership rather than domination system.

One reason that gender relations have to be considered in social analyses is the following dynamic. As the status of women rises, so also does the status of traits and activities stereotypically associated with the feminine: soft rather than hard values, empathy, caring, nonviolence – and men then find it more possible to embrace these values without feeling threatened in their status.

While these societies are not ideal, having moved closer to the partnership side of the partnership-domination continuum has had enormous benefits, vastly improving people's quality of life. They have much lower crime rates and hence lower prison and judicial costs than the U.S. They have longer life spans and much lower poverty rates. And they have a more caring ethos – sometimes referring to themselves as "caring societies."

Finding Solutions to Poverty – and Connecting the Dots

The term quality of life as an indicator of social and economic health itself is a manifestation of the movement toward partnership. However, quality of life measures are only slowly, and in most cases not even that, using data that focuses attention to the connection between how a culture structures the roles and relations of the two halves of humanity – women and men. Nor do these measures generally separate statistics by gender or take into account norms and policies for childcare.

Photo: Jürgen Werner Kremer

Studies show a strong connection between a society's quality of life and the construction of gender roles and relations. A three-year study carried out by one of the authors (Eisler) and her colleagues under the auspices of The Center for Partnership Studies dramatically showed this connection (Eisler, Loye, & Norgaard, 1995). Titled *Women, Men, and the Global Quality of Life*, it was based on statistics collected by established international agencies from 89 nations. Although it is generally assumed that the quality of life for nations is determined by how rich or poor they are, the material wealth of a country does not necessarily translate into a high quality of life for its people. Much depends on whether the distribution of wealth and the governing

system of values orients to dominator or partnership values. And a great deal depends on the status of women.[3]

Understanding – and spreading awareness of – these systems' dynamics is a major challenge for progressive leaders. If we do not meet this challenge, we will continue to hear a great deal of talk about poverty, overpopulation, environmental degradation, and violence, but we will not get to major root causes of these problems – and hence to critical interventions that can make real change.

Let's look at poverty. Given the fact that billions of people are destitute and hungry, this is a key question addressed by the UN Millennium Development Goals and other studies and programs searching for ways to reduce poverty levels. While there are good ideas and tools in many of these studies and programs, there is amazingly little attention given to the fact that worldwide the mass of the poor and the poorest of the poor are those who do the bulk of the caring work: women. And even when this issue of women's poverty is addressed, it is largely through microlending or tiny loans to women. These loans do help with subsistence, and to some degree empower women. But they do not address the systemic problems that keep women, children, and ultimately also men poor. So they are largely palliatives rather than real solutions.

For long-term, lasting, solutions to poverty, we need a new partnership economics (Eisler, 2007). Developing a fully integrated partnership economics includes changing corporate charters, addressing the North and South economic power imbalance, ensuring corporate social responsibility, moving toward the triple bottom line, and other economic reform mechanisms and regulations currently under discussion. But it must go beyond this. It must begin with an in-depth look at the dominator elements of current economic models, rules, and practices, including the systemic devaluation of the most essential human work: the work of caring and caregiving still generally relegated to women for little or no pay.

A first step toward a new partnership economics is changing how we measure productivity. Today GDP counts activities that take life and destroy our natural habitat – coal burning and cleaning up the environmental damage it causes; selling cigarettes and the medical costs and funeral costs of the health damage they cause. These destructive activities are on the positive side of GDP. But not only do these measures put negatives on the positive side; they do not include the unpaid caregiving work primarily performed by women in the "informal" economy, be it in their homes, or in their communities as volunteers – even though these services contribute most to everyone's social well being.

What is not counted is not considered in making economic policy. We have to change this, and we need leaders who are capable of making these connections and develop new partnership economic models and rules that give visibility and value to the stereotypically feminine work of caregiving.

Patterns of Intra-Family Economic Relations

Another important step toward partnership economics is to include in economic analyses intra-household economic allocation. There are many reasons for the strong correlation of gender inequity with a generally low quality of life – for example, female education contributes to child welfare as well as a more competent work force. But one of the main reasons for the correlation between a low quality of life and a low status for women in poorer world regions is the skewed pattern of intra-family resource allocation characteristic of societies that orient to the domination system.

As a result of this skewed pattern of intra-family resources, in parts of Southeast Asia girls are given less food, health care, and education than boys. This, of course, not only severely affects and limits the lives of girls and women; it also negatively impacts the capacity of half the population, which in turn negatively impacts social and economic development. But there is more. It is well-known that children of malnourished women are often born with poor health and below-par brain development. Nutritional and health care discrimination against girls and women therefore robs all children, male or female, of their birthright: their potential for optimal development.

It also affects us all by impeding human and economic development. It directly affects a nation's workforce capacity. It affects children's and later adults' ability to adapt to new conditions, level of frustration, and propensity to use violence. It impedes solutions to chronic hunger, poverty, and armed conflict.

So while males derive advantages from gender inequity, these advantages are outweighed by the disadvantages. Indeed, the toll of the domination system on men is huge – from being maimed and injured in constant wars to being controlled and oppressed by those above them. But, ironically, much of men's suffering stems from the very control dominator systems give them over those below them: women.

There are other negative manifestations of skewed patterns of intra-family resources allocation characteristic of the domination system, as shown by empirical studies of cultures where challenges to traditions of domination have not yet made significant inroads. As Judith Bruce and Cynthia B. Lloyd report in their 1997 analysis, "there is considerable empirical evidence across diverse cultures and income groups that women have a higher propensity than men to spend on goods that benefit children

A key aspect of the movement toward partnership is a redefinition of power and leadership.

and enhance their capacities" (Bruce & Lloyd, 1997). How much higher this propensity can be is shown by Duncan Thomas. In his report "Intra-Household Resource Allocation," he notes that "in Brazil, $1 in the hands of a Brazilian woman has the same effect on child survival as $18 in the hands of a man" (Thomas, 1990, p. 635). Along the same lines, Bruce and Lloyd found that in Guatemala "an additional $11.40 per month in a mother's hands would achieve the same weight gain in a young child as an additional $166 if earned by the father" (Bruce & Lloyd, 1997).

Of course, there are men who give primary importance to meeting their families' needs even in rigidly male-dominated cultures. Often, however, men in these societies are socialized to believe it's their prerogative to use their wages for non-family purposes, including drinking, smoking, and gambling, and that when women complain, they are nagging and controlling. As Dr. Anugerah Pekerti, Chair of World Vision, Indonesia, notes, some fathers seem to have no problem putting their own immediate desires above the survival needs of their children.[4]

So on top of the well-known fact that much of the humanitarian aid to developing nations winds up in the hands of elites who deposit it in Swiss banks, build mansions, and otherwise line their pockets with it, even when funds go directly to the poor, these too often end up not really benefiting their families, or ending patterns of poverty.

Yet traditional economic models, whether capitalist, socialist, or communist, are based on the assumption that the male "head of household" will expend the resources he controls for the benefit of all family members – and that therefore the bulk of aid to people in the developing world should be given to men. Although this is slowly beginning to change, it has been an assumption in conventional economic analyses, which typically treat the household as a unit.

Another common assumption behind policies that channel aid to men is that the male head of household is the prime provider. This assumption too ignores the reality that in many of the poorest world regions women, not men, are the primary providers for the nutrition, health, and other vital aspects of life of their families (Dwyer and Bruce, 1988, p. 526). Even the recent microlending programs that largely target women only provide minimal amounts – a few dollars for tiny enterprises that barely keep women and their children alive – while the bulk of loans go to businesses owned by male elites.

In most African nations, for example, women do the subsistence farming that keeps their families alive. Yet they get only a small fraction of international development aid, and often laws and customs further discriminate against them so that they're not even allowed to inherit land and may be left destitute when their husbands die (Agarwal, 1995).

While the effects on the overall quality of life of these generally ignored patterns of gender inequity are most dramatic in the less affluent regions of the world, they are hardly exclusive to it. The same patterns are evident (except in most economic analyses) in wealthier nations such as the United States, where they become most visible when families break up. Studies have shown that in the United States men's living standards in the first year after divorce go up, whereas those of women and children dramatically drop (Weitzman, 1985; Eisler, 1977).

And there is more. If we look at our environmental crises, we see that the devaluation of nature's life-support activities and women's life support activities is all of one dominator cloth. We can't just tack on environmental responsibility to a fundamentally imbalanced system.

In short, there are underlying systemic reasons for the strong correlation between gender inequities with a generally low quality of life that leaders must consider. One is the hidden system of gendered valuations we looked at earlier in which anything associated with women is given less value than anything associated with men. A second is that male-superior/female-inferior relations are a mental map that

can easily be transferred to all social and economic relations, making relations where members of one group control and are served and members of another group are controlled and do the serving appear normal and even desirable.

These are emotionally charged issues. But they must be taken into account by today's leaders if they are to forge solutions to entrenched patterns of poverty, injustice, and environmental despoliation worldwide.

Ending Traditions of Violence

Power relations in families are not just personal matters. They affect – and are in turn affected by – the larger culture. This reality has important implications for leaders who want to move to a more peaceful world.

We today know from neuroscience what psychologists have long told us: that children's early experiences are crucial to their mental and emotional development, profoundly affecting what they consider natural, normal, and moral as adults. We are learning that what happens in children's early relationships is crucial to nothing less than the neural patterns of their brains, which continue

Photo: Jürgen Werner Kremer

to develop after birth.

This new knowledge must be taken into account by leaders dedicated to building a less violent, more equitable world. Here again, the analytical lens of the partnership-domination continuum is a powerful tool. And here again leaders have the challenge of addressing emo-

tionally charged issues that must be dealt with if there is to be a realistic approach to cutting through cycles of violence.

As mentioned, dominator-oriented cultures are characterized by a high degree of built-in, socially condoned, and even idealized violence. This violence is part of system's maintenance processes. And family violence is where people first learn that it is acceptable, and even moral, to use force to impose one's will on others.

We're sometimes told violence is just human nature – it's in our genes. Certainly humans have the potential for violence. But findings from sociology, psychology, and neuroscience show that a major factor in whether people are violent is what happens during a child's early formative years. Children who are abused, or who observe others in their families being abused, not only often become abusers; their brain neurochemistry also tends to become programmed for fight-or-flight at the slightest provocation.

Fortunately, not everyone from such families becomes violent. In fact, there are those who not only reject violence in their own intimate relations when they grow up but become dedicated to helping to change traditions of violence.

However, it is in our families and in other intimate relationships that we either learn respect for others' rights or we learn to accept abuse and violence. While some people transcend early experiences of violence and injustice in these primary human relations, many carry them into other relations, and come to see violence and injustice simply as "the way things are."

Throughout history the most violently despotic and warlike societies have been those where violence, or the threat of violence, is used to maintain domination of parent over child and man over woman. We see this connection all too vividly in cultures that spawn terrorists where women and children are literally terrorized into submission. And this correlation is not limited to so-called "religious fundamentalists." It was present in the European Middle Ages, in Hitler's Germany, and in Stalin's Soviet Union.

To build cultures of justice, safety, and democracy, we need families where women and men are equal partners, where children learn to act responsibly because adverse consequences follow from irresponsible behavior, where they learn to help and persuade rather than hurt and coerce, where they're encouraged to think for themselves.[5]

Progressives urgently need a new integrated social and political agenda that takes into account both the so-called public sphere of politics and economics and the private sphere of family and other intimate relations. Recent books by one of the authors (Eisler, 2002, 2007) detail this agenda for family, economic, political, and environmental relations, as do a number of articles cited in the endnotes (Eisler, 2005, pp. 27-28).[6]

Spiritual and religious leaders have a particular opportunity, and responsibility, here. Sadly, for much of recorded history religion has been used to justify, even command, violence against women and children. This is still the message of many so-called fundamentalist religious leaders today – leaders who, not coincidentally, also advocate "holy wars." And even progressive religious leaders to our day are largely silent on the global pandemic of intimate violence.

Consider these statistics: Each year 40 million children under the age of 15 are victims of family abuse or neglect serious enough to require medical attention (U.N., 2001). A woman is battered, usually by her intimate partner, every 15 seconds in the United States (U.N., 2001). In China and India, millions of baby girls are killed or abandoned by their parents. "Honor" killings by other family members result in the death of thousands of women in Middle Eastern and South Asian countries (Forum, 2003). Twenty percent of women and 5-10 percent of men have suffered sexual abuse as children (WHO, 2002). Each year, an estimated two million girls undergo some form of female genital mutilation (U.N., World's Women, 2000). Child abuse alone costs the United States economy $94 billion a year (WHO, 2004). If we look at these numbers, we see that while intimate violence gets far less media attention than casualties in wars, the numbers of children and adults whose lives are blighted, and all too often taken, by this violence are actually greater than the more publicized losses.

Only if leaders, particularly leaders with moral authority, take a strong role in making this violence visible, and work to stop it, can we realistically build cultures of peace. Engaging these leaders is an aim of the Spiritual Alliance to Stop Intimate Violence (SAIV, 2009).

Center for Partnership Studies www.partnershipway.org

Partnership Structure: Myth and Reality

We have touched on some rarely discussed matters that need attention if we are to make a significant, and lasting, impact on the chronic problems plaguing our world. We have briefly looked at the social structures the domination system has had in place for centuries. We will now briefly look at what partnership structures really look like.

There is often misunderstanding about the kinds of structures that will support more mutuality and caring in human relations and a more responsible and caring attitude toward our natural environment. Some people believe that what is needed are completely flat organizational structures. Others think that what's needed are organizations where everything is run by consensus.

But neither a completely flat organization nor mandatory consensus makes for a partnership structure. This is important to keep in mind, since when these extreme ideas don't work out in practice — as they usually don't — people will say this failure proves rigid controls from the top must be reinstated.

Although there's a great deal of consultation among all members in a partnership organization and some group decisions are made by consensus, this doesn't mean that all decisions in a partnership-oriented culture must be agreed to by everyone. In fact, requiring that all decisions be approved by each and every person can lead to a new kind of domination. When consensus is mandated, one person can make it impossible for anything to get done.

While linking rather than ranking is a key partnership principle, to be effective all organizations and structures need some hierarchies or lines of responsibility. But these hierarchies are very different in a partnership context. They are *hierarchies of actualization* rather than *hierarchies of domination*. In hierarchies of actualization, managers – as well as teachers, parents, and others in leadership positions – function as mentors and helpful facilitators. And everyone can assume a leadership role, not just those who are "entitled" to it.

In short, partnership leaders empower rather than disempower others. And by modeling this leadership style in all aspects of life – from families to the family of nations – partnership leaders inspire others to develop their consciousness and creativity both for themselves and those around them.

Developing Partnership Leaders

All this takes us back to the Partnership Studies graduate program focus and to the leadership development program we have been developing. Clearly partnership leaders are not interested in simply giving orders that must be obeyed, or coming in with projects that have to be implemented from the top down. They model leadership not as a unique gift of special people but as an activity that everyone can engage in successfully. They are, of course, also interested in their own development. But they see their development as part of everyone else's development, rather than elevating themselves at the expense of others, as in the old domination systems. And they are effective.

This more participatory and empowering leadership style is modeled by President Barack Obama. But one leader or even a number of leaders in policy making positions is not going to effectuate the shift from domination to partnership systems. For this shift we need many dedicated partnership leaders at all levels, in all fields, in all world regions.

The students in our Partnership classes are gaining the knowledge and skills to be active co-creators of our future. These classes offer them opportunities to reflect on the impact of traditions of domination on their own lives and cultures, as well as to apply partnership principles in practical ways.

For example, one student developed a partnership audit to assess and improve the policies and practices of a major U.S. city – and implementing the recommendations in this audit then became a goal of a number of civil society groups. Other students became interns for The Center for Partnership Studies (www. partnershipway.org). One became active in the Spiritual Alliance to Stop Intimate Violence, connecting with grassroots groups and working on a project to offer new parents concise and accessible information on partnership parenting – nonviolent, non-coercive, more effective ways to set limits for children while supporting the development of their self-esteem and potentials. Another is writing a manual for groups that want to start partnership communities.

A number of students are using their knowledge of partnership systems to inform the writing of their theses and dissertations. One master's degree student is applying the framework of partnership in her thesis work on a specific Andean population with whom she lived for a number of years and which practices deep reciprocity. A doctoral student, working in the field of medicine, is looking to partnership systems for ways in which partnership can positively impact patient care outcomes and improve nurse satisfaction in a time of dire nursing shortages.

Another student began development of a multi-media presentation for young men on partnership systems. Several other students are teaching partnership in community colleges and universities, thus multiplying and amplifying the reach of partnership education – and

with this, the development of more partnership leaders.

These women and men show that once the principles of partnership leadership and the realties of the tension between the partnership and domination systems as two underlying human possibilities are understood, we can each play an important role in creating the conditions that support the development of our innate human capacities for love and friendship, for caring and caregiving, for creativity, for sensitivity to our own real needs and those of others. Systemic change requires taking into account the whole social system, going beyond what are conventionally considered

A first step toward a new partnership economics is changing how we measure productivity.

the "important economic and political issues." It requires leaders who understand that real leadership in our time must empower rather than disempower, that we need everyone's creativity and participation, and that working together, we can lay solid foundations on which to build a more sustainable, equitable, and peaceful world culture.

Footnotes

(1) For detailed descriptions of these systems and the tension between them throughout history, see Eisler (1987, 1995, 2000, 2002, 2007).

(2) See Pietila (2001). For a more detailed discussion of these social and economic dynamics, see Eisler (1987, 2002)

(3) Eisler, Loye, & Norgaard (1995). This study was published simultaneously with the 1995 United Nations Women's Conference in Beijing. The nine measures we used to assess the degree of gender equity were: the number of literate females for every 100 literate males; female life expectancy as a percentage of male life expectancy; the number of women for every 100 men in parliaments and other governing bodies; the number of females in secondary education for every 100 males; maternal mortality; contraceptive prevalence; access to abortion; and based on measures used by the Population Crisis Committee (now Population Action International), social equality for women and economic equality for women. The thirteen

measures used to assess quality of life, were: overall life expectancy; human rights ratings; access to health care; access to clean water; literacy; infant mortality; number of refugees fleeing the country; the percentage of daily caloric requirements consumed; Gross Domestic Product (GDP) as a measure of wealth; the percentage of GNP distributed to the poorest 40 percent of households; the ratio of GDP going to the wealthiest versus the poorest 20 percent of the population; and as measures of environmental sensitivity, the percentage of forest habitat remaining, and compliance with the Convention on International Trade in Endangered Species.

When we explored the relation between the gender equity and quality of life variables with descriptive, correlational, factor, and multiple regression analyses, we found a strong systemic correlation between these two measures. These findings were consistent with our hypothesis that increased equity for women is central to a higher quality of life for a country as a whole, and that gender inequity diminishes the opportunities and capabilities, not only of women, but of the entire population. The link between gender equity and quality of life was confirmed at a very high level of statistical significance for correlational analysis. 61 correlations at the .001 level with 18 additional correlations at the .05 level were found, for a total of 79 significant correlations in the predicted direction. This link was further confirmed by factor analysis. High factor loadings for gender equity and quality of life variables accounted for 87.8 percent of the variance. Regression analysis also yielded significant results. An R-square of .84, with statistical significance at the .0001 level, provided support for the hypothesis that gender equity is a strong indicator of the quality of life.

(4) Dr. Anugerah Pekerti, Chair of World Vision, Indonesia, states, "When the fathers are asked why they smoke cigarettes instead of buying food for their hungry children, they say, 'We can always make more children'" Kristof (1998, June 11).

(5) For a more detailed discussion, see Eisler (2002, 1996).

(6) See also http://www.rianeeisler.com.

References

Agarwal, B. (1995). *A field of her own: Gender and land rights in South Asia*. Cambridge: Cambridge University Press.

Bruce, J. & Lloyd, C.B. (1997). Finding the ties that bind: Beyond headship and household. In L. Haddad, J. Hoddinott, & H. Alderman, (Eds.), *Intrahousehold resources allocation in developing countries: Methods, models, and policy*. Baltimore: International Food Policy Research Institute and Johns Hopkins University Press.

Dwyer, D., & Bruce, J. (Eds.). (1988). *A home divided: Women and income in the third world*. Stanford, CA: Stanford University Press.

Eisler, R. (1977). *No-fault divorce, marriage, and the future of women*. New York: McGraw-Hill.

Eisler, R. (1987). *The chalice and the blade: Our history, our future*. San Francisco: Harper & Row.

Eisler, R. (1987, 1995). *The chalice and the blade: Our history, our future*. New York: HarperCollins.

Eisler, R. (1995). *Sacred pleasure: Sex, myth, and*

the politics of the body. San Francisco: Harper Collins.

Eisler, R. (1996). Human rights and violence: Integrating the private and public spheres. In Kurtz, L. & Turpin, J. (Eds.), *The web of violence*. Urbana, IL: University of Illinois Press.

Eisler, R. (2000). *Tomorrow's children: A blueprint for partnership education in the 21ˢᵗ century*. Boulder, CO: Westview Press.

Eisler, R. (2002). *The power of partnership: Seven relationships that will change your life*. Novato, CA: New World Library.

Eisler, R. (2005). A progressive alternative to the 'morality-values-family' regressive agenda. *Conscience*, Summer 2005.

Eisler, R. (2007). *The real wealth of nations: Creating a caring economics*. San Francisco, CA: Berrett-Kohler Publishers, Inc.

Eisler, R., Loye, D., & Norgaard, K. (1995). *Women, men, and the global quality of life*. Pacific Grove, CA: The Center for Partnership Studies.

Forum. (2003). *Ending violence against women: human rights in action* (Proceedings of Forum, December 10, 2003). Boston, MA: JFK library.

Kristof, N.D. (1998, June 11). As Asian economies shrink, women are squeezed out. *New York Times*.

Naisbitt, J., & Aburdene, P. (1985). *Re-Inventing the corporation: Transforming your job and your company for the new information society*. New York, NY: Warner.

Pietila, H. (2001). Nordic welfare society –A strategy to eradicate poverty and build up equality: Finland as a case study. *Journal Cooperation South*, Number two, February 2001, 79-96.

Schlegel, S. A. (1998). *Wisdom from a rain forest*. Athens, GA: University of Georgia Press.

Sanday, P. R. (2002). *Women at the center: Life in a modern matriarchy*. Ithaca, New York: Cornell University Press.

The Center for Partnership Studies (CPS). http://www.partnershipway.org

The Spiritual Alliance to Stop Intimate Violence (SAIV). http://www.saiv.net

Thomas, D. (1990). Intra-household resource allocation. *Journal of Human Resources* 25, No. 4, Fall 1990, 635.

United Nations (U.N.). (2000). *Study on the status of women*. Retrieved from http://www.un.org/womenwatch/daw/

United Nations (U.N.). (2000). *The world's women 2000: Trends and statistics*.

United Nations (U.N.). (2001). *We the children: Meeting the promises of the world summit for children*. Retrieved from http://www.unicef.org/specialsession/about/sg-report.htm

Weitzman, L. (1985). *The divorce revolution: The unexpected social and economic consequences for women and children*. New York: Free Press.

World Health Organization (WHO). (2002). *World report on violence and health*. Retrieved from http://www.who.int/violence_injury_prevention/violence/world_report/en

World Health Organization (WHO). (2004). *Violence creates huge economic cost for countries*. Retrieved from http://whqlibdoc.who.int/publications/2004/9241591609.pdf

World Economic Forum (WEF). (2009). *Competitiveness reports*. Retrieved from http://www.weforum.org/en/media/publications/CompetitivenessReports/index.htm

walking through
the greys and browns
of November woods,
I stop to thank
an especially scrawny tree

Linda Galloway

Previously published in *Modern English Tanka*

Photo: Jürgen Werner Kremer

Bringing Your Spiritual Practice Into Your Work

Roger Harrison

A major reason for writing this paper is my desire to encourage readers to bring their spirituality and their spiritual practices into their work in the world, and to endeavor to create in their organizations a climate hospitable to others who may wish to do so.

Most professionals are reluctant to speak in our organizational and work lives about our spiritual practices. I have experienced a similar reluctance in myself. I have been an organization development consultant during all of my working life, over fifty years so far (See Harrison, 1995, 1995a). I have written a good deal about organizational cultures, issues of consulting practice and the like, but I, too, have avoided express-

Roger Harrison, Ph.D. In a career spanning fifty years, Roger Harrison, consultant, educator, and theorist, has influenced nearly every phase of the birth and growth of the discipline of organization development (OD) - from its beginnings within the sensitivity training seminars of the sixties to its current role in shaping the way organizations respond to the present chaotic times. He is recognized internationally for his conceptual contributions to that field, and his writing has shaped the way two generations view change in organizations. Always sensitive to hidden aspects life in organizations, in recent years Dr . Harrison's work has gone in new and radical directions. Examples are his work on releasing the power of love in organizations and his current preoccupation with bringing one's spiritual practice into one's work. Contact information: 1760 Compass Blvd., Freeland, WA 98249, (360) 331 7646/Phone & Fax, rogerh@whidbey.com.

ing myself in print regarding how I have tried to integrate my spiritual practice with my professional life. However, a major passion during my half century as an organization development consultant has been to encourage my clients and colleagues to pay attention to the shadow aspects of organizational life, those that are usually unspoken. For example, in the face of warnings by some colleagues about possible consequences to my reputation, I first wrote in the eighties about the importance of accessing the power of love in organizations (Harrison, 1983, 1987), So far as I can tell, my professional image suffered no harm as a result. Now it seems appropriate to take another step in that direction, and, perhaps, to contravene another taboo by exploring ways of bringing one's spiritual practice into one's work.

I have for a long time been interested in possibilities for knowing and doing that are not mediated by our five senses. Examples of these might be

* The uses of "positive thinking," affirmations, synchronicities, and other approaches to manifesting desired outcomes of our projects and intentions.

* Non-traditional approaches to healing, such as Reiki (Haberly, 1990), energy healing, healing prayer, and Kything (Savary & Berne, 1988).

* Using kinesiology (muscle testing, pendulum, dowsing, etc.) to access inner knowing.

* Communicating and partnering with non-physical guides, allies and helpers, including various forms of meditation and prayer.

In recent years a growing number of books, articles and web sites devoted to these matters have surfaced, and people are becoming more open in speaking about their beliefs and practices in working with things unseen. Now, having given talks on this subject to other consultants that were warmly received, it's time for me to write about it.

First let me say a little about what I mean by spirituality and spiritual practice. Here are three definitions from a paper on teaching spirituality to business students (Pielstick, 2001).

Oxford Desk Dictionary, The quality or condition pertaining to the nonmaterial, higher moral qualities, or the sacred.

Mitroff & Denton (1999, p. xv), The desire to find ultimate meaning and purpose in life, and to live an integrated life.

King (cited in Gibbons, 2000, p. II-13), The search for direction, meaning, inner wholeness, and connectedness to others, to non-human creation and to a transcendent.

When I use the term, I am referring to experiences of the sacred, and to practices that may lead to such experiences.

Present in each of us there is an inherent drive to move toward wholeness in the course of our evolution as persons. In consequence, if both one's work and one's spiritual life are vital and alive, one will begin to experience a need to bring them into congruence with one another, and, indeed perhaps to speak freely about them. In the work cultures many of us live in, there are perceived and sometimes real costs and consequences of being open about these matters.

The views I present are based upon my own experience as a consultant, mostly with private sector organizations. During that time, I have come increasingly to value wholeness in my inner life and my work experiences. I have found that the inner and outer can each enrich the other when I bring them together.

Along with many members of my generation, I was trained early to avoid conversation about sex, religion, or politics in most social gatherings. In the circles in which I now move, the prohibition against references to sex has been relaxed much more than those regarding politics, religion and spirituality. I have

more—doing the latter with as much empathy as I can muster—and when I am able to avoid judgmental thoughts. Come to think of it, that holds true for conversations about most things!

In this paper, I intend to describe my personal journey in bringing my work and my spiritual life into harmony and congruence with one another. I know from others who have entered into such an undertaking that they have had similar or analogous results to mine. I suspect many others have taken on a similar task to mine, have proceeded in very different ways, and have obtained equally satisfying results. I believe that whatever one's religious or spiritual path, it can offer rich opportunities within it to affect one's work and one's workplace for the better, whether that be through following one's basic spiritual principles and values in work, through prayer and meditation, or through engaging in specific practices intended to furnish guidance, assistance and blessing to the practitioner and to others by spiritual means. I hope that my story may be useful to others by opening up options and possibilities to consider from the

in a family of scientists and engineers, I had little spiritual or religious training. Although I often experienced feelings of awe and transcendence in the natural world, I did not interpret those feelings as in any way spiritual. My awakening to things spiritual began when, in my early forties, I realized on a transatlantic flight to the US from my then home in London that I had no burning ambitions or desires, having come pretty close to achieving most of those I started with, both in my personal life and in my work as a consultant. I mused that if the aircraft were to fall into the ocean, there would not be too much left unfinished, and yet I expected to live as long again as I had to that point. The journey behind me was full of bumps, dead ends and steep places; the one ahead seemed flat and rather empty.

The time was the early seventies; I had heard something of eastern spiritual practices, but knew nothing about such matters, except that meditation was reputed to be an antidote to the feelings of meaninglessness and emptiness that I was then experiencing. Having always been highly achievement oriented, I

In working with organizations, I now tend to think of myself as establishing a co-creative partnership with the essence, spirit, or soul of that organization.

found in conversation with others that a surprising number of people are engaged in bringing their spiritual beliefs, values and practices into their work, but they often feel isolated and alone or lonely in doing so. We have come, it seems, to identify the principle of religious and spiritual freedom with a prohibition against speaking publicly about what we do and think in our spiritual lives. Perhaps one reason for that is the fear that one will be judged by others who do not agree with one's utterances, even, especially, when the others do not voice their negative judgments.

I probably push the boundaries on speaking about my spiritual practice more than many do, and what I have found is that such conversations go along best when I talk less and listen

standpoint of one's own understandings and inclinations.

I shall also suggest here that practices for working with the being, soul or essence of an organization in a spiritual way can be of value to consultants and leaders, and indeed to any member of an organization. I shall give examples of such work from my own practice, and suggest ways in which the work may be approached.

I shall also briefly address the difficult issue of when and how to share one's own spiritual practices and experiences with others. That is a growing edge for me, and indeed, writing this paper is part of my learning process in that regard.

My own experiences and practices

Having had a very secular upbringing

began a spiritual search that over the next seven years included Transcendental Meditation, the Arica forty day training,[1] and a variety of other excursions into the esoteric. Then came a night in 1978 when I was walking home from a session at the Nyingma (Tibetan) Institute in Berkeley, wondering why all this searching was such a lot of work. It came to me that I had been striving to get into highly exalted states of consciousness, but I wasn't really what I thought of as a good person. I didn't always tell the truth; I viewed the law as something to be respected only when someone was watching. I was avaricious, striving to get at least my share, and often more than my share, in my business dealings. I seemed to be aiming for an advanced degree in the practice of spirituality, but

I hadn't yet passed Decent Personhood 101.

Starting then, my aspirations became more modest. I directed my attention to the basics of integrity, generosity, kindness and open-heartedness—often making progress, sometimes backsliding. I expect to continue that process, along with other spiritual practices I have encountered that serve me and others, for the rest of my life.

During the early nineties, when I was about 60, I began to work with an energy healer at a time when I was having a difficult time recovering from the termination of an intense love relationship. She introduced me to the use of flower essences for self healing, and to kinesiology as a way of communicating with my body as to which essences would benefit me at a given time. Wright (1988) describes both the use of flower essences and of kinesiology.

This work stimulated me to embark on an exploration of ways of receiving information from non-physical sources. I began with some success to use Wright's methods to complement my reason and my intuition in dealing with difficult issues in my consulting practice, as well as in my life generally. More recently I have expanded my understanding and my practice through study with David Spangler and the Lorian Association.

Wright provides detailed methods for obtaining practical guidance on whatever activity or project one is engaged in, through accessing a combined "team" composed of devas, nature spirits, "The White Brotherhood"[2] and one's higher self. Such a team may be enlisted for immediate assistance with health, business, relationship or other issues, or may be asked to enter into an ongoing relationship in support of an ongoing life issue or project.

David Spangler's work encompasses what he calls "incarnational spirituality," and includes a detailed cosmology. A central idea of incarnational spirituality is that while the material and non-physical realms are different in quality, the non-material is not "higher" and certainly not more sacred than humanity or the everyday material world we inhabit. David Spangler, through The Lorian Association, gives an online course specifically oriented to working with non-physical allies (2008).

Here are some experiences I've had with these approaches:

When I'm writing professionally I invite a connection to inner allies for

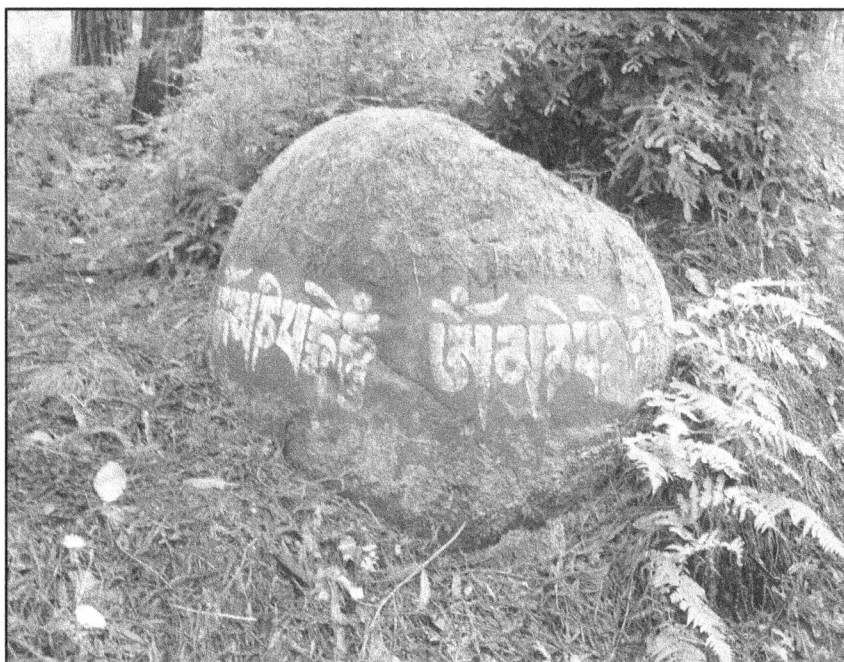

Photo: Jürgen Werner Kremer

inspiration and guidance, using the practices advocated in Machaelle Small Wright, 1990, 1997. While that connection is in place I may use a pendulum to test whether something I'm writing is understandable by my intended audience and likely to be well received. Working this way in co-creative partnership often leads to being "in the flow," a condition in which I often feel as though the material is being sourced elsewhere, although it is completely congruent with my own values and intentions. An example is the writing of my professional autobiography (Harrison, 1995) in which I was frequently assisted in moving through stuck places by establishing a co-creative partnership with unseen allies.

In my personal life I have had good results with similar approaches. My spouse and I have set up non-physical teams to assist us in such projects as these: deciding on relocating ourselves from the Bay Area to the Pacific Northwest; finding the right house to purchase; planning vacation trips; working with health issues; and deciding financial issues such as responding to requests from non-profits and from family members for financial support. If nothing else, the process of framing appropriate questions and focusing our attention on the details of these issues has enabled us to make better decisions. However, we believe we have received more support than that: when we work with the support of a non-physical team, we seem to be blessed with more than the usual number of fortunate synchronicities, in which events come together in ways that make our lives easier, safer and more successful. We also note that none of the decisions we have made in this way have turned out badly.

I have pondered the question of when to invite such guidance and when to avoid doing so. The stance I have come to take for myself is that I best serve myself and my clients when I limit myself to inquiring how best to do something, or which of several approaches will most likely lead to the result I or my clients want. I have not always limited my inquiry in this way, sometimes asking "should I do this or that?" and I know I can obtain answers to almost any question I ask. I have come to question the wisdom for myself of asking "should I or shouldn't I?" questions, unless I am first clear about my own intention in the matter: who or what I want to serve, or what desired state I want to achieve. I place these limits because I want to practice assuming personal responsibility for what I do in the world, although I am quite willing to seek assistance in the ways and means for doing what I have decided upon. However, there are times when I feel confused, helpless or dependent and do go beyond my self imposed limits on the questions I ask. When I do this, I am careful to be clear about who I am asking for guidance, because I want to increase the likelihood that what I receive will be for the highest good for all.

There is another reason why I find it useful to access spiritual forces for assistance with ways and means, rather than inquiring what one should do. I have found that the discipline of deciding what I want, and then making a clear statement of my intentions assists me in maintaining focus and direction. According to Wright (see her publications on working with "soil-less gardens," 1990, 1997, 2007) it greatly assists one's non-physical allies if one writes a concise, clear and unambiguous statement of "definition, direction and purpose" (DDP) for one's project before initiating an inquiry. I find that doing so also assists me greatly in removing ambiguity and inconsistency from my intention. My preferred practice is to write down a statement of intention for the project for which I want help. I try to be both specific and brief, so that I focus on the essence of my purpose and desired outcomes. As I move through a project, I will often come back to my DDP, ask myself whether it still represents my intention, and then change it if necessary. Having made a clear statement at the outset, I can use such a review to track my progress. I find it satisfying and encouraging to remember where I was at the outset in relation to my intended results, and see how far I've come.

Having developed a clear and precise statement of the essence of my intention, I then focus on that essence, and invite allies to join me, following Wright's suggested procedures (1990, 1997, 2007) or choosing some other process. For example, I may use processes I have learned from David Spangler's work on partnering with spiritual forces (Lorian Association, 2008). Wright's work is easier to apply, because she gives explicit and detailed directions for accessing assistance, and I am glad I could follow a set of explicit directions when I began my explorations into what initially seemed to me to be very esoteric matters. I have now had enough experience that I can venture beyond the somewhat rigid directions that Wright insists one follow, but I find working within Wright's framework to be quite comfortable.

Spangler gives the practitioner a lot more space to use one's own intuition, personal preferences and creativity in working with non-physical beings. Critical to Spangler's work with allies is developing and using one's "felt sense." Spangler has defined the felt sense as "A

Our spiritual life in an organization involves our values, our myths and our vision, all those ideas, images and emotions that together make up our sense of what it means to be a member of the organization.

capacity grounded in our bodies and felt as a physical sensation as well as a mental and/or an emotional one to identify and experience subtle forces, energies and beings... It is related to the familiar idea of a 'gut feeling' or a 'physical hunch.' This can be developed with practice and attention to what our bodies have to say about the world around us."[3] For me it means being open to associations, bodily senses, intuitions and imagery that may arise while I am focusing on my intention. When I sense the presence of an ally or allies, I then focus on my intention and my questions about the project and remain alert for what may come to me through my felt sense.

Spangler (2004, 2008) has also published a step by step process for manifesting desired outcomes, which I have found provides a useful and viable way of focusing attention and intention on a project. As noted above, it relies heavily on using one's felt sense, but it does so within a more formal structure. One thing I like about it is that the method provides a framework and process for becoming clear about one's intentions and desires, a feature that I find missing in Wright's work. One can thus start out from a place of less clarity and focus, and become much more clear as one goes through the process.

It's true that I do not always go through elaborate, highly structured processes when I want a bit of assistance. I will often use kinesiology to decide on the spur of the moment, some question that is puzzling me. Kinesiology lends itself to "yes" or "no," questions. In my case I make use of a pendulum because, like a number of others I have talked with, I find that if I use the kinesiology process advocated by Wright (1988) I get unreliable results. I also make use of a pendulum when I have set up a formal connection with allies and am seeking yes or no answers to questions about whether or not a particular act or course of action is likely to lead towards my intended outcomes.

When I first did this, I had to get over my prejudices about the kinds of people who use pendulums, or dowsing, as it's often called. However, the practice yields reliable results for me.

Like any practice that taps into one's intuitive knowing, outcomes are subject to influence by wish or fear on the part of the practitioner. That is why, when I am working on something important, I prefer to focus my intentions, and to invite allies who may protect the integrity of the process. It can also be helpful to ask someone else to check the answers I receive by repeating the process. For example, in making decisions about family matters, such as making charitable donations, making gifts or loans to family members, planning a trip, and so on, I invite my spouse, Margaret Harris, to join me and take an independent reading on the questions posed. On the infrequent occasions when we don't track one another, we then inquire more deeply into how each of us is interpreting the meaning of the question we have asked. Such a process is only appropriate, of course, when the second person is properly attuned[4] to the project or decision under consideration.

I have evolved theories and beliefs about how and why this all works, but I have to say that I hold them lightly—I don't pretend to really know. In spite of the fact that I come from a family of engineers, and much of my formal education was in the sciences, I do not feel greatly distressed by my lack of certainty. When exploring beyond the boundaries of what I think of as science, I use a kind of naïve empiricism; I believe one is doing well just to find practices that work reliably and produce desired results. Having found some such practices, I feel that it would be disempowering indeed not to use them, just because I don't have a scientific explanation for how they work. It would feel limiting to me not to explore and experiment with processes for which scientific explanations are lacking. How else are we to go beyond our current paradigms and world views?

Experiences in working with the soul of an organization

Since I have been a consultant to business organizations for such a long time, in trying to integrate my spiritual practices with my work it has seemed natural to look for ways in which connections with non-physical allies could support making good decisions in business. In this, I take as my starting point the idea that a good decision is one that serves the good of the whole. By "the whole," I mean something akin to the totality of the living systems that are impacted by a decision.

I have sometimes indulged myself in dreaming of a world in which we all enlist the assistance of non-physical beings when dealing with the very complex issues for which we cannot foresee all or even most of the consequences of our actions. I have occasionally had a vision of the Board of Directors of a company in a strategic planning session. They spend a few moments attuning themselves to the soul or essence of their business, and then, after staff presentations, followed by full discussion of the issues, they ask for guidance on the different aspects of their strategic plan. In my fantasy, they are sitting around the conference table tuning into their felt sense, or using kinesiology to ask, "Will it benefit the whole for us to downsize our business this year? Is it for the highest good for us to merge with one of our competitors?" And so on, each one reaching a sense of what is for the best,

Photo: Jürgen Werner Kremer

using their own approach to receiving information and guidance. When they do not agree, they deliberate further, then attune more deeply and try again. At the end of the day, off they go to their homes, secure in the knowledge that they have used all the resources available to them, seen and unseen, human and angelic, to ensure the future well being of their business and of the Earth!

My decision to focus on the good of the whole is based on values, not practicality. I do believe it is possible to receive assistance from spiritual allies in projects with a narrow or self-oriented focus—for example, making an advantageous investment. I have occasionally used spiritual connections to try to gain financially, and I have found that for me, it doesn't feel good to focus my work with the sacred on pecuniary gain, especially when that may occur at the expense of others. It is also true that the methods I use to receive information and guidance from non-physical realms are less subject to distortion by wish or fear when I can maintain a fairly detached attitude towards the outcome. Such detachment is difficult for me when my financial security is involved.

In working with organizations, I now tend to think of myself as establishing a co-creative partnership with the essence, spirit, or soul of that organization. When working in this way I will invite a connection with that essence and ask for information and assistance in my work.

The first time I experienced such a connection, it was through the agency of another consultant. We were both at a gathering in which the conversation turned to the difficulties several of us were having in bringing our spiritual lives into our work as consultants. This individual mentioned that he was able to do psychic readings of the organizations he worked with. I asked him if he could do a reading of one of my clients, an electric utility where I was having some difficulty in seeing how to move forward. He agreed, and asked me to lie down so he could put his hands on me. After a short time, he said he was getting an image of a giant, muscular being, similar to the one represented by Rodin's sculpture, The Thinker (c. 1880). This being was endeavoring to hold a heavy hammer aloft, but was strained to the limit of its strength by the hammer's weight. If the hammer should fall, destruction would follow, and the being would then have failed to keep a sacred trust.

I found this image provocative, although I could not imagine what it meant. The experience stuck in my mind, and some weeks later, I decided to take the risk of sharing the story with the Vice President for Engineering, in the hope that the image would mean something to him. To my utter amazement, he was able without hesitation to give me a meaningful interpretation. He told me that the company had decided some while ago to postpone investment in additional generating capacity, due to the high cost of capital. As a result, this old line utility, which, as business expanded in its territory, had grown up and prospered together with its customers, was dangerously stretched to meet the growing demand for electricity, causing fears of an area-wide blackout similar to the one in New York City in 1977.

Because my work was with Customer Service, I was not involved with the generating side of the business, so I had had no idea of this. As my work with the utility unfolded, I found the event and conversation helpful to me in better understanding the essence of the organization, with its strong dedication to traditional values of public service. It was also the first time I had an inkling that the idea that an organization had a "soul" might possibly be more than a metaphor.

A couple of years later, I had a powerful experience involving a possible non-physical being associated with an organization. I had been invited, together with my then partner, to a conference

being put on by the Findhorn Foundation, called "From Organization to Organism." The invitation came from Roger Benson, a co-leader of the Findhorn Community. Knowing of my work with organization culture (Harrison, 1972, 1987; Harrison & Stokes 1992)

Photo: Jürgen Werner Kremer

Roger asked if I would be willing to undertake a diagnosis of the Findhorn Community's organization culture, an invitation I was glad to accept, because the organization was so clearly different from those I had previously experienced.

Following the conference, my partner and I conducted numerous interviews with members of the community, including its leadership, its teaching staff, long and short time residents of the community, and one of its founders, Eileen Caddy. When the interviews were complete, we had about a day and a half to collate and do a content analysis of our data, and to create a presentation to the assembled community after dinner that evening.

This would have been plenty of time if the data had mapped nicely to the model of organization culture that I had by then been working with for years (Harrison & Stokes, 1992). We would not have been surprised when this very different community did not fit my model exactly, but we were not prepared for the degree of discrepancy we found. We tried to come up with a model that did fit the data, but found that quite difficult. This led to a difference of opinion between us as to whether we should go with a modified version of my original model or persist in coming up with a new one. Meanwhile, our available time was shrinking fast, and our anxiety was rising.

Finally, in some desperation, we resolved to seek help. From our interviews I knew that the community members often turned to the "Angel of Findhorn" for guidance. We went over to the Sanctuary, a circular room built for meditation that was fortunately unoccupied at the time, and I lay down in the center. I then asked the Angel of Findhorn to help me to understand the data we had collected and to create a model of Findhorn's organization culture. I lay quietly for a few minutes, and quite suddenly and clearly a model came into my mind, one very different from anything I had worked with before, and one that seemed to fit our data. As I recall, the work of organizing our interview findings then flowed along easily, and we were able to complete our flipchart presentation just as the bell rang for dinner. Following the meal we made our presentation to the assembled community members, whose comments on our offering by and large confirmed the congruence of our model with their lived experience of Findhorn's culture. (This event is described in Harrison, 1995, pp. 139-141).

Being semi-retired, I have not been practicing organization development professionally for a while, and am limited in the examples I can give from recent practice as a consultant. I have been a board member for non-profit organizations, however. I find that after so many years as a consultant, I tend to bring a consulting orientation to my board work. I can report that I have found it very helpful to establish connections with non-physical allies when faced with decisions as to how best to assist a board to move forward with its work. I have found such connections valuable in deciding when to confront and when to support, when my usefulness on a board is at an end, what is the right timing for raising an issue, which board tasks to volunteer for, how to address a difficult issue, and so on.

Allying oneself to the soul of one's organization

David Spangler (2004) has written of "inner citizenship," the spiritual aspects of being an American. He speaks of attuning oneself to the highest aspects of our country's collective being, and he describes the practice of living as a citizen in ways that are congruent with that vision. When I read Spangler's work on this,, my immediate thought was, "This idea is directly applicable to the spiritual aspects of one's relationship with an organization, whether as an employee, a manager, or a consultant." I have been inspired to build on his work so that it applies to the spiritual practice of living in an organization. (Spangler & Harrison, 2005)

Our spiritual life in an organization involves our values, our myths and our vision, all those ideas, images and emotions that together make up our sense of what it means to be a member of the organization. The aggregate of what is held on that level by all the organization members can be thought of as the collective psyche of the organization. Although that psyche has a good deal of consistency, it can also shift and change based on market events, management changes, the ups and downs of our own careers, and how fearful or powerful, successful or frustrated, contented or disaffected we may be feeling.

There is a deeper level yet that is not just a psychological one, but a spiritual level, a level of essence or soul. (In exploring the possibilities that may

open to us through sensing and working with the soul level of an organization, I ask that readers accept its existence as a proposition testable through experience, not as a matter of faith or authority.)

In some organizations it is fairly easy to arrive at a "felt sense" of the organization's soul. I remember in particular a visit I made to the Lima, OH plant of Procter & Gamble in 1986. The Lima, OH plant was P&G's first venture into using the "high-performance systems approach" elements of which are self-organizing teams and participative management. In this approach, everyone in the organization, especially those at the shop floor, is trained in the skills, understanding and processes they need to make their own decisions on behalf of quality and business success, and given the authority to do so. The flow of information and influence in the organization goes laterally, as well as up and down the

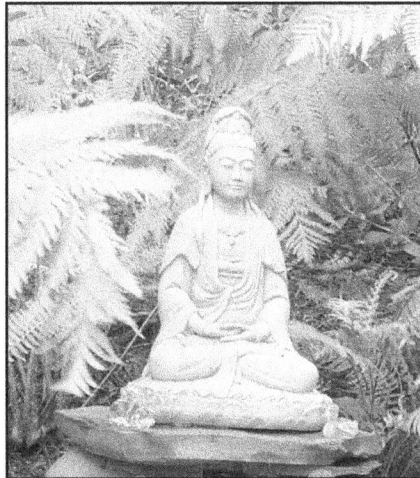

Photo: Jürgen Werner Kremer

hierarchy, instead of having all the ideas and commands flow from the top.

On my arrival at the plant, I was greeted by the Plant Manager, who had assembled a group of employees and managers to brief me and answer any general questions I had, prior to a plant tour. The first thing I noticed was that I couldn't tell the managers from the workers by the way they dressed. The second thing I noticed was that I couldn't tell the difference between management and workers by the way they talked, either. In my previous experience, workers have tended to talk about their jobs and about company policies which affect them; managers talk about technical sys-

tems, production goals, improvements they are endeavoring to make in the technical or people aspects, and the like. I experienced a palpable sense of good will and camaraderie in which everyone seemed to participate, a sense of caring and support that appeared not to be in conflict with lively competition between work teams on productivity and quality. I came away with a strong sense of what I now think of as the soul of the organization, which was characterized by love, service, cooperation, innovation and creativity, and which seemed to permeate all of its doing and being.

It is certainly true that many of us spend a great deal of our lives in organizations that seem to lack anything that we could characterize as "soul." And as we look from the outside at many organizations, some of whose names are household words, we find it difficult to imagine them as having a soul. Organizations can be ruthlessly exploitative, lacking in integrity, and seemingly without any kind of heart. Organizations may be confusing, full of contradictions, inconsistent and lacking in clear purpose, so as to defy our attempts to know their deeper essence.

It is with organizations as it is with individuals. We may be inconsistent, seemingly without purpose, hard hearted, and we may do evil. Yet there is always something deeper, finer, and more constant behind our behavior. The existence of soul does not depend on outer manifestations, and the latter may either reflect our soul or obscure it.

An organization's soul comes into being through human choice and will, initially that of the founders. It begins as a kernel of focused energy, around which additional energy can collect and achieve coherency and an organizational pattern or structure may form.[5] We may look for the genesis of the organization's soul in the founding story. Christina Baldwin in her wonderful book, Storycatcher describes a fine approach to doing this work (Chapter 8 in Baldwin, 2007)

As others join the organization and give their own energy and will to manifesting the organization's core purposes, collective mental, emotional and relational patterns evolve, which have both conscious and unconscious components.

These form the culture of the organization, which begins to exert a will of its own, felt by organization members as norms and pressures to behave, think and hold values that are congruent with the collective. These collective tendencies might be called the "personality" of the organization. It reflects the energies of organization members, and at the same time the collective is more than the sum of those energies. The corporate personality begins to act as a being with its own unique qualities.

Then the organization can, if it is sufficiently organized and attuned to being of service to life, hold the energy of the soul level. I think of the soul of an organization as expressing its will to do some kind of good—as Spangler puts it, to bring a blessing into the world. At this point, the organization's life transcends the will of the founders, and it is much more than the sum total of the organization's members. Soul generates life force. It is a nurturing field for the people in the organization, and to a lesser extent, its customers, suppliers, and the wider community. Thus it is a force for good, both within and without, and that to me is a reason why as organization members or consultants, we should wish to work in partnership with an organization's soul, because it represents the highest and best vision of the organization in its environment.

Organization soul can differ from the organization's culture and personality, which may be strongly affected by other human motives such as fear and greed, by the environment within which the organization operates, by technology, markets, business cycles and the like.

The focus of consultants, executives and managers in their efforts to change and direct the organization, and to enable it to deal with its internal and external problems and opportunities, is, I think, rarely directed towards the soul level of the organization. Usually, attempts to change and manage the organization are at the level of personality, culture, technology, markets and finances and the like. This is demanding enough for most people, and the organization's soul remains implicit and often unconscious. There are those who do concern themselves with the congruence between the organization's being, and its strategies

and tactics, and I believe there to be strategic benefits in doing so.

Strategic benefit is gained when we enlist the cooperation of an organization's soul in co-creative partnerships for the good of all, using whatever approaches are comfortable for us when working with spirit. The example I give above in which I invoked the Angel of Findhorn is a case in point.

It is possible to enter into active dialogue with the soul of an organization. Instead of treating the organization as a mechanistic environment that we—or anyone else—manipulate for our own ends, placing the full responsibility on ourselves for directing and "fixing" it, we can enter into a personal and intimate relationship with the system. Our role then becomes less that of a mechanic and much more that of a sensitive and receptive gardener, who endeavors to understand the unique growth patterns of each plant, shrub or tree, through the full range of its life cycle or evolutionary path. I suggest you try the exercise below:

1. Go within yourself in a brief meditation. See if you can get a felt sense of the presence of the soul or spirit of an organization with which you are associated. Be aware of any images, sounds, words, kinesthetic feelings or intuitive ideas that may arise that connect you with something that feels like the soul or spirit. Write these down.

2. Inquire of that being: What is your vision for this organization? What is your work to do in the world? What benefits are you meant to bring? Write down whatever comes in response to this question.

3. Ask: What interferes with this purpose? What is needed from me/us to support your evolution at this time? As before, take notes on what you receive.

Asking such questions can bring group members to a new and deeper understanding of their organization's purpose, and this understanding may enable them to "come back on track."

For example, in a recent Board retreat conducted by the author and Freya Secrest for a small non-profit, revisiting the founding moments of the organization resulted in the realization that both an educational and an activist thrust had been part of the founding vision.

As the organization had evolved, however, the educational mission came to dominate the consciousness of its members, and the activist aspect was forgotten. Remembering the original vision brought new energy and understanding into the Board, out of which new initiatives are have been undertaken.

It is important to understand that getting in touch with soul of an organization has consequences. The soul carries within it patterns for the transactions of the organization. When we draw upon that connection, we shall find ourselves moved to take on responsibility for other entities, not just engaging in transactional relationships with them. Soul business is business with integrity, and more than that, with a sense of the connectedness of all to all. One consequence of this, for example, is that if we tend to be preoccupied with the organization's internal issues, frequent enquiry of its organization's soul may direct our attention outwards towards the organization's relationships with its stakeholders.

Note that when we are connected to soul, the consequences of negative behavior become more potent. The energy of the soul level tends to magnify the impact of the organization's acts, for better or for worse, thus raising the costs to the whole of our doing harm.

The founding story is a good place to start looking for the organization's soul, but it is not static. Subsequent stories may become more pertinent. Different narratives give differing viewpoints on the soul. The original narrative may become too narrow a way of understanding the soul. Organizations develop wisdom and understanding over time. To me, however, it is usually crucial to an understanding of the essence of an organization to know the founding story, at least in outline. That is because, when the energies and impulses that brought the organization into being become overlaid or distorted by subsequent influences, personalities and events, those energies do not go away, but continue to have a presence. Losing touch with that presence is a kind of soul loss, and may contribute to organization members feeling that they have lost their way, and are in some way rootless and ungrounded. The founding story may become part of the Shadow of the organization, and may need once again to be brought into the open and made a conscious part of the organization's life.

Consider how organizational soul becomes autonomous from founders' souls. For example, the founders may incubate the soul of the organization. We not only look at the founders' intent, but also at how that intent might have evolved to the present day, given the circumstances that now exist. What were the deeper principles underlying their intent, principles that might lead to rather different conclusions and actions today, if we can become aware of them?

Organizations have two identities. The first is what the organization does in the world, e.g, offering goods and services. The second is the organization's ecology, the community in which it takes part. Both play a part in the ongoing evolution of the organization's soul. The soul doesn't stay apart on a higher plane and just beam good energy to the organization. It seeks to express its qualities as practically as it can, and those qualities manifest through behavior.

If our own behavior as managers, organization members, or even as consultants, is thoughtless or negative, we can cripple the soul in expression, e.g., through fostering a culture of fear, greed, personal ambition, narrow agendas, short sighted expediency, and so on. We are then expressing soul in a dysfunctional manner. There are forms of human expression that can bind the soul and prevent it from manifesting its qualities; the end result is that the soul is more or less crippled.

If we live in an organization where the governing principle is fear, it can result in binding the souls of those in the organization and the soul of the organization in very tight ways. The life energy of the soul can be weakened, obscured or diffused, but it is still present as a part of the organization's life and potential. When soul is obscured in this way, it often helps to look back at the organization's founding story for clues to the soul's qualities and capacities.

We can ask the organization, "Within the context of this organization, how can we nurture the greatest freedom, open up space for people to be more creatively expressive, more secure, more safe—things that release some of these bind-

ings." How that is best done depends on the nature of the organization: an army would do it differently than a consulting firm would; a partnership would be different than a multi-national corporation would; a non-profit would be different than a for-profit organization.

Organization soul brings a connection to a wider community of souls. The implication of such connections is that an organization's soul seeks ways of stimulating the organization to be a responsible player in the larger environment.

Soul vs Culture: Organizational culture is mostly transactional; soul is radiant, giving. It grows in the depth of its connections and availability of its energy if it is given a chance. The founding story of an organization can be rather narrow, e.g., "We'll make these goods and provide these services, and we'll make a lot of money." But other possibilities become evident to organization members through time that are beyond transaction, e.g., giving to the community. Organization soul can deepen by expressing its highest vision in a growing number of ways. It deepens through additional possibilities and capacities. Culture is what happens when you cope with the world. Soul is what you want to infuse into everything you do. Also, culture is specific and possibly measurable. Soul is not.

In mergers and acquisitions, we end up with "hybrid organizational soul," in the same way that we may evolve a hybrid culture. The more congruent are the culture and soul of two organizations, the less sense of loss and confusion organization members will experience during the transition. By the same token, when two organizations come together, both with strong and well developed soul and culture, there will be more conflict than if the soul qualities of one of the partners is relatively undeveloped or weak.

As a manager, executive, or consultant, nourishing the soul of the organization is one of my major responsibilities. That doesn't mean we have to nurture all parts of the organization. Sometimes parts have to leave or die. What it does mean is that whatever we do is done in integrity and in congruence with the highest values. For example, in cutting costs, integrity may be served by execu-

tives taking a pay cut and sharing in the suffering.

As organization members in touch with the organization's soul, we need to be mindful of nourishing it, and of not doing things that jeopardize the soul or our connection with it. There is thus a spiritual dimension to one's responsibilities that is added when you begin working with soul. No longer just concerned with the bottom line, we are also concerned with what might be called the "top line."

If different parts of an organization can agree on what is the highest and best that they have in common, that can inform choices they make about how they work together. You are always looking for the balance between the good of the part and that of the whole. Even when you are making a decision to downsize and eliminate a part, you do it in such a way as to empower the part that is separated.

Once you get into the rhythm of soul work, you find that it is supportive of doing things that way. However, it requires a good deal of attentiveness at the outset, and until that rhythm is established. It's not so different from what happens when one cares for one's own soul, rather than simply nourishing parts of the personality. One takes on a new set of priorities. Those new priorities may at times restrict choices, because we are putting additional requirements on ourselves. At the same time, working with organization Soul opens up new vistas and possibilities for expression, as in the example above of my work with the small non-profit.

It is worth noting that organizational soul is not identical in its genesis to an individual's soul. Organizational soul emerges, develops and becomes more complex as the organization develops. But you are still talking about that spiritual dimension, one of quality and meaning. It makes sense to look at that development, and ask of each phase, "What might this period have contributed to the soul of the organization?" Whereas with a person, you might ask, "What did this period reveal, provide access to," the implication being that the person's soul was always there as a latent quality ready to take form when it is called forth.

I want to speak briefly here about the work of Mitch Saunders and Craig Fleck, with whom I have been associated during the last couple of years. This work, sometimes called Sensing and Shaping the Future (Saunders, 2008) has strongly influenced my thinking about working with an organization's soul. Saunders would not, so far as I know, describe his work as a spiritual practice; therefore, a detailed treatment of it is beyond the scope of this paper. I consider the approach to be implicitly spiritually oriented, however, so I describe it in outline here.

For me, the essence of the Sensing and Shaping approach is in the kind of relationship we establish with a living system, such as an individual, group or organization. We can choose to relate to the system as an object to be planned for and acted upon, or as a being in its own right, with whom we can establish a relationship, a co-creative partnership. This is reminiscent to me of Martin Buber's (1996) distinction between "I It" and "I thou" as the two fundamental ways we can relate to another.

Saunders and Fleck speak of such a co-creative partnership as "coming alongside" a system, working with rather than on the system. As leaders, consultants, or organization members, we view the system as having its own unique path of evolution, and we see whatever is going on in the system as attempts to be of service to the life of the system. Then we observe what is unfolding, and endeavor to understand how that is related to the evolutionary needs of the system in its life cycle, and we work with the system's own energy to shape its responses in ways that are in service to its life.

The reason I briefly mention the Sensing and Shaping approach here is that I believe it is more congruent with the principles implicit in working with an organization's soul than any other I have seen in my own reading. At the same time, it is not an explicitly "spiritual" approach. Speaking or writing about it is unlikely to evoke the prejudices held by some towards anything that is avowedly spiritual in nature—even though people who think very concretely might have some difficulty with Sensing and Shaping. Therefore, it lends itself to working

with an organization's soul in one's inner life, while publicly pursuing a less controversial approach.

Spirituality into Work

What I have said about my own practice, and about working with the soul of an organization is, of course, based upon my own worldview, which is a product of my experience and intuition, and is also deriving from the teaching I have sought out in my quest for understanding. There is no need for one to share that worldview in order to attune oneself to the spiritual aspects of one's work. Each path of which I am aware encourages those who tread that path to seek the highest and best in all they do, and to work with love. After Kahlil Gibran (1923) I hold that "Work is love made visible. And if you cannot work with love but only with distaste, it is better that you should leave your work and sit at the gate and take alms of those who work with joy."

Whatever one's preferred way of connecting with Spirit—meditation, prayer, ceremony and ritual, or simply through inquiry of the heart, information and assistance are available to help us on our way. The difficulty comes when we contemplate venturing beyond our own minds and hearts, seeking to engage in dialogue and deliberation with others. Whether and under what circumstances to do this can be a difficult decision.

My own reason for even considering taking such a step is that I feel that such dialogue can be encouraging and supportive to those who engage in it, and I have found that to be so for myself. When, in the eighties, I first began to want to make my work as a consultant congruent with my spiritual life, I was greatly encouraged and supported by meeting regularly with a group of others who had similar longings. The support of that group enabled me to take the first step into publicly sharing my somewhat controversial thoughts about the importance of attending to the workings of love in organizations (Harrison, 1983, 1987).

My own experience of engaging in public conversations about bringing one's spiritual practice into work has been encouraging, although limited to groups of organization development

consultants. My earliest experience of this kind was with a session titled "Deepening OD Practice with Spirit: Accessing the Power of the Unseen" which, together with Sandra Florstedt, I offered at the 1995 national conference of the Organization Development Network. I have also offered such sessions to other consultants. Here are some of the things I've learned.

I take pains to create a safe space in which people can share as openly as they are ready to. I first set up the seating in a circle, where each has a view of the others.

One example of how I endeavored to create a safe space is, first, to invite a show of hands in answer to the question, "How many of you have a personal relationship with something you consider sacred? That could, for example, be God, angels, saints; a teacher or prophet like Jesus or Mohammed, and so on?" Most raised their hands.

Then I asked, "If you do have a relationship with the sacred, would you raise your hand if that relationship has an effect on how you do your work?" Fewer raised their hands, but it was more than half.

Then I asked, "How many of you consciously use your relationships with the sacred in ways that are intended to help you with your work?" A smaller but still significant number acknowledged that they did.

Finally, I said, "Are any of you willing to tell us about some ways you do this?" There was silence for few moments, and then someone spoke up. This was followed by more silence, and then another volunteered something. As more people shared, the space between their offerings grew less and less. It reminded me a bit of popping corn, where as heat builds the popping goes faster and faster.

Some of the contributions were quite moving, and it seemed as though a field of trust was being created in the room as more people took the risk of speaking up. When everyone who wanted to had shared, I gave a short talk about how I bring my spiritual practice into my own work. I then moved on by inviting people to sit in groups of three or four and to share whatever else they wanted to with the others in their small group. It was actually difficult, once those conversations got under way, to stop them so that we could close the session in a timely fashion by forming the large circle again and talking a bit about how the experience had been for them.

I was struck in this experience by the number of people who later expressed gratitude for having an opportunity to speak of these matters. A number of times during the remainder of the conference, people came up to me and wanted to share more, or to say how glad they had been to find that they were not alone.

Subsequently, I have experimented with sharing my own story as a way of creating a safe space that others can enter. I don't really have enough data to tell which order of sharing works best; so far, in fact, there has been no discernable difference. While my belief is that I can create more trust by listening than by talking, I am sure that for some, it reduces the risk when I share first. When I do, I take pains to make it clear that my experiences are my own, and that they are in no way intended to be prescriptive for others. That seems to build trust as well. Most of the people in the circles I move in prefer not to be preached to.

In my experience, people have a hunger for this kind of conversation, and it is not difficult to start a dialogue. People in these sessions were surprisingly willing to speak about their spiritual practices, and, if they used them in their work, how they did so. The first times I offered such a session, I was full of anxiety and trepidation about how it would go, and what would happen to my credibility in my profession as a result. On the basis of my experience thus far, I am far more inclined to take such risks again, although I could not say that my fears are completely allayed. The reason it seems worth some risk is that I believe that when the space is a safe one, such conversations can be highly supportive and empowering for those who engage in them, as well as enabling the participants to learn from one another. To me, such a game is worth the risks it entails.

References

Baldwin, C. (2007). *Storycatcher*. Novato, CA: New World Library.

Buber, M., (1996). *I and thou*. New York: Touchstone.

Cornell, A. W. (1996). *The Power of Focusing:*

A Practical Guide to Emotional Self-Healing. New Harbinger Publications, Oakland, CA, 1996. See also www.focusing.org/index.html.

Gibran, K., (1923). *The prophet*. New York: Knopf.

Haberly, H. J. (1990). *Reiki: Hawayo Takata's story*. Olney, MD: Archedigm. See also http://en.wikipedia.org/wiki/Reiki

Harrison, R. (1995a) *Consultant's Journey, A Dance of Work and Spirit*. San Francisco: Jossey-Bass. The book has been republished and is available from http://www.authenticitypress.com/ComingSoon.htm

Harrison, R. (1995b). *The Collected Papers of Roger Harrison*. San Francisco: Jossey-Bass.

Harrison, R. (1995c). A model of community culture: Organizational diagnosis in a new age community. In R. Harrison, *The collected papers of Roger Harrison* (pp. 263-268) . San Francisco: Jossey-Bass.

Harrison, R. (1987). *Organization culture and quality of service: A strategy for releasing love in the workplace*. London: Association for Management Education and Development. Republished in R. Harrison (1995b).

Harrison, R. (1983). Strategies for a New Age. *Human Resource Management*, *22*(3), 209-234. Republished in R. Harrison (1995b).

Harrison, R. (1972). Understanding your organization's character. *Harvard Business Review, 5*(3), 119-128.

Harrison, R., & Stokes, H. (1992). *Diagnosing organization culture: An instrument*. La Jolla, CA: Pfeiffer & Company. (Now available through Wiley & Sons.)

Harrison, R., Consultant's Journey, A Dance of Work and Spirit. San Francisco: Jossey-Bass, 1995. This edition is now out of print.

Footnotes

[1] For further information see http://www.arica.org/

[2] The White Brotherhood is a name sometimes used to refer to "ascended masters," "bodhisattvas" and other highly evolved beings who have been in human form and may or may not be currently incarnate. These beings are said to have chosen to serve life on earth and in particular, humanity.

[3] For detailed instructions for developing one's felt sense, see Ann Weiser Cornell, 1996.

[4] I use the words "attune" and "attunement" from time to time in this paper. I find that the Merriam-Webster Online Dictionary definition of "attune" is quite close to what I mean by the word. That is,
1. to bring into harmony
2. to make aware or responsive <attune businesses to changing trends>

[5] My thinking about working with the soul of organizations has been greatly influenced by my conversations and correspondence with David Spangler, and also with Freya Secrest and Sophia Frowert.

www.ingramcontent.com/pod-product-compliance
Lightning Source LLC
Chambersburg PA
CBHW081156270326
41930CB00014B/3179